Lories and Lorikeets

Lories and Lorikeets

The Brush-tongued Parrots and their Care in Aviculture

Alison Ruggles

Colour photographs by Dennis Avon

Line illustrations by Pippa Mayell

BLANDFORD

A BLANDFORD BOOK

First published in the UK by Blandford
A Cassell Imprint
Cassell plc, Wellington House, 125 Strand, London WC2R 0BB

Copyright © 1995 Cassell plc

Text copyright © 1995 Alison Ruggles

All rights reserved. No part of this book may be reproduced or transmitted in any form or by any means, electronic or mechanical, including photocopying, recording or any information storage and retrieval system, without permission in writing from the copyright holder and publisher.

Distributed in the United States by Sterling Publishing Co., Inc.,
387 Park Avenue South, New York, NY 10016-8810

Distributed in Australia by Capricorn Link (Australia) Pty Ltd
2/13 Carrington Road, Castle Hill, NSW 2154

British Library Cataloguing-in-Publication Data
A catalogue entry for this title is available from the British Library

IBSN 0-7137-2268-1

Typeset by Keystroke, Jacaranda Lodge, Wolverhampton

Printed and bound in Great Britain by Biddles

Contents

Foreword by Tony Silva 7
Acknowledgements 9

1 Introduction to lories and lorikeets 11
2 Early historical sightings 15
3 Habitat 17
4 Lories in the wild 21

Part I Care in aviculture 24

5 Accommodation 24
6 General management 37
7 Diet and feeding 47
8 Sexing 65
9 Breeding 68
10 Incubation 75
11 Hand-rearing 82
12 Studbooks 94
13 Conservation 97
14 First aid 108
15 Diseases of lories and lorikeets co-written with Peter Scott MSc., BVSc., MRCVS, MIBiol., ACOArb. 118

Part II Genera and species 128

16 Classification 128
17 *Chalcopsitta* 131
18 *Charmosyna* 142
19 *Eos* 161
20 *Glossopsitta* 173

21 *Lorius*	178
22 *Neopsittacus*	194
23 *Oreopsittacus*	199
24 *Phigys*	201
25 *Pseudeos*	203
26 *Trichoglossus*	205
27 *Vini*	234
Bibliography	241
Index of scientific names	243
Index of common names	245
General index	250

Foreword

Specialist books, dealing with a particular genera or group of closely related species have become the norm today; just a decade ago, the majority of books dealing with the parrot family covered very broad groups. This trend towards specific groups reflects the way in which aviculture is presently pursued: specialist collections are quickly outnumbering the 'Noah's Ark' collections which were typical of the past. By specializing, far more is learned about the group being kept. Fortunately, some of these specialist aviculturists have written books in recent years. Noteworthy among these books is the one for which I have the great pleasure of writing this Foreword.

Alison Ruggles is a specialist aviculturist: she keeps the brush-tongued parrots – the lories and lorikeets as they are commonly referred to in aviculture. She has not only concentrated on this group, but has studied them with great intensity. I first met her in 1990, when she attended the 2nd International Parrot Convention in Tenerife, Canary Islands. Our meeting was not casual; she approached me to ask some questions about the collection at Loro Parque, where I was then curator. Little did she realize at the time that the previous day I had watched her for some time admiring the collection of brush-tongued parrots at Loro Parque. She was just not looking at them as the average aviculturist admires a group of birds – she was deeply concentrated in her observation, enjoying the antics of the birds unlike most of the other aviculturists gathered in the Park at the time. She had clearly selected the group which she enjoyed most, and as a specialist in that group, was making her observations on species which she did not have, in order to broaden her knowledge.

All of the knowledge that Alison has gained over the years can be found in the following pages. This is the most complete work on this group published to date – and, to my mind, it is the most valuable. She shares her personal knowledge and at the same time provides such extremely valuable data as clutch size, incubation period, fledging age, age at which maturity is reached, ring size and the management of the species, to mention just a few areas covered. All of this data is occasionally augmented by the observations of other aviculturists. This book will surely become the bible of the aviculturist specializing in brush-tongued parrots. I would also urge aviculturists interested in other groups of parrots to acquire a copy of this book, as it has many valuable lessons to teach; it will undoubtedly guide the aviculturist with collections comprised of many species, and it will teach the specialist to become much better at what he or she does.

I commend Alison for her excellent work and wish this book all the success in the world.

Tony Silva
INTERNATIONAL AVICULTURAL CONSULTANT

Acknowledgements

My aim with this book is to offer a little help to all those interested in lories, their management, their breeding in captivity, and their place in the wild, and for it to be of use to anyone contemplating keeping them. I am very grateful for all the help I have received from many quarters while writing it.

First and foremost my thanks go to those at home: my husband John, for his tolerance (many burnt meals) and support; and, in the same vein, my daughters Karen (my Australian contact) and Suzanne (for allowing Pippa time to work with me on the diagrams).

Many thanks also to:

Dennis Avon for taking and supplying the original colour transparencies for the book, for producing the maps, and for his patience in working with me to produce the colour diagrams of Rainbow Lorikeets and Black-capped Lories;

Pippa Mayell for her time and enthusiasm spent on the descriptive diagrams and line drawings. (And to Little Chef and Happy Eater for allowing us to sit for hours each fortnight over cups of coffee working on these!);

Peter Scott for his help on many subjects and particularly for his help with Chapters 14 and 15;

Trevor Buckell and Jos Hubers for their generous advice and help: Trevor in particular for help with distribution and Plates 52 and 53, and Jos in particular for help with ring sizes, weights and Plate 53; Roger Sweeney for his correspondence regarding the management of various lories in the tropics; and Tony de Dios for the photographs which he sent for reference;

Kevin Evans for supplying transparencies from Taronga Zoo's collection in Australia; Cees Scholts for his transparencies from Holland; Jan van Oosten for his transparency from the USA and to Karen for her transparency (the author's birds are depicted in Plates 4, 10, 11, 17, 19 and 31);

Gunter Endeler in Germany and Mervyn Weston of Nekton for their nutritional advice and Peter Holsheimer of Aves in Holland for his comments on the subject.

Almost last but not least my thanks to Stuart Booth, my editor, and Cassell for producing the book, for their support and gentle nagging (which was very necessary).

Absolutely lastly, but probably most importantly, my thanks to my lories – my inspiration. My hope for the book is that there will be something of use or interest to be found in it for everyone.

Alison Ruggles
Sussex, 1995

1 Introduction to lories and lorikeets

Lories and lorikeets are members of the parrot family (Psittacidae) and, in recent years, have been classified in the subfamily Loriinae.

I think they are without doubt the most beautiful, fascinating and intelligent birds in the world. It is not, however, their beauty alone that attracts those of us whose passion is lories. It is also, perhaps primarily, their characters, which are many and varied. They are lively, full of fun, inquisitive, loving and always up to something.

Aviculture as we know it has been practised for just over 100 years but many of the species that are now kept in aviaries have only been available commercially for the past 20 years or so.

The expression 'lories and lorikeets' is analogous to 'parrots and parakeets'. Lories, like parrots, are generally the larger, with proportionately shorter, more rounded tails, and lorikeets, like parakeets, are comparatively slender with longer, more pointed tails. I use either term to refer to the group as a whole.

Geographically lories range across the tropics, from Bali in the east, across the Pacific, with its landmasses and literally thousands of islands, to Henderson Island in the west. From the north they range from the Philippine Islands south across Australia to Tasmania. Many centuries ago, most of the islands in this vast area would have been joined, which may account for the number of quite similar subspecies that are nowadays found so far apart across great expanses of water.

Topographically lories resemble other parrot-like birds but have one distinguishing characteristic: an elongated proboscis-type tongue, with bowl and brush-like papillae at the tip. This feature led to their being known as *brush-tongued parrots*. This tongue can clearly be seen when any confiding lory explores some proffered titbit or, as trust builds up, your fingers or face. At preening time lories commonly extend their tongues, which can reach from ear to ear. Most of the time the tongue is retracted and they look like any other psittacine.

Their tongues are especially adapted for feeding on pollen and nectar – the lories' staple diet in the wild. Examination of the crop contents of field specimens has revealed that they also eat fruit, insects, some seeds, buds, flowers and other plant parts. In aviculture there are probably as many lory diets as breeders.

Lories are generally very brightly coloured, with sleek, tight-feathered, shining plumage. Some are clad in delicate shades and others in daringly bold attire; the colour variations defining the subspecies are often very subtle (see Plate 53).

I do not think a day goes by without some antic in the aviaries making me laugh. There are a couple of characters – siblings, now kept in aviaries well apart – which raucously join in the laughter, while others chip in with their limited vocabulary. Another couple bounces up and down on the wire in anticipation of attention. Another pair is engrossed in ablutions, in which both take enormous pleasure, and from which they emerge totally bedraggled and unable to fly. Yet others are completely preoccupied with courtship: flashing their eyes, hissing, fanning their wings, and seeming quite unaware of my presence. One individual hangs from a swing by one leg while his mate dangles from the other, swinging round and round or nipping him playfully. If the nip goes too far, one or both will utter a furious squawk and hurtle towards the ground. Then there is the actor (who does not fool me), guarding and peering frequently into an empty nest while his mate quietly broods in another. There are also the clowns, like comedians in a pantomime which, with heads lowered and big, precise, laboured steps, slowly pound their way from one end of the perch

INTRODUCTION

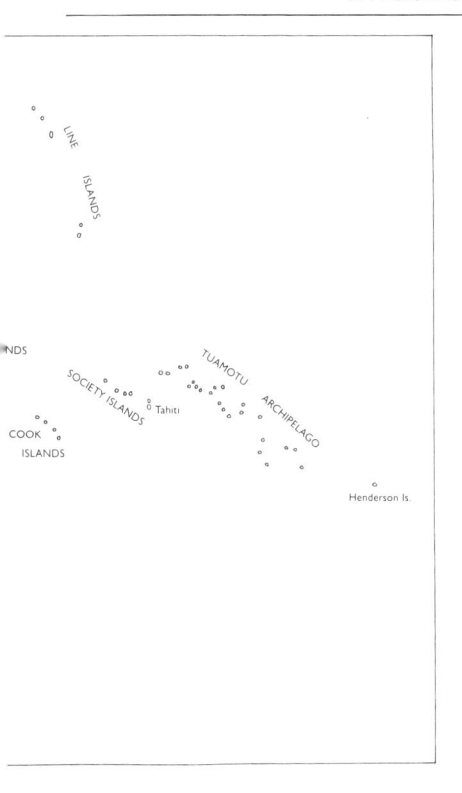

The Pacific distribution of lorikeets

to the other, letting out a hiss on arrival and turning jerkily to start off again in the other direction. When two are involved in this game, synchronization is required or there is some loss of dignity when one or both misjudge and take a tumble.

If there are problems involved in keeping lories, they can mostly be overcome:

(1) *Feeding* Lories *do* need feeding twice daily.
(2) *Noise* Not all lories are noisy. As a general rule, the larger the bird, the greater the noise but this can vary from pair to pair and even from bird to bird.
(3) *Droppings* Liquid comprises the major part of the diet and what goes in generally comes out at much the same consistency, and the distance which these droppings can be ejected is considerable.

Many years ago I used to keep about the same number of Australian parakeets and softbills, as I now keep lories. I found the workload about the same – just different.

Happy, healthy lories are always communicating in some way, with you or with each other. Each species has its own requirements and

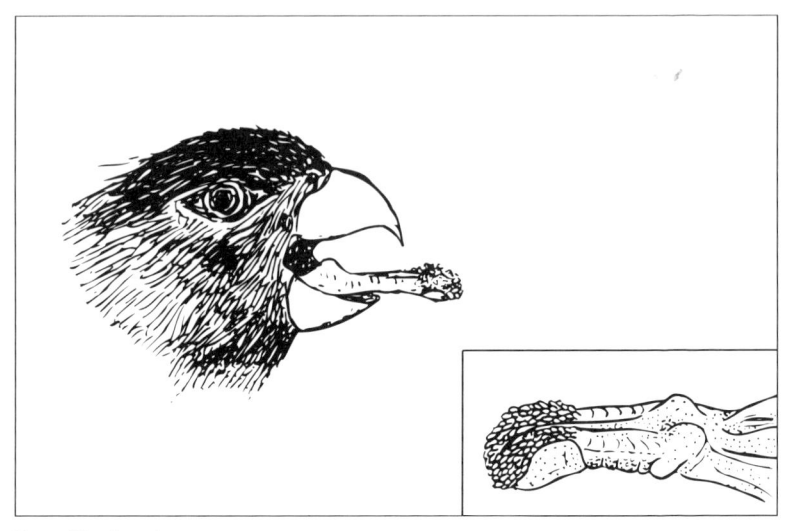

Fig. 1 The brush tongue.

aviculturists should be vigilant, constantly observing and trying to meet these demands as nearly as possible. The joy which the lories give is limitless, but there is also a challenge.

The rainforest is shrinking. Some subspecies of lory are on the verge of extinction. For a few it is already thought to be too late and, for many, the future is hanging in the balance. No longer can we freely acquire birds from the wild. We can, however, learn to manage and breed them with more purpose than in previous years, and this we must do if we want to have lories in our aviaries in the future. Aviculture is an absorbing hobby and we must constantly update our knowledge. There is still so much to learn and probably always will be. Not all the species available in aviculture can be described as being well established; thus breeders have plenty of scope to achieve something worthwhile. It is essential in aviculture no longer just to 'collect' but also to learn how to maintain and reproduce all the species we have to more than one generation. The effects of weaknesses or any shortcomings in diet and dietary supplements do not always become apparent in the adult birds and may not appear until at least the second generation reproduces. We know relatively far less about lories in aviculture than about any other psittacine, and we still know very little about them in the wild.

There are hopes, still a long way off, of one day returning to the wild a proportion of the birds that are bred in captivity, when and where it is deemed safe so to do.

2 Early historical sightings

Compared with the amount of early research into other members of the Psittacidae (parrot family) relatively little was carried out into lories, despite their accounting for almost one-sixth of the whole family. Here are just a few instances, from the last two centuries or so, of their having been known and admired, or kept as companions and pets.

As long ago as 1734, Seba described the Purple-capped Lory (*Lorius domicellus*), and so did Edwards in 1750. An accurate drawing of this species appeared in 1800. Records show that the Ornate Lorikeet (*Trichoglossus ornatus*) was sketched in 1747.

The early Australian settlers were interested in 'the parrots' mainly for sport or the 'pot'. Government officials in the late eighteenth century were usually both sportsmen and naturalists and the skins, when mounted in glass cases, found a ready market in the drawing rooms of England.

In Australia the Rainbow Lorikeet (*Trichoglossus haematodus moluccanus*), or Swainson's Lorikeet as it is known in England, was first described in 1789, in *The Voyage of Governor Phillip to Botany Bay*. It was then known as the Blue-bellied Parrot. This beautiful lorikeet has the distinction of being the first Australian parrot species to reach England alive. The bird in question was the special pet of Sir Joseph Banks (1744–1820), the English botanist, and had originally belonged to Tupia, a Tahitian who sailed with Captain Cook on the *Endeavour*.

Probably the first illustration of an Australian parrot was a very good representation of a Swainson's Lorikeet that appeared in Brown's *New Illustrations of Zoology* (1774). Another drawing of Swainson's Lorikeet was produced by Buffon in 1783. In 1863 a pair of these lories was sent to London Zoo. Regular importation into the UK began in about 1870. It was about this time that Captain Arthur Phillip, Governor of Australia, described having seen the Musk Lorikeet (*Glossopsitta concina*), which he called the Pacific Parroquet.

In 1857 Alfred Russel Wallace (1883–1913), the Welsh naturalist, described large flocks of Moluccan Red Lories (*Eos bornea bornea*) on flowering trees on Amboina.

Luigi d'Albertis in 1872 was the first European explorer and naturalist to penetrate any distance into the daunting interior of New Guinea. He was a crack shot and states in his diary that: 'Every shot brings down a bird of a new species'. By giving them trinkets, he enlisted the help of the natives, with their spears and arrows. In 1878 he returned to Italy with a unique collection of specimens, having been the first white man to travel the full navigable length of the Fly River (360km/580 miles), on the 9 tonne steam launch *Neva* which was provided by the New South Wales Government.

In 1881 the German naturalist and explorer, Friedrich Herman Otto Finsch (1839–1917) noted that the Cherry-red Lorikeet (*Trichoglossus rubiginosus*), a friendly and fearless lory, was being persecuted for taking fruit on Ponape.

Recently I managed to acquire two old prints by Pieter de Bevere, dated 1735–1750. The subjects are not named, but are recognizable as the Black-capped Lory (*Lorius lory*) and the Red Lory (*Eos bornea bornea*). A Dutchman, de Bevere lived almost his entire life in India, which poses the question of how he came by his subjects.

Early pioneer explorers and zoologists were making expeditions to Java and New Guinea before 1820. Kuhl after whom the Kuhl's Lorikeet (*Vini kuhlii*) is named, made his last expedition, before his untimely death, in 1822. The French vessel *La Coquille*, with zoologists Lesson and Garnot on board, went on an expedition between 1822 and 1825 after which Lesson wrote of his findings, which included lories.

There were further voyages to the south pole between 1837 and 1840 and more sightings were recorded by zoologists Hombron and Jaquinot during this voyage. Two United States expeditions took place, in 1838 and 1858, with the ornithologist Peale on board, and from 1873 until 1876, Peale also took part in the scientific expedition of HMS *Challenger*.

Arthur Philip, the ornithologist, accompanied an expedition to New South Wales, and also one to Botany Bay, Port Jackson and Norfolk Island, and a zoological collection was made during the voyage of HMS *Alert* by the English ornithologist Richard Bowdler Sharpe (1847–1909). *Jottings* compiled by the English ornithologist and entomologist, George Robert Gray (1808–1872) on a cruise of the South Sea Islands on HMS *Curaçao* in 1865, added to the knowledge gradually being built up.

Mention should also be made of the voyages and expeditions of Salvadori, the Comte de Buffon (1707–1788), Brisson, Müller and Ludwig Koch, and many more, all of which contributed to our knowledge of lories, as well as providing the Natural History Museums at Tring, UK, and Leyden, Holland, among others, with skins; these formed the bases for all research done to this day. Many of the specimens have never been seen in captivity, and all this was well before 1900!

In 1896 St George Mivart produced his magnificent monograph *The Loriidae*. He worked on it for more than 30 years, drawing on the literature from the above-mentioned expeditions and his own travels, among other sources. Since he finished his manuscript, up to the present day, only six species of lory have been described as 'new'. This monograph is still a valuable reference book.

3 Habitat

New Guinea, which was known to the Portuguese in 1562, but not to other Europeans until the mid-1800s, is the second largest island in the world. It sprawls like a giant reptile to the north of Australia. The western half of the island is Irian Jaya and the eastern half is the independent state of Papua New Guinea, which alone is surrounded by 600 offshore islands. The mainland is dominated by lofty mountains, which form the backbone of the island, and whose slopes provide a series of climatic zones:

(1) *Lowland rainforest* This extends up to 1200m (4000ft) where the big buttress-rooted trees reach 50m (165ft). The sub-canopy has layers at about 16m (50ft) and 11.5m (37ft); various shrub-like plants thrive under 6.5m (20ft). Below them is the ground layer of seedlings, ferns and mosses, where small skinks scuttle through the leaf litter, together with snakes (not all deadly) and spiders, of which there are about 3000 indigenous species, some edible to birds but one, the 'bird-eating spider', definitely not. This spider does not prey on live birds, but will devour those that are ailing or dying. One bite will incapacitate a person for days.

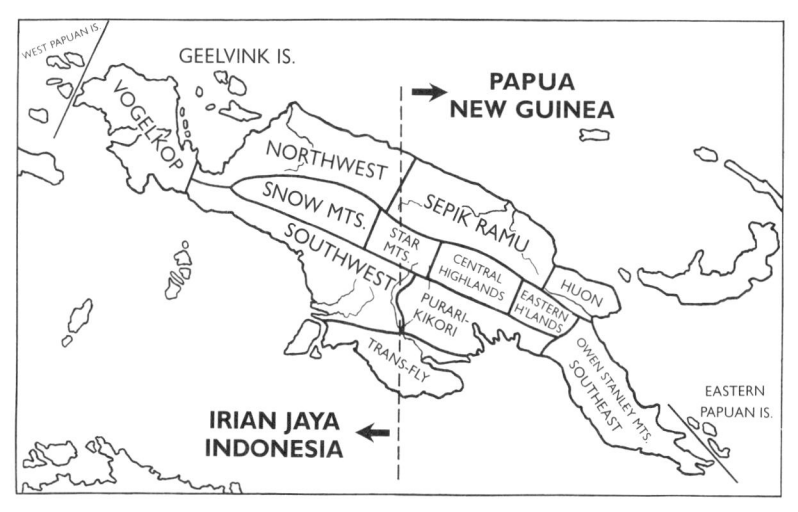

New Guinea ornithological sub-regions

Crossing the tiers of luxuriant, dripping, moss-covered canopy from the forest floor to the crowns are many climbing, looping, creeping lianas, bamboos and rattans. Here and there the green is alleviated by the profuse scarlet blossoms of the flame of the forest creeper (d'Albertis creeper, named after the Italian explorer), and by the pandam palm, with its fruit the size of pineapple, and the okari, whose fruit resemble lemons; the fruits of both are filled with edible seeds. Ever-present are eucalyptus, cycad ferns and climbing palms and the whole is perpetually enshrouded in mist.

(2) *Lower mid-mountain forests* Oak is found in this forest, which extends from 1200m (4000ft) up to 2750m (9000ft). Here the scene is one of myriad streams, cascading waterfalls, narrow gorges and wide rivers, which with no warning disappear, becoming subterranean. Here, as everywhere, crocodiles may be found, although only those larger than 1m (3ft) are considered dangerous.

(3) *Cool mountain forest* Lying between 2750m (9000ft) and 3750m (12 000ft) this consists mainly of conifers.

(4) *Alpine grassland and rocky summits* This extends upwards from 3750m (12 000ft).

Most birds inhabit lowland and mid-mountain forests. Oddly, the vivid colours which are so attractive, function as camouflage amid the colourful flora of the jungle canopy. Some 12 000 species of flowering plants have already been catalogued in New Guinea but, as botanists explore the more remote areas, new specimens are frequently being discovered and a more realistic figure would probably be half as many again; a number of them bear edible fruits.

The whole region is the largest constantly wet area in the world, being exposed to 10 months of moisture-bearing winds: the northwest monsoons from December to April and the southeast trade winds from May to October. It lies well within the equatorial belt and New Guinea itself is just 650km (400 miles) south of the equator; nevertheless several of the highest mountains in Irian Jaya are permanently snow-capped. The highest is Castenz Toppen at 5022m (16 500ft). The annual average rainfall is 1500mm (60in) of rain and, in places, as much as 7000mm (280in) has been recorded.

In contrast to the forest is the open savannah which appears drier and drabber than many deserts. Visiting the savannah at midday when the forest becomes silent as the heat sears, has been described as 'just like going into an oven'. Here there is little rain for eight months of the year. Port Moresby, the capital of Papua New Guinea, is situated in savannah, that stretches inland for 30km (20 miles). In the wet season most areas of savannah become swamp, like much of the lowland forest. Dusk falls swiftly in the tropics and, at this time, the forest erupts with bird song.

The area around the River Ramu and River Sepik, much of which is to this day uncharted territory, is the home of many lories; the Sepik (Josephine's) Lorikeet (*Charmosyna josefinae sepikiana*) is found at altitudes of between 762–1829m (2500–6000ft), often in the company of Musschenbroek's Lorikeet (*Neopsittacus m. musschenbroekii*). The swamplands are permanently awash. This is the hottest and most humid region, with air that is both dense and heavy; birds depart for higher altitudes in order to roost.

There are also caves, with sink-holes descending more than 90m (300ft). Many contain prehistoric paintings. These are home to bats and swiftlets, which find their way in the dark by sonar, as well as bird-eating spiders and birds themselves in huge numbers. The ground is inches deep in pungent guano.

The frequent earthquakes in this region are a sign of the geological instability of this part of the earth's crust. Nearly all the volcanoes, with the exception of a few mainland vents, are located offshore in two main arcs, one off the north shore of New Guinea, curving up through New Britain, and the other starting in Bougainville and continuing south through the Solomon Islands. In 1937 Vulcan was a low pear-shaped island off New Britain. There was an eruption there on 28 May 1937 that caused the island to rise 213m (700ft) from sea level, and to become attached to mainland New Britain. Already the peak is thickly covered with forest!

In some virtually inaccessible areas, forest tribes still practise cannibalism. In the villages people tend to live communally in stilt-houses built of sago palm and bamboo. The main living-room walls are adorned with skulls as well as the breastbones of animals and plumes of many birds. All around are narrow windows from which arrows can be shot, both in defence and for food. Things have moved forward considerably in the town but, as the human population expands, there is an ever-increasing need for areas of garden land on which to grow food; this is one reason for habitat loss.

In their book *The Trees of Paradise* Richard Edmunds and Nigel Hughes, two modern-day explorers, describe their journey deep into the interior of the Sepik Region of Papua New Guinea. They tell of the several attempts which they made before finally arriving at their goal – the primal forest (forest untouched by man). They had to hack their way through the rugged and inhospitable terrain step by step, encountering swamps, ranges of apparently never-ending mountains, and deep ravines, many interspersed with rivers which had to be crossed. On these mountains, in dank, humid splendour, hung the forest – not all primal. Clouds of mosquitoes constantly covered the two men. They caught malaria, were attacked by leeches, and suffered from lack of food, stomach upsets, exhaustion and dehydration. The Papua New Guinea natives were very helpful and hospitable but were quite frightened of white people (who were seldom encountered away from Port Moresby and the coast); these people never travelled far from their villages, except to hunt. Countless promises of trips in dug-out canoes, escorted by hunters – the only way to journey for many miles – were followed by countless changes of plans, and then by red tape as officialdom became wary of their activities.

When they finally reached the primal forest, they found it comprised gigantic trees towering over lesser trees and layers of undergrowth, all with tangled, creeping ropes of aerial roots trailing to the matted, swampy undergrowth; the sky could not be seen and it was very dark. They heard, but never saw, lories, although this is the home of many species. Out of the breeding season several species forage and travel together in huge flocks, but they are invariably too high up to be seen. Nigel told me that their sighting of a Bird of Paradise was definitely one of the highlights of the expedition, despite trees rather than birds being their main objective.

Richard Edmunds has recently returned to represent the people of the Sepik Region (i.e. the inhabitants of the valleys of the Sepik River) to the Papua New Guinea Government in an attempt to help them resist the offer of temporary wealth from logging. Propaganda about this is constantly being pushed at these people, who have no concept of what loss of forest means, and are therefore very vulnerable. Governments cannot resist these opportunities and are pressing the people to accept and, basically, give away their heritage and their future. Alternatives need to be found. Some things are being done, e.g. the promotion of eco-tourism, but this, at best, is a drop in the ocean. Logging, however, is living for the short term. If any rainforest is to survive in the long term, it may have to be preserved as National Park areas. The work of Edmunds and Hughes has halted the indiscriminate felling of one large area of primal forest by making young land-owners aware of the consequences of cropping trees. These landlords will now only agree to the felling of the largest ones, leaving trees and birds to live to see another day.

One example of the effect of logging is the Solomon Islands; here logging is already well under way and it is estimated that these islands will be 60 per cent deforested by the year 2000. Much more habitat is similarly threatened. However difficult the terrain in Papua New Guinea, and the area that Edmunds and Hughes visited is still largely uncharted territory, logging *will* start. It is just a matter of time and scale. (See also Chapter 13.)

Time ran out before we realized it for the Mitchell's Lorikeet (*Trichoglossus haematodus mitchellii*). Suddenly the trees were gone and with them the lorikeets . . .

4 Lories in the wild

Lories and lorikeets, as previously mentioned, are distributed over a large part of the tropics. There have been few resident ornithologists beyond Australia and relatively little has been recorded outside that country.

These birds are largely arboreal, feeding, sleeping and breeding in trees. They clamber in great flocks all over the trees, chattering deafeningly all the while. Then, suddenly, it is time to roost and as one they all depart or, in the case of some, such as the Cardinal Lory (*Chalcopsitta cardinalis*), the Red and Blue Lory (*Eos histrio*, some subspecies of which are almost certainly extinct) and the Blue-crowned Lorikeet (*Vini australis*), set off for another island altogether. Most small-to-medium lories are strong, swift fliers.

Lories are highly sociable birds and spend all their time on the move. Large flocks of several species swarm together noisily over flowering trees, foraging among the blossom, which they pollinate while they feed. When every morsel is finished they will depart quite suddenly in a screeching cloud, in search of another tree to denude, and probably will not be seen in that vicinity again until the tree next blooms. All that will be left as evidence of their presence will be a carpet of blossom on the ground. In the aviary I find the flowers that I give them are treated in much the same way. My birds take great delight in exploring them with their tongues, extracting what they wish, then sucking or crushing the rest, before abandoning the remains on the ground. Vast numbers of flowers are required to be of any dietary significance and I give them as often as I can, largely for the joy it affords them as a plaything (see also p. 60).

Because of the irregular flowering of the trees, in particular their favourite – the gum – lories are nomadic. They search mainly for pollen which is rich in energy-giving properties and is thus vital for such active birds, and also for nectar; generally these are obtainable at different times. Many types of flower are enjoyed, e.g. eucalyptus, karri, gums, coconut palm, banksia, casuarina, grevillea, erythrina, depending on season. In Australia they also enjoy buds, insects, some grasses, seeds and even cereals, such as maize and sorghum. They also feed on paperbarks growing along the banks of creeks and waterholes and some are fond of caterpillars and larvae.

Generally, in the wild, lories dislike descending to the ground but they have been observed there, heads lowered and jerkily bobbing or jumping

Fig. 4 In the wild.

sideways, much as they do on the pebbles of my aviaries. They do descend to bathe in shallow pools, where these occur, and have been seen quickly darting in and out of streams in order to avoid becoming waterlogged. In a shallow aviary pond, which no doubt affords them a feeling of security, they will flap for quite long periods and even play together, often until they become saturated and have to climb up the netting to a perch. In the wild they much prefer to lap water from an overhanging leaf or reach for any water trapped in an open petal or palm frond. I have observed them doing virtually the same in the aviary, licking raindrops from their flight roofs, particularly in hot weather.

In all there are just seven Australian species of 'lorikeet' (so-called because they all have longer tails). Fig parrots are quite different, although they are sometimes called lorilets; the Swift Parakeet behaves like a lorikeet, as well as having a crude brush-tongue, but anatomical indications dictate that it is more correctly classified as a parakeet.

In 1974, when lorikeets began visiting and destroying his flowergarden, Alex Griffiths started a sanctuary at Currumbin in Queensland.

Nowadays thousands of lorikeets arrive from the forest at feeding times, much to the joy of the many spectators who proffer dishes of honey-soaked seed and sponge, or watch them splash in the concrete baths provided. (Recent research there has indicated that this early diet was not entirely suitable for lorikeet maintenance.)

Lories almost invariably nest in holes high in trees. There are a few exceptions which prefer ground- or low-nesting. Inevitably, as the world has evolved, this preference has brought about the decline of these species in one way or another. The Collared Lory (*Phigys solitarius*) is one species that has experienced a decline in numbers since the introduction of the mongoose to Fiji. Rats have had a similar effect on the Tahitian Blue Lorikeet (*Vini peruviana*) which is extinct on Tahiti itself, although small numbers remain on certain other islands. A similar situation exists in the case of the Ultramarine Lorikeet (*Vini ultramarina*) from the Marquesas Islands. (See also Chapter 13.)

I know of one or two ground-nesting lories in aviculture, not the species mentioned above – among them a pair of Green-naped Lorikeets (*Trichoglossus h. haematodus*) in my possession about 15 years ago, which tunnelled under an upturned beer-barrel – the base for a large, thick, hollow tree which I found in a timber-yard. Being of little use for timber, it was not hard to persuade the yard to part with it. However, it was an enormous task to transport it home, saw down the centre in order to get it through the aviary door, and then to wire it together again, cut an entrance hole at the top and finally fit a revolving roof. All this only to find that the birds nested underneath my labour of love for them! I was able to inspect the eggs only by lying flat on the ground. They reared youngsters there but were only safe from predators because the aviary was on a concrete base.

Lories in general, and the island species in particular, are under threat from shooting, introduced predators, the collection of feathers for jewellery and ceremonial affairs, trapping as pets and for export and, mainly, loss of habitat resulting from the needs of an expanding population and deforestation. In the past, if proper steps had been taken in time, it is very likely that the Paradise Parrot (*Psephetus pulcherrimus*) of Australia (which some people think may still exist in small numbers) and the Carolina Parakeet (*Conuropsis carolinensis*) of the USA could have been saved. Some things are being done in this day and age for our beloved lories, both in the wild and in aviculture, but there is much more still to learn and to do.

PART I Care in aviculture

5 Accommodation

The accommodation offered by aviculturists will affect their birds. The amount of thought put into the design of aviaries and how well they are put together will mean the difference between the birds' comfort and discomfort, possibly between their life and death and between excellent and poor breeding results. How often have we all fallen into the trap of spending money on another pair of birds, when we have nowhere to put them, rather than spending the money on the aviaries?

Types of aviaries and cages

Traditional full-height aviary with shelter (Fig. 5a)   The dimensions should be approximately 1.8, 2.7 or 3.6m × 0.9m × 1.8m high (6, 9 or 12ft × 3ft × 6ft high). A suitable house or shelter for a single aviary would be 0.9m square (3ft square).

Bank or range of traditional aviaries with shelters (Fig. 5b)   By arranging the above aviaries in adjacent rows, ten flights for example can be serviced from the same walkway; this affords safety to any escapees and speeds up feeding and servicing ponds and floors. One house can be divided in the same way to give ten shelter sections, as well as space for servicing nests and safe indoor feeding. There must be double netting between flights to avoid damage to the birds' feet.

Suspended aviary (Fig. 5c)   Favoured by many aviculturists in hot countries, including Australia, South Africa and the Philippines, this type of aviary was designed by Ramon Noegel in Florida in the 1970s. Such aviaries are possibly more hygienic because faeces and discarded food drops through the base wire. Certainly aviaries for lories have to be constructed with the management of copious amounts of excreta in mind. Suspended aviaries are easy to clean because they are usually made just of strong mesh. One main disadvantage is catching the birds, particularly in a long flight. A long-handled net is required and there is a greater risk of escape. If the aviaries are bolted or clipped to a framework of legs they are relatively light and easy for two people to carry into a building, where catching is safer, or to unclip and move the base to a fresh area to allow

ACCOMMODATION

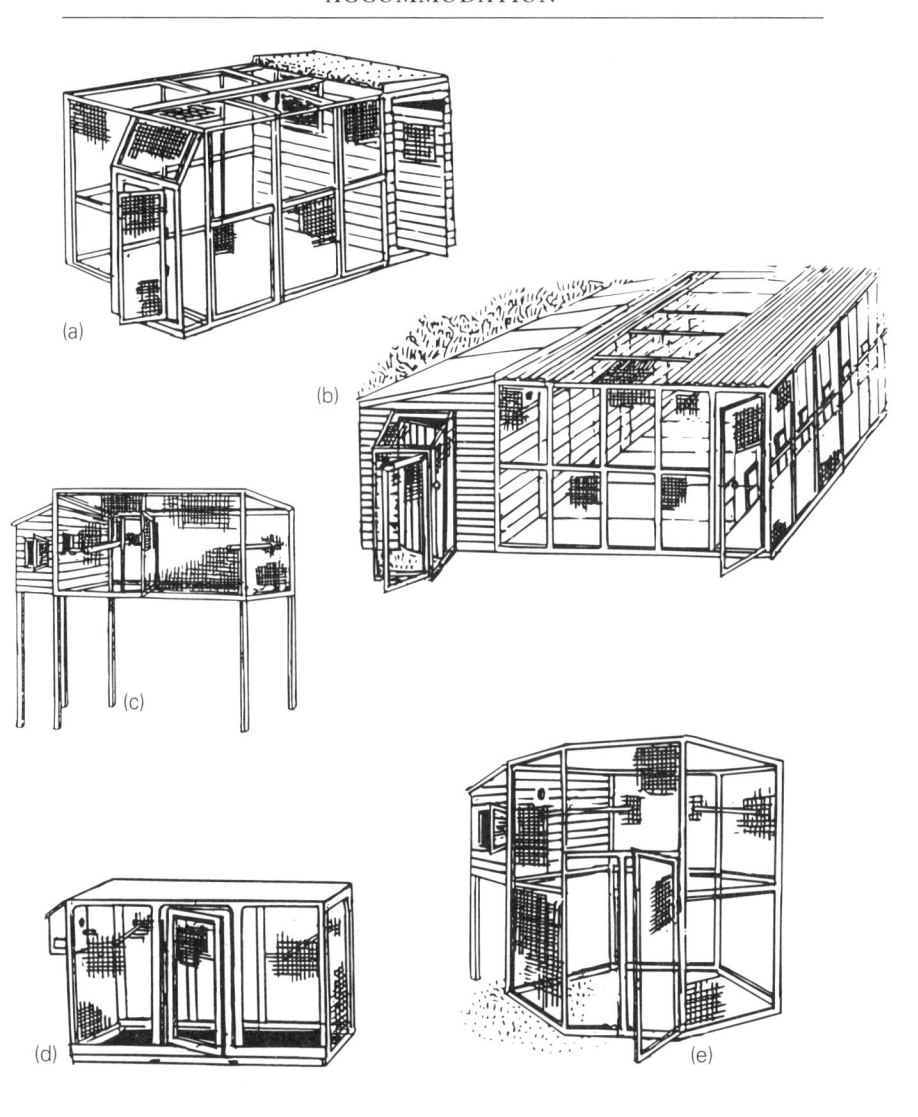

Fig. 5 Aviaries; (a) Single 2.74m × 1.8m (9ft × 6ft) aviary, easily adapted to make a double aviary. (b) Range of aviaries serviced by a safety porch and walkway. (c) Suspended aviary 1.8m × 0.9m × 0.9m high (6ft × 3ft × 3ft high) plus house. The house can be dispensed with and one end covered in, in which case the aviary can be placed on legs as shown, suspended by a chain from the ceiling if used indoors, or clipped on one side and hung on a wall.* (d) Internal aviary 1.5m × 0.6m × 0.9m high (5ft × 2ft × 3ft high); three sides and top and bottom could be solid. (e) Hexagonal aviary (an octagonal aviary would take up less space).
*A full-height house and safety porch could be incorporated.

the ground beneath to recuperate. There must still be a sheltered area for the nest, perch and food containers and a sheltered area or house section is also necessary.

Indoor aviaries (Fig. 5d)   These can be housed in a spare room indoors for those delicate species requiring greater heat; this can be a basement, as is common in certain parts of Europe, or in the house section of an aviary.

Barn or purpose-built construction   This houses a bank of full-height or suspended aviaries and is a method favoured where noise is a big problem, because it can be controlled with certain insulating materials, and in countries where it becomes very cold in winter or extremely hot and humid; in the latter instance, cooling the building will control to some extent, the speed at which food sours and nests become damp and infected with fungus and bugs.

Hexagonal or octagonal aviary   This type of aviary is for socializing adolescent lories, or colonies where applicable (see Fig. 5e). It is a type of aviary that has the merit of affording the opportunity for the current year's young, whether parent-reared or, particularly, hand-reared, to learn to socialize with others of their own kind. Feed must be placed at various points in such an aviary, and a close watch kept to make sure that all the birds are eating and none is being bullied or denied access to the shelter section. Plenty of 'toys' should be placed in the aviary – swings, hanging bells, ladders, trailing willow branches and ponds – and creeper overhanging part of it will encourage the investigation of leaves and insects, as well as giving some shade.

Siting

Aviaries in the northern hemisphere should face south, away from the prevailing wind, or east if they are well protected. Ideally they should not face west or north because, in winter, they will take too long in the morning to warm up, as well as receiving less sunlight overall. I have identical blocks of seven aviaries facing east and west and maximum/minimum thermometer readings in the morning show that the west-facing block is always about 5°F (3°C) colder and, in winter, this block receives no sun in the flight until mid-morning at the earliest. Pond-water freezes much more quickly and also takes longer to thaw in this situation. The house should be situated at one end of the flight. I believe the nest should be situated in the house for a number of reasons:

(1) protection from draught,
(2) additional protection in the cold for winter laying,

(3) protection from rain, i.e. so that the nest does not become drenched either on top or at the back in heavy rain or rain and wind,
(4) provision of a refuge where a bird may hide away, take a secluded nap, or retreat to brood in peace should visitors come to the aviaries,
(5) ease of inspection. I have yet to find evidence that the occasional extreme heat in the house affects hatching eggs or chicks in any way.

Materials

Suspended flights usually comprise all-metal mesh clipped together to make an oblong box, with a door clipped approximately centrally. Popular originally in Australia and also now in Europe, although expensive, are flights of aluminium frames and mesh and, being introduced to the UK, are all-steel aviaries which are easily moved and reconstructed, and from which parasites, such as red mite, are more easily eliminated. These aviaries do not rust and are virtually indestructible.

For conventional aviaries bricks or concrete blocks, although the most expensive materials, are also the most substantial, warm and long-lasting. Recently I obtained some quotes for replacing the house part of a block of 15 aviaries in both the above materials. It came out at about three times the cost of wood. Eventually I decided that, rather than buy new wood, the cheaper course of action was to strip down to the shell, replace or reinforce rotten sections of main beams, re-use any old cladding and incorporate it with new, and re-line the whole with an Australian, water-proofed, white-faced eucalyptus board.

Wood is still the most popular material in the UK (but its life, even if the birds are regularly moved for re-treating the timber, appears to be about 12 years) with welded mesh for the flights. For the flights I would suggest timber 32mm (1¼in) square planed and prepared. For lories, the mesh most commonly used on wood frames for flights is 18 gauge, 12mm × 38mm (½in × 1½in). This can be bought as rolls 90cm (3ft) wide, of various lengths for attachment to the existing framework or as ready-made panels, 1.8m × 0.9m (6ft × 3ft), which can be purchased individually to make the required size. Door sections and house sections clad in tongue-and-groove can also be purchased in these dimensions.

All woodwork should be treated with preservative prior to use. All mesh should be scrubbed with vinegar and water and then hosed off to obviate the chance of the birds eating any droplets of zinc (and lead) left from the galvanizing process. If ingested, both can prove deadly (see Chapter 14).

In the case of individual aviaries, pop-holes from the flight to the house shelter can be sliding or hinged. It is more difficult with blocks of aviaries; the pop-holes in mine cannot be closed in such ways but they are very small and can, on occasion, be plugged individually (e.g. with old squares of hessian or towel which can later be washed). I do this for the most delicate species during prolonged severe freezing conditions, when a hen is laying, or when a bird does not appear quite itself.

Corrugated Perspex should be put over the perch area at one or both ends of the flight. This provides a protected area where the birds can sit out of the rain and feed. A pond positioned here is less likely to become contaminated by wild birds and rodents.

Roofing

Roofs should be sloping and can be entirely of wood, with double, overlapping roofing felt plus sealant, or can incorporate sections of double Perspex for added light. Lining and/or insulation is well worth the cost, both in cold and hot weather. The roof should be higher than the flight at the front and overlap it all round to protect the walls. Gutters can be placed at the back further to protect the walls from damp and thus give extra life to the aviary. A water barrel or soakaway can be placed below the downpipe from the gutters.

Floors

Concrete is the most hygienic surface for flooring although the initial cost of laying it is high. Blocks of aviaries are best positioned on slightly sloping concrete which can be hosed and disinfected. The floor of the house should be higher than that of the flight so that it can be hosed down without dirty water backing up under the wall to the house. This will not only rot the house wall but will also allow fungus to take hold. For the same reason, it is worth noting that the walls of the house should overlap the base.

The house sections of blocks of aviaries can be of the suspended type to facilitate hosing underneath. It is worth making provision for this at the time of construction by sloping the floor towards the centre and also towards one end, where there should be a covered drainhole to the outside. In my house sections, I now have removable shuttering under the suspended internal flight sections. These sections are 60cm × 90cm × 90cm high (2ft × 3ft × 3ft high) and shavings, which can be raked and changed, are placed in them. The shuttering can be simply lifted out for disinfecting as necessary. It also keeps the house warmer. Cat-litter, the type made from compressed wood, can also be used; it is very absorbent and stays dry far longer than wood shavings. It is, however, more expensive and on no account should lories be allowed to come into direct contact with it because it swells on ingestion. Some people use sand, but it is heavy to handle. If there is only one pair of lories to a house, you can have a wood floor and line it with newspaper. These individual aviaries can be of full height or of the half-house type used in conjunction with suspended aviaries (see Fig. 5a).

In the flights concrete floors are hygienic but they can look clinical and appear dirty within a day or two of being hosed down. Concrete paving slabs are cheaper but, although they are excellent on free-draining soil, they are hopeless on clay. Dirt collects between them, only to emerge during hosing-down, or in a downpour when the site often becomes a lake due to the slow drainage. One of the best surfaces, I believe, is pebbles. These can be 2.5–5cm (1–2in) in diameter and should be laid to a depth of 5–7.5cm (2–3in). They can be placed on concrete, slabs, or directly on the earth, but bear in mind that, without the precaution of sinking wire or sheet metal around the edges of the aviary during construction, rodents can enter. Aviaries can be underwired and pebbles placed on top; some weeds may grow through but this can be prevented by placing black polythene below the wire. Care should be taken that no polythene is accessible to the birds. Hosing will keep the pebbles clean and any particles of mouldy food will be washed out of the reach of the lories. Damp-loving worms, who feast on this, stay well below the stones and, by and large, totally out of the reach of lories. Gravel is another option but some pairs of lories collect it and 'bomb' their nest and eggs. I do not favour sand in case it is ingested. Grass and earth are not a good idea either because of fouling and the presence of worms, which act as an intermediary host for parasites (as do beetles, slugs and snails).

Heating

Depending on the species kept, the climate and personal preference, heat in some form may be deemed necessary. In an aviary kept at a minimum temperature of about 7°C (45°F), the nectar will not freeze; the lories which it houses can therefore eat more than those in unheated houses. This is my personal preference. Tubular heaters of different lengths, or in banks of two or three together, can be fitted to the walls; I have some 30cm (1ft) long in individual 90cm (3ft) square half-houses. They have a sloping shelf above and are netted in all round, and provide slight background heat in the most inclement conditions; they are turned on as required from waterproof switches outside the individual houses. In blocks of aviaries I find oil-filled, thermostatically-controlled radiators best. Be sure to choose a type where the controls are not likely to be soiled by faeces, or make a cover for them. Ideally a maximum/minimum thermometer should be kept in the aviary (be sure it is out of the reach of the birds who may chew the glass and get at the mercury). From a daily reading you can decide at what temperature to set your radiators as conditions alter. I prefer to give most of my birds the choice of sitting in a draught-free, slightly warm house or going out in the elements.

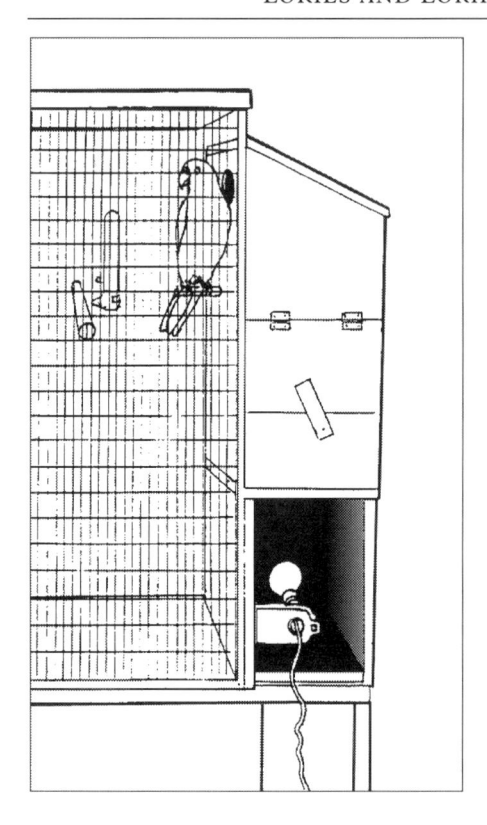

Fig. 6 Additional nest heat will benefit many of the small delicate species which are housed indoors (as used by Carole Day).

Light and ventilation

Wherever possible aviaries should receive the maximum amount of daylight. All windows need to be netted. They can be fixed purely for light, or have removable screwed-in Perspex; this facility is preferable because it allows for washing and additional ventilation. It is important to site these windows so that draughts are avoided. Another option is to insert panels of wired Perspex in the roof but these let out considerable heat even if they are double-skinned. In my baby-bird-room I have inserted a Ventelux roof window around which a netting box has been constructed; both this and the window itself open by means of a pole with hook. In the case of individual houses, where it is not appropriate to have opening windows, Perspex can be used; this can be unscrewed to give more ventilation in the warmer months but lets in light all year round.

In bird-rooms and blocks of aviaries some form of extended daylight is desirable. Strip-lighting may seem best, except for the difficulty and cost involved in using it in conjunction with a dimmer. With conventional or long-life bulbs, a dimmer can be set on a timer. I think it is also advisable to leave a low wattage night-light on all night for the following reasons:

(1) The risk of night-fright injuries is reduced.
(2) Birds can find their way back to their nest after disturbance.
(3) Parent birds with chicks can feed during the night.

I have bulbs attached to a dimmer and timer to give a couple of hours extended light before dawn; it is set to dim at about 10 p.m.

Outside the aviary a sensor (or time clock), low-wattage, external bulkhead light fitting is an investment against night-fright injury and also a deterrent to thieves. The advantage of a sensor is that, in excessively dark daytime conditions, the light will come on. Bulkheads can now be obtained to accommodate the differently-shaped long-life bulbs that, although expensive to purchase, pay for themselves in the long term.

In bird-houses, buildings housing suspended flights, and in the house section of blocks of aviaries, there is a need for constantly changing air to prevent fungus spores from settling. If a safety porch is attached to the door, positioned, for example, at the back (see Fig. 5b), and the windows are also at the back, with the birds' quarters at the front, both can be opened for periods to change the air. In this respect an ionizer is a useful addition but care must be taken to avoid it pointing directly at any birds and creating a draught. Some ionizers deal with bacteria as well as dust and fumes. Certainly, on routine cleaning, I have found that a huge number of particles have been attracted to the filter.

Access and safety

Access to flights and houses can be gained by small half-doors. Full-size doors are not really suitable in the case of lories, which will probably fly to welcome your arrival. It is preferable to build safety porches wherever possible or, for blocks of aviaries, to have walkways (see Fig. 5b). Fastenings are needed on the inside as well as the outside of all doors. Time spent routinely oiling hinges, checking woodwork and netting pays dividends.

Security

It seems vital to me to secure the house and/or flight with a padlock. If you have a block or bank of aviaries, it would be sufficient for just the safety-porch door to the house and the walkway to have padlocks, while internal doors to each individual aviary had quicker fastenings. It is possible to have a number of padlocks all opened by the same key.

A security system of some kind seems vital in these days. Indeed many insurance companies will not give or renew cover unless one is installed.

Light is an additional deterrent to thieves, as are the presence of dogs or geese, noisy gravel surrounding the aviary, a high screening and/or dense, prickly hedging of hawthorn, holly, brambles, gorse, roses, berberis or pyracantha.

Electric fencing is another good deterrent against intruders whether human beings, foxes, dogs or cats. Double netting on external panels and a roof overhang can be helpful, particularly against cats and foxes.

Ponds, sprinklers and sprays

Some form of bathing water must be provided. A pond on the ground is the most usual but should not be sited beneath or within aim of perches and, in small flights, this may not be possible. A draining shelf for the pond can be placed at the desired height. Another consideration is that, if a pond is in the open, it can be filled by rain but can also be fouled by starlings; this can cause listeriosis, among other things, as I have found out to my cost. I now site home-made hanging ponds under the Perspex.

Many people now install sophisticated sprinkler systems but it is cheaper to run a perforated hosepipe over the aviary and turn the tap on for the desired period. Bacterial contamination of the pipes and fittings, while a worry, can be overcome by flushing them periodically with specialist proprietary solutions, or a chlorine solution. This should be done approximately fortnightly and meters to test the level of chlorine for safety can be purchased. During this cleansing period and subsequent flushing, the birds should be shut away. Sanitizers can be purchased to add to the water and thus keep it free of this problem; in the recommended dose, these are

Fig. 7 Spraying is good for plumage (water should be fresh). It encourages young birds to preen and bathe and is important for the well-being of every bird.

ACCOMMODATION

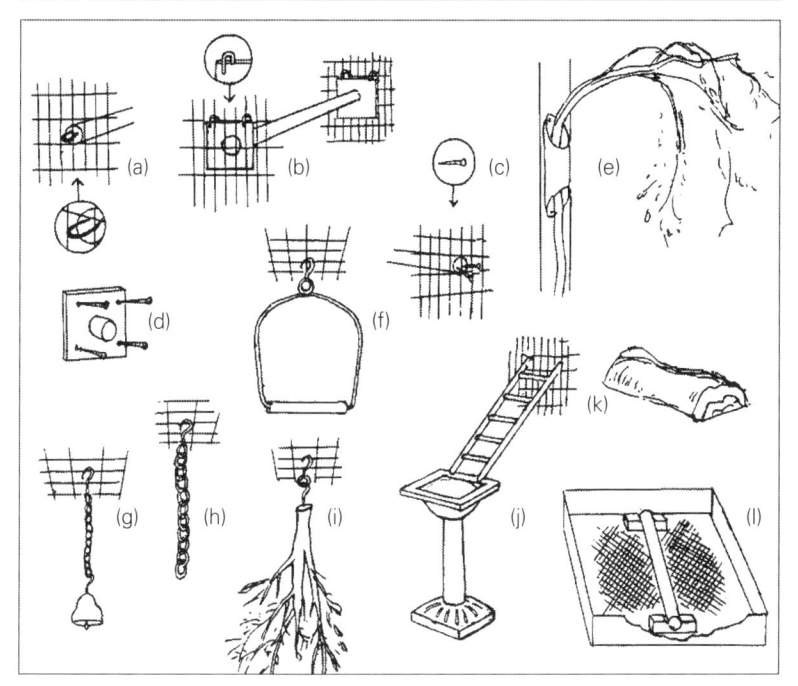

Fig. 8 Perching. (a)–(e) show methods of securing perches: (a) A staple straddling the wire. (b) 15cm square by 1.25cm thick (6in square by ½in thick) blocks of wood with hooks attached. Holes are made with a drill attachment. (c) Two nails straddling the wire. (d) Similar to (b) but for fixing in the house section. (e) Copy of a system used at Loro Parque in Tenerife. Plastic drainpipe can be sawn to allow access for nails or screws. (f)–(j) A mixture of perching and 'toys'. (k) Low form of perching for insertion into a hospital cage (burn after use). (l) A design for training chicks to perch. The perch is glued into the holder and can be used in a brooder or cage.

safe for the birds. In the absence of any of the above, or in addition, and certainly while training youngsters to bathe and preen, a hand-held spray is a bonus and enjoyed by most.

Draught

The avoidance of draught is one of the most important considerations of the accommodation. If you live in a particularly windy situation, or you keep some semi-delicate species with no heat laid on, it is a good idea to have panels of clear Perspex or PVC cut to size which can be screwed into position for the worst months.

Perches

Perches can be bought in as dowelling and cut to size, or you can cut them yourself from suitable trees; place one at either end of the flight to allow for maximum flying and insert others, as desired, for enjoyment. They should not, however, be too near the house wall because of fouling (particularly important with *Charmosyna* spp.). Perches need to be secure but easy to change (see Fig. 8), or mating will probably not be successful. They also need to be of sufficient diameter for the birds' toes not to hang down and get frost-bitten, but not so large that the toes are continually stretched. They should be of a wood that can be chewed safely and they must be changed frequently. There should be perches just outside and inside the pop-hole and, inside the house, there should be a perch well away from the entrance so that the bird can sit out of the draught.

Nest-boxes

Nest-boxes come in many different shapes and sizes (see Fig. 9) but should be of untreated wood, say 19mm (¾in) thick for insulation against both heat and cold. Many birds are tolerant of a wide variety of nest-boxes: I have seen Goldies (*Trichoglossus goldiei*) nest in an open-fronted box meant for finches and in one intended for a pair of Blacks (*Chalcopsitta a.atra*). The common denominator is that the boxes should be sited under cover and be protected against the elements. The nest-hole should be just large enough for the bird's shoulders to pass through as this gives it a sense of security; 100mm (4in) for the largest species, 75mm (3in) for medium species and 50mm (2in) for small species is a guide.

Fig. 9 Nest-boxes (opposite). (a) Large: 25cm square by 50cm high at the front and 43cm high at the back (10in square by 20in and 17in high), with a 7cm (3in) diameter nest-hole and an inspection door either side. (b) Small: 20cm square by 38cm high at the front and 33cm high at the back (8in square by 15in and 13in high), with a 4.5cm (1¾in) diameter nest-hole and an inspection door. (c) Large L-shaped: 22cm square by 50cm high (9in square by 20in high) with an 18cm × 22cm (7in × 9in) nesting toe containing an inspection door and 7cm (3in) diameter nesting-hole. (d) Small L-shaped: 15cm × 18cm by 47cm high (6in × 7in by 18½in high) with a 10cm × 15cm by 16cm high nesting toe containing an inspection door, and a 5cm (2in) diameter nest-hole. (e) Large slanting: same dimensions as (a) but with inspection door on the upper side. (f) Horizontal: 18cm × 34cm by 20cm high (7in × 13½in by 8in high) with half-open front. (g) Porch variety: 34cm (13½in) wide overall, with porch and nesting area 16cm × 21cm by 20cm high (6½in × 8½in by 8in high) and a 4cm (1½in) diameter nest-hole. (h) Hollow log: of any size or depth. (i) Adaptation for extra heat: this model can be adapted for any size of nest-box with hooks on the base.

ACCOMMODATION

The nests should be easily accessible for inspection without undue disturbance. Nesting material should be dry and 5–7.5cm (2–3in) deep; in my opinion it should not consist solely of shavings which, when dry, are too light and allow eggs to fall through and be lost. A mixture of shavings and untreated wood chippings forms a stable base while giving some species the chance to chew and form the tilth they desire. Peat, rotten wood and even a sod of earth can all be added to the above although, with the last two, there is some risk of infestation. Sawdust should on no account be included in case it is inhaled. A ladder of either mesh or wooden pegs is a must, to avoid broken eggs and damaged chicks, and a replaceable piece of glued or screwed-in wood gives the parent bird something to do and thus helps to prevent it from becoming bored while brooding.

Nests for *Charmosyna* spp. can be horizontal, giving them a larger area for nesting; there is thus a chance that they will stay dry for longer, and that defaecation may take place through the nest-hole. An L-shaped or sloping nest is a bonus for nervous birds which dart straight in and drop down. These can be adapted in many ways to suit individual needs; e.g. a shelf can be placed inside, with the nest cavity below, or a tunnel-like drainpipe can be attached to the outside of the nest-hole. I have had lories nest in canary pans, finch boxes, food-pots, flowerpots, drain-pipes, on the ground under tubs and in drainpipes, and between house walls and insulation board. One thing is important: if a pair of birds takes to a nest-box make sure they keep it. At annual spring-cleaning time, I mark the nest-box and its lid with the aviary number to ensure this. The other important thing is that, if you are going to touch anything in a nest – eggs, chicks, etc. – be sure to roll your fingers in the occupants' nesting material first; in this way you convey their smell, not yours.

Cover

Cover, in the form of surrounding plants, can enhance the appearance of an aviary as well as offering the birds seclusion and shade. Overhanging trees, e.g. willow and the creeper polygonum, can afford seclusion and give an interest to the lories as they climb about sampling items; those plants with flowers will be enjoyed through the netting and also attract insects. Care must be taken to choose only well-tested species.

6 General management

Obtaining Lories and Lorikeets

There are five main sources of lories and lorikeets:

Importers This way is becoming less significant because the stream of wild-caught birds has all but dried up.

Dealers While no longer obtaining birds from importers direct, dealers are still buying in some lories. Unless the bird has a closed ring and/or a sexing ring from which to check its number and determine its history you will probably be unable to determine its blood-lines. In the case of first-time lory-owners, this may not matter, but it will become increasingly important when new pairings are required after a loss. (You could be buying your hen's grandson for instance and looking for new blood is vital. If you are breeding with inferior stock, this will not improve things, but if you have a good breeding pair you will want to purchase a bird of an equal but unrelated standard.)

Lory groups, societies and magazines All will probably lead to the next path.

Breeders This is probably the most satisfactory route to a purchase, and it is best to make an appointment to view the bird and collect. This is not always possible and, in my experience, Amtrak in the UK are reliable, overnight transporters of livestock. The bird should have a ring and the owner should be a participant in the appropriate studbook so that you can check the relevant details. After your initial viewing of the bird, when you have probably approached it too quickly, causing it to sit up and tighten its feathers, ask if you may return and view it again, unobserved by the bird itself.

Things to look for are:

(1) Is it 'fluffed'?
(2) Are its wings and/or stomach drooped? This is a bad sign.

(3) Are its eyes closed? It might be sleeping or it might be unwell. Look further.
(4) Has it tucked its head away? Again it might be sleeping, but look at its stance.
(5) Is it standing on both legs? This is a bad sign; sleeping on one leg is normal.
(6) Is its breathing fast, laboured, wheezy or rattly? Any of these is a bad sign but remember that if you approach quickly, the breathing will speed up somewhat naturally, particularly in the presence of strangers.
(7) Is there any discharge from the eyes or nostrils? This is a bad sign.
(8) Is the vent clean and dry, as it should be, or caked or dripping with excreta?
(9) Are there lumps (possibly malignant growths), cuts or scabs (possibly indicating an excitable nature or fighting)?
(10) Examine the areas either side of the breastbone. These should be well covered. If they are not, but the bird is a youngster, I would not necessarily rule it out, but it would form part of the picture. A grossly fat bird can be just as worrying. Certain Black-capped Lories (*Lorius lory*) can be somewhat idle and need special management in this respect.
(11) Boxing or well-covered caging is a less stressful form of transport for a bird that does not know you.

Having purchased the bird, you should then find out how the vendor has been managing and feeding his birds. Follow his procedures closely, introducing any changes gradually in order to reduce stress to a minimum. When you arrive home with the bird, it is a wise precaution to quarantine it before introducing it to your other birds. In this way:

(1) The bird can relax and settle after the journey.
(2) You can observe and note how and what it eats, and its faeces.
(3) Probiotics and electrolytes can be administered and, after a rest, any other treatment, e.g. worming, can be carried out.

In due course introduce the bird to its new mate. It is wise to let the newcomer have the flight to itself for a day or so, during which time the original occupant can be caged. This gives it time to find the food, which should be placed both in the house and in the flight. It is a wise precaution to shut the newcomer in the house for at least the first night, if it does not go there of its own accord. When the original bird is introduced, try to watch unobserved.

Importing your own birds It is becoming increasingly important to keep the gene pool wide and, in order to gain unrelated blood, it may be necessary to do your own importing (or to have someone do it for you). The Ministry of Agriculture, Fisheries and Food in the UK, or the equivalent in other countries, should be approached for documentation and guidance on quarantine and the various regulations; these must be strictly adhered to. Someone other than yourself must run the quarantine and the Ministry will visit it before giving approval for each individual importation. If you get the go ahead, it will take approximately one month to obtain the documents. When the birds arrive a Ministry veterinary surgeon will visit on days 1 and 35 of the quarantine period.

After a long journey the birds will be tired and stressed; they will need peace, warm food near both perches, some fruits and possibly sponge, so that there is a choice to maintain their interest, plus honey-water with electrolytes. Next day, if all is going well, a pond of warm water can also be given. This should not be given on arrival because the birds may well be sticky and dive in, only to become chilled. If they are very stressed they may benefit from an infra-red light beside one perch to warm them right through to the bone. Fresh newspaper (not shavings) should be placed daily under the quarantine cages so that your assistant can note any changes in the droppings. Any deaths must be notified immediately.

At the end of this time, if all is going well and weather permits, the birds will be ready for gradual acclimatization into your collection. Remember that new birds are likely to pick up from your collection infections to which they are not immune, and this also works the other way round. This is one of the disadvantages of importing. This question of infectious organisms that cause no problem in one environment but create relative havoc in another, is a risk we take each time we buy in birds, even within our own countries. New arrivals are additionally at risk because of the stress factor which can depress their immune system to varying degrees. Probiotics should be offered in the nectar, I would suggest at 2-weekly intervals, to help balance the gut flora. Quarantine cages are best constructed entirely of metal and walls and floors should be easily cleanable.

Observation This is possibly the most important aspect of aviculture. Probably the worst thing that can happen to loriculturists is the management of their lories allowing them no time to sit, observe and enjoy their birds, or preventing them from visiting others to watch their birds and share and gain knowledge. A little quiet time spent observing your birds each day is not a waste of time; it is not only pleasant but essential. There are a number of things to watch for:

(1) Signs of illness (see p. 37).
(2) Loss of appetite, which might indicate illness, the approach of laying, newly hatched chicks, some disturbance, or a dislike of the food (I have experienced this with some pairs when I have included coconut in the nectar).
(3) Signs of aggression or bullying (see p. 41).
(4) Preferences for certain feedstuffs; offering a variety of foods will reveal which are preferred.

(5) Feedstuffs preferred when there are chicks. This varies.
(6) Long absences of a hen from her chicks. As a result chicks may become too chilled or weak to call and thus may not be fed. Supplementary feeding may be the answer or, if the problem continues, the chicks may be taken in for hand-rearing.
(7) Pining after the loss of a partner. This is not always a problem but, in excess, pining may lead to death. The company of a spare member of the opposite (or even the same) sex may occasionally remedy the situation. It may also have the reverse effect. Observation will tell you the best solution to offer.
(8) Behaviour of flights of adolescent birds. I keep up to 20 young of all sorts together and believe that this time is very valuable for them. I do not anticipate trouble, and have never experienced any, but the birds have plenty of room, several feeding stations and lots of toys. Additional young are introduced only in batches and are watched closely for a day. Every so often it becomes apparent that one or two are being bullied and that is the time to move them. I say 'them', because a bird will pine if moved without a sibling or a 'special friend' from the brooder. Thus two or more should be moved to another situation. The choice lies between moving the most dominant or the most nervous pair. Observing the situation as a whole should make the selection obvious (see p. 39).
(9) Boredom can be relieved by the introduction of toys, branches and similar items to stimulate the birds' minds and provide fun and interest. This applies not only to youngsters but also to adults. New branches, particularly ones that droop (see Fig. 8) are appreciated. All my adult pairs have a swing and most play endlessly on it. Ponds, of course, afford hours of fun. So does a length of hanging big-link chain, or a dangling bell, if it does not drive you mad. Last season I provided my adolescents with a long swing made from an apple branch held up by two old dog-leads. The daily undoing of the dog-leads provided as much fun as the swinging. It reminded me of children throwing toys out of the pram for the joy of seeing you pick them up time and again. External plants which enhance the look of an aviary will provide leaves, flowers, and bugs for the birds to investigate and chew; they can only get at the bits that poke through the wire so the plants will not be spoiled. Choose varieties that are hardy and safe for all birds. It cannot be assumed that, because native wild birds eat, e.g., yew, it is safe for lories; it is *not*. Wild birds have the facility to extract what is safe and regurgitate the poison.

Compatibility

Pairing This can be as easy as just putting two birds together. Nevertheless it is advisable to put the pair in an aviary which is new to both of

GENERAL MANAGEMENT

them and to provide them with two food-pots and two nests. Unobtrusive viewing will tell if they are preening, eating out of the same bowl and both going into the house and/or nest at night.

Incompatibility and aggression The birds may ignore each other or, worse, the cock usually chases the hen from food. An extra pot of food placed well away from the original one may be the answer. The birds may still fight but, if this only lasts a few seconds and they go to opposite ends of a perch, there is still hope. It is worth allowing a little time for them to settle if the situation does not look too dangerous, but it is not advisable to leave a pair that are behaving in this way. If, within an hour or so, their behaviour has not become harmonious, it will most likely develop into aggression. Even so, this may not be the end of things if swift action is taken. I suggest catching the aggressor and putting it in a cage from where it can view its prospective mate in the flight. Keep them apart and try again in a day or so. Things may improve but, if not, one of the aggressor's wings can be clipped (see Fig. 10). A running pole, i.e. a perch that runs the full length of the flight, can be supplied so that the dominant bird can get into the house and to the pond but the passive bird can generally fly out of harm's way. Should the passive bird be cornered and attacked, try a lengthy separation, keeping the aggressor in a cage, preferably away from other birds. After some weeks starved of company, re-introduction may prove harmonious. If none of these strategies is successful, I usually give in and try another pairing.

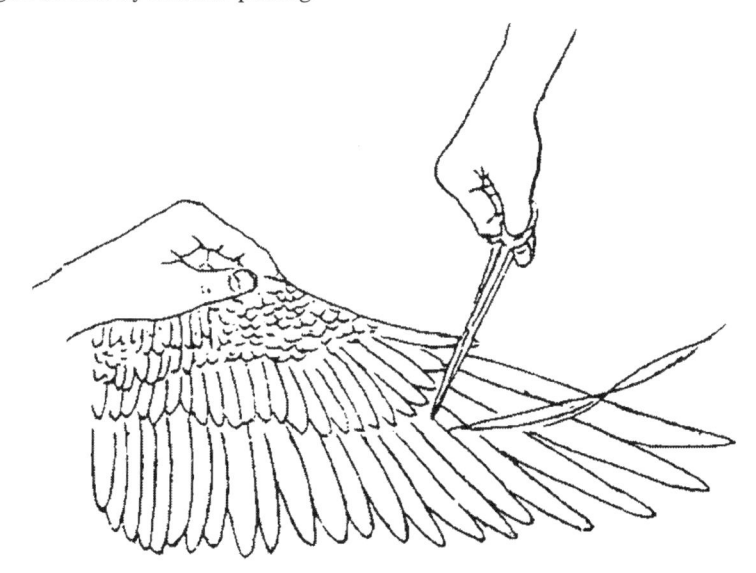

Fig. 10 Wing clipping, showing the angle at which to cut.

Hygiene

Thought and attention to this most important aspect of management can save a lot of expense. Poor hygiene leads to illness, or even death, and the accompanying bills from the vet.

(1) *Food and water containers* (even in water bacteria multiply quickly) should be emptied and washed daily. Each week they should be soaked in anti-viral, anti-bacterial and anti-fungal solutions, or a solution with all three properties.
(2) *Discarded food*, on which bacteria and fungus will quickly begin to grow, should be removed frequently.
(3) *Pond-water* should be changed daily and the ponds themselves should be frequently scrubbed and soaked in antibiotic solution.
(4) *Aviary disturbance* can be bad for breeding pairs and I will not 'thorough out' when pairs are breeding. I believe 10 minutes in a house is long enough for a pair to be off eggs or chicks in warm seasons but food-pots, perches and ponds can easily be dealt with in this time, even if only at the rate of one or two per day, and hosing of stones is not disturbing if the nests are in the house. When there is no nesting, e.g. October or February possibly in the northern hemisphere, the inside of the house can be 'spring-cleaned' and 'thoroughed' with Ark-Klens, or an equivalent.
(5) Nests should have all the substrate removed and the interior cleaned after each clutch has fledged. During rearing, frequent topping up and, from time to time, removal of all nesting is necessary; this should be done quickly and a little of the old, dirty material should be mixed with the new, fresh material, so that the birds recognize the scent as theirs. October may well be the best time for the annual 'Spring-clean'. This involves labelling each nest-box and lid with the aviary number, removing all the substrate, thorough scrubbing and scalding with boiling water. After soaking each box in Ark-Klens leave it to dry, then dust thoroughly with anti-mite powder such as Rid-Mite, leave it for a day to air, then top it up with fresh substrate and return it to the appropriate aviary. I try to take no more than 2 days for the whole process as the birds hate not having their nest but early October is not cold. If any birds are still brooding, their nests will have to be done at a later time.

Management in weather extremes

Heat In hot weather remember the following:

(1) Drinking water must always be available.
(2) Food goes rancid quickly, so extra feeds will be needed. If this is

not possible, provide extra dry diet, water and fruit, which do not deteriorate so speedily.
(3) Ventilation should be increased, if possible, e.g. by opening windows and doors, or removing Perspex windows.

High winds Provision against high winds, where these are likely, should be made at the time of construction.

(1) Secure aviaries to the ground.
(2) Provide reinforcing attachments to roofs and Perspex sheeting.
(3) Plan to avoid draught and thus cut down the effect of wind.
(4) Install hedging and/or wooden windbreaks.

Freezing conditions The availability of warm water is the main consideration.

(1) Nectar freezes quickly and, when lories are housed with no heat, it is particularly important to give extra warm feeds; the most important is the morning one. It is also helpful to bring forwards the time of the second feed of nectar.
(2) If water is unavailable it would be dangerous to give extra dry diet; extra fruit and sponge, both dry and soaked, is advisable to increase the birds' energy and to give them something to chew at and possibly extract some fluid.
(3) The heating systems may be struggling to keep houses above freezing and, although every few degrees help, warm nectar can be particularly beneficial at this time. Extending the hours of 'daylight' is also advantageous now, particularly for small species which, without light, will not feed, and, without feed, will lose body heat and energy.
(4) Ponds are a big headache in freezing conditions. For a day or so topping them up a little provides at least some water. Once there is no space left, and if the ponds cannot be removed and thawed, small pots of water can be given. The birds will chew the ice and snow to some extent.

Powercuts Loss of light, cooking facilities and heating where relevant can have drastic effects on the birds and alternative arrangements must be available.

(1) From a nectar-making point of view, it is important to make some provision in the form of a stand-by cooking/heating system. An Aga cooker is a great boon if space is available and a generator might be ideal, but financially both are beyond most of our means. A relatively cheap camping-gas unit which will boil up one kettle at a time (slowly) is better than nothing.
(2) Some provision must also be made to warm up sick birds. In

the absence of an Aga or open fire (by which to put a cage), a hot-water-bottle placed in the bottom of a covered cage can be helpful. I have gone so far as to put a severely chilled individual in a loose 'bra' until more suitable heating arrangements were put in motion – and I succeeded in saving it.

(3) In aviaries with electric heating the first move is to plug the pop-holes in order to keep in what heat there is. Birds will probably suffer from extended freezing conditions. If possible, hang a torch in the aviary so that the birds can see to eat and so they will not panic if you top up their nectar with hot water to encourage them to eat.

(4) In larger houses or blocks of aviaries a portable Calor-gas unit can be used.

(5) A simple alarm can be fitted to a socket in the house which warns of a powercut. Otherwise, if this happens during the day, when the lights are off, this may not be noticed.

(6) A brooder full of chicks will not cool disastrously immediately so keep all ventilation holes shut for a while. A hot-water-bottle can be inserted, but the chicks' feet must be protected from burning; surround the bottle with folded layers of plastic mesh (Netlon) so the heat can filter up but does not come in contact with the feet. Warm feeds are beneficial, but must be balanced in the equation of the cold atmosphere if there is no heating. Consider a loose 'bra', if only to transport them to the house of a friend where there is no powercut. A polystyrene box is a good standby; a hot-water-bottle in this will keep warmer for longer than it will in a brooder.

(7) Eggs in an incubator can be treated much like chicks in every aspect but the feeding mentioned above. It is possible, although risky, to transfer any particularly valuable eggs to a sitting hen. She will probably desert if you increase her number of eggs and they must be well rolled first in her nesting material.

(8) An inverter, for me at any rate, is a must because I have lost eggs due to constant powercuts. These did not all last long but they disrupted the development of the eggs, some of which were hatching, but days late, when the birds body clocks were telling them to abandon sitting. My inverter takes one incubator and one brooder (care must be taken in choosing types that are not too powerful for the inverter). It is attached to a 12-volt battery and the mains. When a cut occurs it switches automatically to the battery.

(9) A surge-breaker should be attached to the inverter; without this some appliances will reach about 44°C (112°F) for a few seconds, which spells disaster another way.

Repairs and maintenance

A time should be set aside for annual maintenance and repairs. Since the escape of a pair of birds through a revolving feeder, I now do this every November. Netting, wood, ladders and nest bases should be checked, hinges oiled and chew blocks inserted into nests. Bases which fall out when breeding is commencing may result in broken eggs or, if a repair is done, the birds may be put off sitting, and the insertion of a spare nest at this time will not be accepted. Woodwork may need re-treating, and it is as well to give severe-weather, stand-by equipment a trial run (boring but well worthwhile).

That vital spare aviary

Spare accommodation is essential for those occasions when a bird, or a group of birds, need to be separated from the rest.

(1) Some provision must be made for fledging birds: aviaries during the summer and indoor cages during the winter. More than one enclosure is advisable because a pecking order will inevitably develop and the birds will have to be split into batches. It may not be possible to sell all your young at once, particularly if they are all the same sex, or you may decide to keep a couple back for future stock.
(2) If bullying occurs, consideration will have to be given to separating birds.
(3) After injury or hospitalization a sick bird should be transferred to a spare cage or flight for the recuperation period. If the bird has to be confined for more than a day or two, it will probably not be able to move out again until late spring.

Transport

Wherever possible birds are best personally accompanied. If tame they may prefer to travel in a cage but otherwise a box, containing some food, should be provided for the journey. If a courier is to be used, or if the bird is to be imported or exported, the box must conform to the regulations on dimension. Travel boxes can be bought or home-made. Overcrowding must be avoided or losses can occur. Probably one or two birds per compartment is ideal and each compartment should be long enough to accommodate them beak to tail plus an inch or two, and high enough to allow them to sit on a perch without having to crouch. Plastic mesh covering the paper or shavings will keep the base dry. Two-thirds of the front should be mesh and all the other sides should be solid, drilled with a few holes high up for ventilation without draught (see Fig. 11).

Adequate food for the duration of the journey plus a bit extra should be provided. Fruit can be placed on the floor and a 'D'-pot can be secured to the mesh and half filled with bread and/or sponge and nectar or water added. This should not spill with careful handling. A 'Live Bird – This Way Up' label should be stuck to the top as well as a label bearing the destination (name, address and telephone number); somewhere on the box put your name and telephone number as sender. Notify the recipient well in advance of the expected time of arrival.

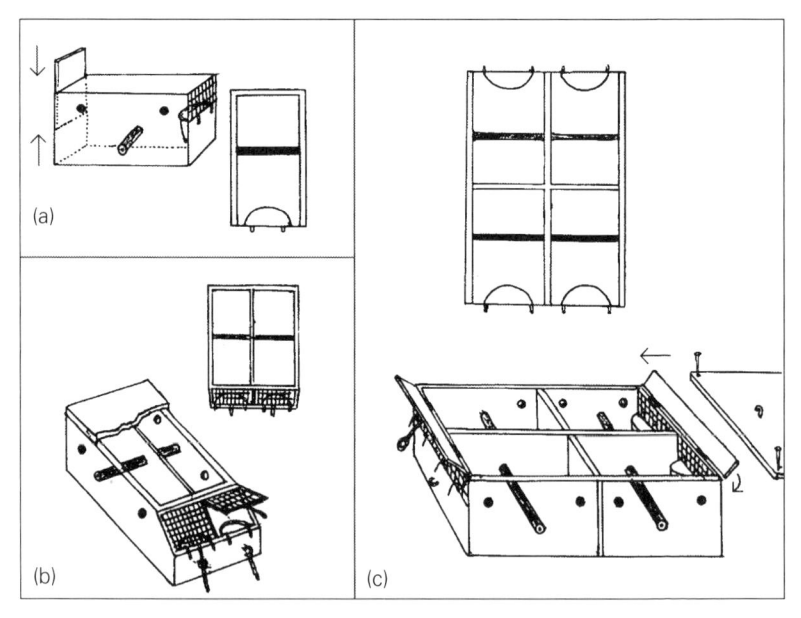

Fig. 11 These transport boxes have perches just off the ground with layers of plastic mesh (Netlon) and paper beneath and a food-pot. (a) and (b) Suitable for one or two individuals. (c) Suitable for transporting four pairs internationally. The flaps can be kept closed in cold conditions or secured open in hot conditions. A call to the handling agent will ensure that the flaps are adjusted if required. Nectar is routinely given in airport quarantine provided that pots are supplied.

7 Diet and feeding

The importance of diet

Why is diet the most talked about subject in loriculturist circles? Because, in all honesty, none of us, as yet, has much idea at all about this subject. How could we? So little is known of what lories eat in the wild, and from what they derive any benefit. We know that they forage for pollen and nectar; the former is high in protein (depending on plant species) and the latter is high in carbohydrates, a vital energy source for these highly active, nomadic and opportunistic feeders, which travel vast distances in search of their next feed. Their needs in captivity are totally different.

Relatively few specimens have been killed to ascertain the contents of their crops and virtually none has been taken outside Australia. The contents of the crops show that, in addition to the above, buds, leaf and flower parts, fruits, seeds, grasses, insects, grubs and larvae are eaten. This livefood may have been taken intentionally or accidentally, while harvesting pollen and nectar. (Generally, these are available at different times, even on the same tree, but lories need to take thousands of flowers a day to satisfy their dietary needs.)

Recent research has shown that a bird requires almost 50 different nutrients for perfect functioning. The absence of only one will lead to illness. In aviaries fresh branches in particular are commonly stripped in search, I believe, for something just under the bark. But for what? From time to time I hear of lories in earth-bottomed aviaries scratching for something in the soil. But what are they looking for? Incorrectly-fed horses often dig, scratch away the grass, then lick the soil in much the same way as lories but, because much more is known of their nutritional needs, this signal is immediately recognized by most owners, and certainly by equine vets, and routinely rectified. We are still a long way off this situation with lories, but fortunately more people are specializing in this field, so let us hope that it is just a matter of time.

Then there is feather-plucking, which is more or less universal in some subspecies, e.g. Edward's (*Trichoglossus haematodus capistratus*) and Forsten's (*T.h. forsteni*) Lorikeets. Can these subspecies need something different from, say, the Green-naped Lorikeet (*T.h. haematodus*) or Swainson's Lorikeet (*T.h. mollucanus*) which, I believe, do not do this to any great extent? Perhaps the first two species are more nervous, or more bored? This does not strike me as being the case. *Charmosyna* lorikeets seem to need a different, more easily-digested diet, and *Neopsittacus* spp. require a different diet again. Yet they are all lories and lorikeets. It is a confusing picture.

Ann Brice is an American scientist and Ph.D. of the Psittacine Research Centre in the USA, where many birds are kept for research purposes, including studies on 'the use made of pollen by lories'. She has found that only 4 per cent of pollen eaten is utilized by adult birds – most of which is digested overnight; this percentage rises considerably when they are rearing young; the rest is passed out undigested. More research into this is currently taking place under Ann's direction.

Major dietary components

Gerry Dorrestein of the University of Utrecht, at the ARA Conference in London in 1992, said: 'Food is often the underlying and/or primary cause of disease'. He went on to say that it is not as simple and straightforward as percentages of protein; importantly, it depends on the quality, type and source of pollen, as well as the bird's ability to extract protein from it. For this, the ratio between proteins, carbohydrates and fats is important.

(1) *Proteins* These are used by a bird for body maintenance, cell and feather formation and cell regeneration. They cannot be stored in the body in the same way as carbohydrate and fats. Not all proteins are suitable for every species. This means that the value of the diet should be judged not by the amount of protein which it contains, but by its amino-acid content and, moreover, the ratio of carbohydrates and fats to protein is significant in order for the diet to be well balanced in protein.

'If a product contains say 20% protein, it can be *useful* or *very harmful*, depending on the quantity of nutrients it contains. Do you know why wheat with the same quantity of protein as rye can be used in poultry diets at up to 50%, and rye at not even 5%? No? Therefore specific knowledge of products is necessary, not only the protein content.'
[Peter Holsheimer, personal comment]

(2) *Carbohydrates* The major part of dietary energy and fat is provided by carbohydrates. Their energy value is measured in *calories*. Birds have a high metabolic rate and therefore burn calories very quickly.

(3) *Fats* These store reserves of dietary energy, as well as aiding healthy skin and plumage, although an excess leads to obesity and a slowing of digestion.

(4) *Fibre* Muscle tone and strength are maintained with the help of fats.

(5) *Moisture* By weight, lories consist of approximately 70 per cent water and moisture is obviously vital, as it is for all living things.

Vitamins

Vitamins are responsible for the smooth functioning of the metabolism and make up a quarter of the vital nutritive components. Vitamins, minerals and amino acids must be present and available to birds in correct proportions. They are important catalysts in food metabolism. The body cannot break down and convert food into energy, body tissue and feather without them. Minerals and trace elements are constantly secreted and thus need continual replenishment, but the relationship between the two is important.

Vitamin A This vitamin is essential for the metabolism of proteins and fats. Young birds are less able to store it in the liver than adults and, because lack of vitamin A weakens the immune system, are more susceptible to disease. It predisposes the bird to candidiasis, liver necrosis, aspergillosis, sinusitis and respiratory distress, to mention only a few diseases.

B Vitamins These cannot be stored by the body and therefore a constant supply is needed by the bird. There are a number of B vitamins, each of which is essential for a particular aspect of metabolism:

B1 Necessary for the growth of cells and nerves and the metabolism of carbohydrates, an increase of this vitamin is recommended during illness.

B2 Tissue building, the metabolism of oxygen and other gases carried by the blood, and the release of energy from food.

B6 The chemical reaction concerned with the metabolism of proteins and fats is aided by this vitamin.

B12 Essential to the metabolism of most food, without which skin, feathers and hatchability will be affected, this vitamin also helps build proteins.

Biotin Also known as vitamin H, this benefits feather growth. Like niacin, it is part of the vitamin B family.

Vitamin C Directly involved in amino-acid metabolism this vitamin helps the bird cope with stress and the moult, fights disease, and controls the balance of the blood. Birds produce their own vitamin C from glucose when the correct enzymes are present to allow this.

Vitamin D3 Of the D vitamins, only D3 can be utilized by the bird. Birds with access to sunlight manufacture their own Vitamin D3. Those housed indoors must be given supplements but be aware that an overdose of vitamin D3 can be toxic. For healthy bones calcium, phosphorus and vitamin D3 should all be in balance. A deficiency of D3 leads to rickets.

Vitamin E Essential for the development of skeletal muscle and the nerve cells of the brain, the maintenance of protein in the blood and the fertility of the male bird. Vitamin E is necessary for the absorption of vitamins A and C.

Vitamin K This vitamin is concerned with blood clotting.

Minerals

Calcium The major component of bone and muscle. Calcium is essential for nerve and heart function as well as the manufacture of egg shell. Calcium is needed especially prior to breeding and for growing chicks. A hen can usually produce at least two eggs using her own calcium reserves. Unless these are replenished, egg-laying will decline, the eggs may be soft-shelled, and she may produce dead-in-shell or weak chicks – or egg-laying may cease altogether. If blood calcium levels are low, the production of the hormone which initiates egg production is inhibited.

Iron This is the main constituent of haemoglobin, which is found in red blood cells and is associated with the transport of oxygen. Deficiency results in anaemia.

Phosphorus Together with calcium, phosphorus is responsible for the maintenance of healthy bones. Although the diet is unlikely to be deficient in this mineral, it cannot be utilized properly unless sufficient calcium is present.

Potassium and magnesium Both these minerals are concerned with the conduction of nerve impulses and the proper functioning of the muscles.

Amino acids

These play a vitally important role, being the building blocks of proteins, as well as being involved in the metabolism of carbohydrates. They aid the resorption of vitamins and minerals. It is thought that birds cannot get enough of these from their diet and therefore well-balanced supplements seem vital.

Some amino acids may be unavailable to the bird because the protein in the diet cannot be completely digested. There are about 24 amino acids in all, some (e.g. lysine and methionine, important for first feathering in chicks) must be provided in the diet but others can be synthesized by the bird.

Binding

To further complicate the picture, there are certain items that, when taken by the bird, bind (make unavailable) other substances, e.g. raw egg binds biotin and cabbage can bind calcium (as can excess fat, tetracyclines and other antibiotics). Calcium, along with sulpha drugs, binds vitamin K. To this complex jigsaw puzzle must be added variables such as chemistry of the water, sunshine levels, humidity, changes in food requirements, day length, extremes of heat or cold, population density, the extent to which the immune system is working and exposure to stress, disease and infection.

Attempting to get this balance somewhere near right may seem like walking through a minefield and obviously no lay person can really do so satisfactorily. As scientists establish the proper relationship between the chemicals of which food is composed, it is becoming known that a scanty but well balanced diet is better than a lavish but unbalanced one. We are learning more all the time, but surely it is time for nutritionists, scientists, manufacturers of nutritional items, fieldworkers, researchers and lay people to collaborate on this matter.

What diet should we choose?

'The principle of a lory diet is that it should be nutritionally complete, have a certain quantity of metabolizable energy, and with that a balanced mixture of say 42 nutrients. It should be water-soluble and stay in emulsion for a certain period.'
[Peter Holsheimer (animal nutritionist with the Dutch Ministry of Agriculture and manufacturer of Lorinectar), personal comment]

It is possible to judge the quality of the diet by results. If a breeder's birds look well, and are cheerful and active, and if most of those of reproductive age are breeding successive clutches of chicks, which are hatching, and thriving well and, in turn, breeding well, then the breeder probably has the diet about right. On the other side of the fence, a breeder might have birds which sit rather still and silent, with tatty, possibly fluffed feathers, and make no attempt to breed. If they do try, they may well produce one or two infertile, soft-shelled or dead-in-shell eggs. If these eggs hatch, the parents may stop brooding, fail to rear, or breed for one season only. These young, if they reach maturity, may fail to reproduce or rear their own young. My guess is that most of us fall somewhere between these two extremes ('optimists', my polite name for those who tell us about their 100 per cent success rate, aside). If the diet given is, on the whole, yielding satisfactory results I would say stick to it. Other options are to study what many breeders feed and choose the good points from each, or to copy one person's diet exactly, or to buy a 'complete lory diet'.

My diet

I have attempted to analyse exactly what I feed to my lories. I am sure it is not the best nor the only régime, but I hope it will give some 'food for thought' and that the amounts may prove a baseline for experiment. I prefer to mix my own diet and balance it with scientifically proven supplements.

Many of us cook 'by feel' – a handful of this and that – and so it is with my lory diets. I have often been asked: 'But exactly how much of this and that?' For the purpose of this book I have forced myself to weigh that 'handful' and I have bullied some friends into doing likewise. It has proved quite interesting to me, because most loriculturists, broadly speaking, feed the same sort of things; it is the amounts that vary enormously, and that may make the difference. I include here three different diets from three different breeders; each should be mixed with 2 litres (3½pt) of water.

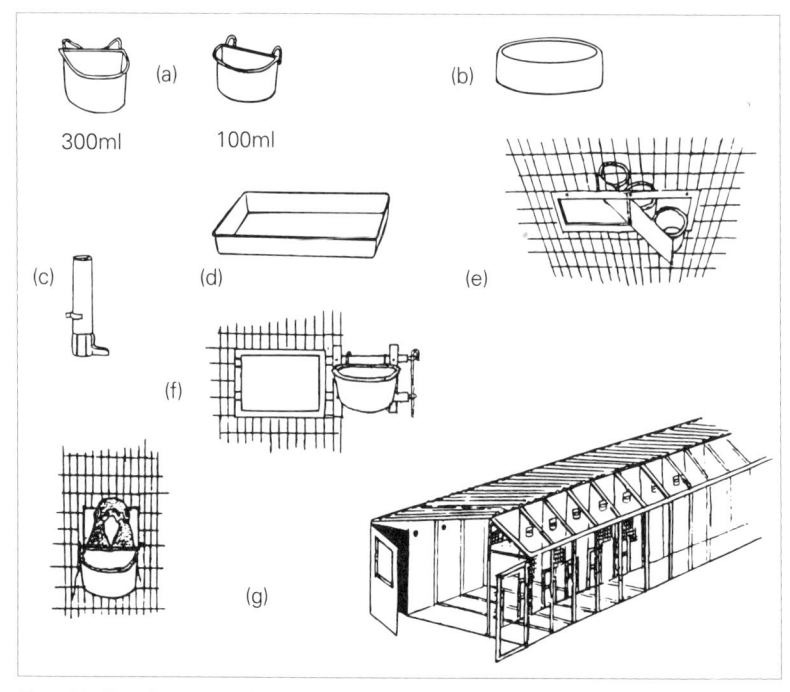

Fig. 12 Feeding utensils: (a) 'D'-pots. (b) Heavy untippable dog-food bowl. (c) Nectar tube. (d) Fruit-pot. (e) Revolving fruit- and nectar-pots (recommended for pairs that bite). (f) Heavier alternative to (e). (g) A method for speeding up the feeding of a large number of lories in a range of aviaries; the hole size is varied according to the type of lory. Shown left is a close-up of how it works; the hole should be large enough for the head but not the shoulders. This idea came from Jonathan Powell.

DIET AND FEEDING

Diet 1 (High sugar content)
2 litres (3½pt) water
60g (2oz) Muscovado sugar
50g (1¾oz) glucose
50g (1¾oz) Milupa
10ml (1 dessertspoon) Nectarblend
Pinch of vitamins and minerals

Diet 2 (Equal dry food and sugar content)
2 litres (3½pt) water
50g (1¾oz) assorted sugars (four including glucose)
50g (1¾oz) dry mix including Milupa
1ml (¼ teaspoon) vitamins and minerals

Diet 3 (High dry content)
2 litres (3½pt) water
40g (1½oz) white sugar
40g (1½oz) glucose
120g (4½oz) Milupa
15ml (1 tablespoon) Nectarblend

Bear in mind that only the nectar contents of the diets are given above. The second diet appears to contain less nutrients but, with additional food items, the picture alters. I have found the following to be a useful guide (see Table 1).

Table 1 A guide to quantities of nectar

Container	Capacity	Sufficient for:
Bottle	2 litres (3½pt)	6–7 pairs large lories 10 pairs medium lories 15 pairs small lories 20 pairs Musschoenbroek's, Emerald Lorikeets
1 large 'D'-pot	300–350ml (10½–12¼ fl. oz)	1 pair large lories
⅔ large 'D'-pot	220–280ml (7¾–9¾fl. oz)	1 pair medium lories
½ large 'D'-pot	125–200ml (4⅜–7fl. oz)	1 pair small lories
1 small 'D'-pot	80–100ml (2¾–3½fl. oz)	1 pair Musschoenbroek's Emerald or Iris Lorikeets

LORIES AND LORIKEETS

FILTERED WATER

DRY BIN
Milupa:
fruit 1 part
wheatgerm 1 part
cereal 1 part
Farex 1 part
Readybrek 1 part

HONEY AND EXTRA PROTEIN

SUGARS
Muscovado 1 part
fructose 1 part
Demerara 1 part
glucose 1 part
OR honey

WHOLEMEAL BREAD

VITAMINS + MINERALS

AM ONLY

HONEY 45g (1½oz, 1½tablesp.)

80g (2¾oz, 5½tablesp.)

¼ slice

PM ONLY

EXTRAS
Spiralina 2 days a week
probiotics 1 day a month
calcium 1 day a fortnight

FOR 6–7 LARGE PAIRS
(TWICE DAILY)

2 litres (3½pt)

300–350ml (10½–12¼fl. oz)
220–280 (7¾–9¾fl. oz)
125–200 (4⅜–7fl. oz)
80–100 (2¾–3½fl. oz)

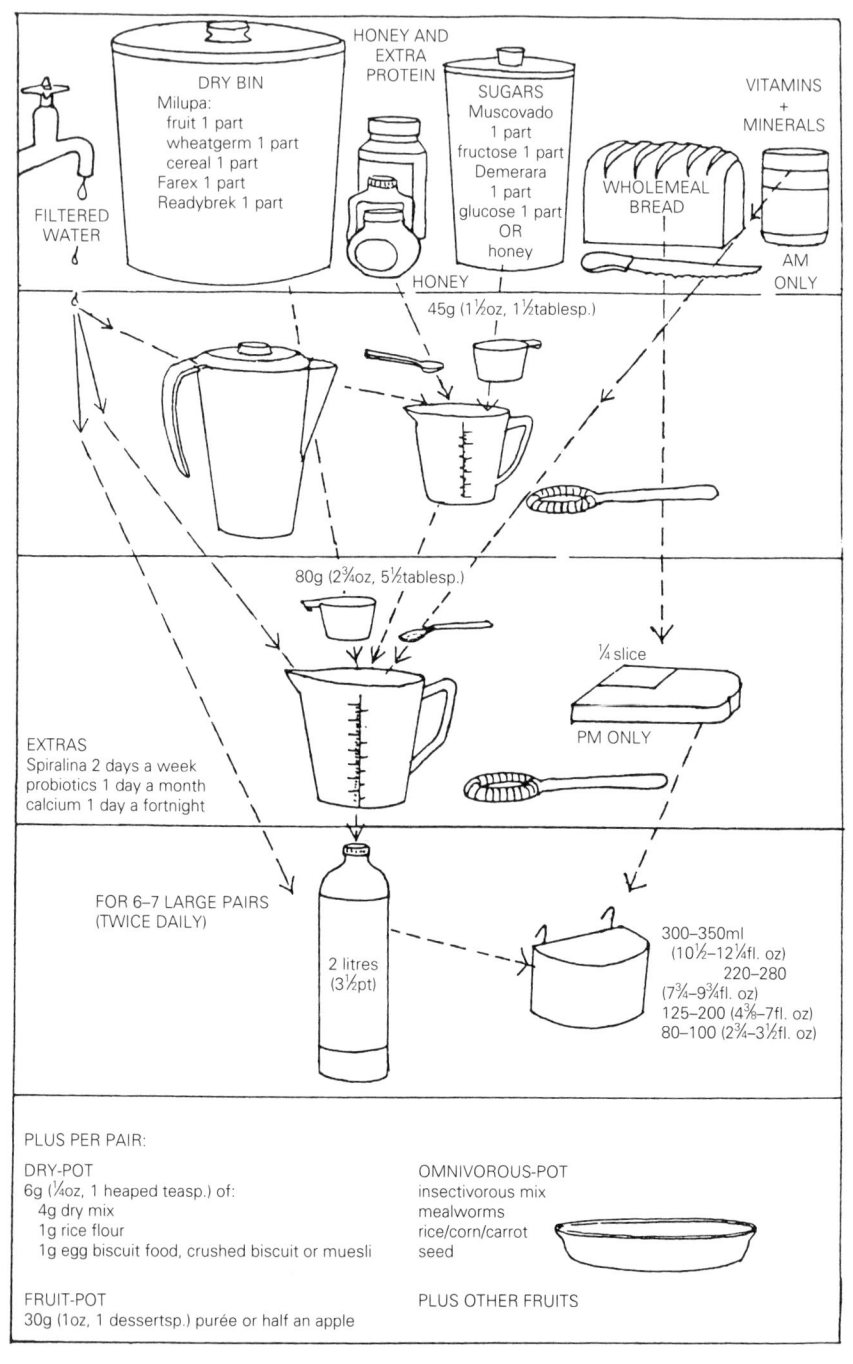

PLUS PER PAIR:

DRY-POT
6g (¼oz, 1 heaped teasp.) of:
  4g dry mix
  1g rice flour
  1g egg biscuit food, crushed biscuit or muesli

FRUIT-POT
30g (1oz, 1 dessertsp.) purée or half an apple

OMNIVOROUS-POT
insectivorous mix
mealworms
rice/corn/carrot
seed

PLUS OTHER FRUITS

Fig. 13 My own lory diet.

DIET AND FEEDING

General diet My general diet for adult lories consists of nectar, dry food and fruit (Table 2). The nectar is given twice a day, in the morning and afternoon, but honey is substituted for sugars at the afternoon feed. Table 1 shows the numbers of birds which will be fed by a given quantity.

Table 2 General diet for adult lories

Nectar-bottle: morning	2 litres (3½pt) water 80g (2¾oz, 5½ tabsp.) dry ingredients 45g (1½oz, 1½ tabsp.) sugars Vitamins and minerals (amount dependent on brand)
Nectar-bottle: afternoon	2 litres (3½pt) water 50g (1¾oz, 3 tabsp.) dry ingredients 45g (1½oz, ¾ tabsp.) honey *¼ slice wholemeal bread per pair
Dry food-pot	6g (¼ oz, 1 heaped teasp.) per pair: dry mix, egg biscuit food (18 per cent protein, lysine, vitamins A and D3), Fruitavit, glucose, ground biscuit, pollen, rice flour, wheat germ
Fruit-pot	30g (1oz, I dessertsp.) per pair of purée: apple, carrot, papaya (and, possibly, banana, blackberries, courgette, marrow, melon, pear, plum and tomato), with a little added sugar; raw or lightly cooked then liquidized. Alternatives: half an apple, pear or other fruit, e.g. grapes, hawthorn berries, rosehips, depending on availability; plus cobcorn, rice, seed – sprouted and/or hulled, or sultanas; greens (usually broccoli, celery tops, cress, lettuce, radish tops, spinach). Cooked marrow is only tolerated when flavoured with fruit, although the pips are welcomed. Beetroot and peas are welcome in any form.

*Given to birds which have finished their morning rations. Birds with chicks are given bread, or sponge, both morning and afternoon.

Most small lories require a weaker form of the above nectar, or the *Charmosyna* diet.

Special diets Special diets are required for *Charmosyna* spp. and for Musschenbroek's and Emerald Lorikeets. One 2-litre (3½-pt) bottle is sufficient for seven pairs of Stella's Lorikeets or ten pairs of smaller birds.

Table 3 Diet for *Charmosyna* spp.

Morning: for breeding pairs	2 litres (3½pt) water 60g (2oz, 3 tablesp.) Nekton-Lori
Morning: for youngsters	2 litres (3½pt) water 30g (1oz, 1½ tablesp.) Nekton-Lori 15g (¾oz, 1¼ tablesp.) Farex or baby rice (no milk)
Afternoon	15g (½oz, approx. ¼ fruit) liquidized papaya 200ml (7fl. oz) any fruit juice plus half-strength normal nectar Vitamins as required so as not to unbalance Nekton-Lori

Table 4 Diet for Musschoenbroek's and Emerald Lorikeets

Nectar-pot	80–100ml (2¾–3½fl. oz) normal nectar ¼ slice wholemeal bread, ¼ digestive biscuit or cube of sponge per pair
Seed-pot	Soaked assorted seed Millet spray
Fruit-pot	As for general diet (see Table 2)
Omnivorous-pot	A selection of at least two of the following (a small spoonful of each): boiled egg, boiled pulses, cheese, cobcorn, insectivorous mix, rice, sprouted seed, sultanas, Valumix (complete dry dog food); and mealworms (six, more when rearing)

Note that the omnivorous pot is filled with most items every day when rearing is in progress. This food can and should be given to other species which are considered omnivorous, and may well be beneficial to all lories. I am beginning to think that this is the case.

All our lories receive insectivorous mix, mealworms and sprouted or hulled seed in their fruit-pots once or twice a week. They all have vitamins and minerals from the Nekton range, or Nutribal and Ace High from Vetark, for five days and on two days they have Spiralina. No additives are given on the seventh day except honey-water in the afternoon, possibly with fruit juice. Breeding birds are given normal nectar as well.

My rearing formula This comprises boiled water, 2 parts Farex, 2 parts Nekton-Lori, 1 part Heinz Fruit Purée and, once a day, 1 part Heinz Bone and Beef Broth.

DIET AND FEEDING

Table 5 Hand-rearing diet

Day	Feed	Number of feeds
0–1	1 drop cooled, boiled water and/or electrolytes	8
1–3	Rearing, formula (possibly plus probiotics)	7
4–10	Rearing formula (plus vitamins at one feed)	6
11–21	Rearing formula (plus crumbled sponge at one feed)	5
22–24	Rearing formula (plus adult nectar at two feeds)	4
43–	Adult nectar, fruit-pot and bread	3
Weaning	Adult nectar, fruit-pot and bread	2

It is interesting to note that my nectar is composed of roughly the same amounts of solid as some proprietary brands but mixed with more fluid. When I have fed my lories on nectar made up with a smaller amount of liquid, as recommended on a packet of a complete food, the consistency of their droppings alters dramatically to that of milk of magnesia. The provision of an additional pot of water might enable them to take the goodness from the more concentrated feed and then top up as required with water.

It is important, if the food separates, that the pot is licked out by the birds. For this reason I prefer to make a slightly thicker nectar in the morning and this is the feed that is supplemented. In the afternoon we decide, according to how much has been eaten in the morning, how much an individual pair will receive in the afternoon. Should the nectar go off before it is changed, bear in mind that the birds still have their dry mix, water and fruit, etc.

I am against a seed diet *alone* for lories (fortunately few people now feed them in this way); the long-term effects spoke for themselves. I am also against dry mix *alone* for lories. This method of feeding is not natural and has not been around long enough for us to have determined the effects on more than one generation.

Choice seems to me to be the best option for lories. It helps alleviate boredom and affords obvious pleasure: wild lories search long hours for food. Certainly the same pair of birds, when given a choice, prefer different items at different times. One pair of my Musschenbroek's never touches nectar except when rearing. Others at this time leave the nectar and consume more fruit and dry food, or the extras such as rice, sponge, bread and worms.

During laying the total food consumption of some pairs drops off for a day or two, as it does during illness. Others change their preference for no apparent reason from day to day.

Dietary constituents from around the world

The following items have not been scientifically tested but other lory breeders tell me that they have been using them over the years. Many ingredients I have used for years; some I have abandoned for one reason or another and no doubt, with more research, there will be changes.

Table 6 Some examples of dietary constituents from around the world

Juices	Blackcurrant cordial; fruit juices; Robinson's Barley Water
Milks	Condensed; dried; evaporated; skimmed; soya; avoid whole milk
Water	Bottled; filtered; tap; well
Sugars	Demerara; fructose; glucose; granulated; icing; Muscovado (dark and light)
Conserves	Fruit jams; golden syrup; honey; karo syrup, molasses
Dry foods	Biscuit, egg and cheese crumble; biscuits, digestive; biscuits, ground; brown rice; Complan; cornflakes, crushed; cornmeal; egg biscuit food; Farley's Baby Food; Horlicks; maize flour; Milupa Baby Food; oatmeal; pancake mix; pea, rice and pulse crumble; peameal; porridge; Readybrek; rice flour; Sainsbury's Oat Cereal, semolina, sponge cake; Weetabix, crushed; wholemeal bread
Fruit and vegetables	Carrots, blanched; chickweed; coconut, ground, dry; flowers; berries; fruits; fruit cocktail, tinned; fruit purées; grasses; herbs; papaya; spinach, liquidized; vegetables; vegetable purées; weeds
Seeds	Ground; hulled; soaked; sprouted
Prepared animal foods	Complete dog foods; fructivorous mix; insectivorous, mix; parrot pellets; puppy foods, ground; Purina trout chow; Vetreplex pigeon food
Supplements	Abidec baby drops; brewer's yeast; Collocal D; cuttlefish bone; enzymes; ginseng; pollen; SA 37 dog vitamins; salt; Spiralina
Other	Casilan (now known to be dangerous for chicks); Cytacon; Milomino; Sandoz syrup; yoghurt

Almost every time I meet a different lory breeder, I can add to this list. I cannot vouch for many of these ingredients – indeed some are not universally available. Some, such as Casilan, I believe to be detrimental to chicks.

Note that any change of diet should be introduced in a controlled fashion, i.e. to only part of the collection at a time. Make only one change at a time and keep the birds on the amended diet (unless it has disastrous results) for at least six months. It may take at least two years for the ensuing young to reach reproductive age before any valid judgement can be made.

Plant materials

Various fruits, vegetables and wild and cultivated plants are a valuable source of nutrients.

Table 7 Nutrient content of some commonly fed fruits

Fruit	Nutrient content
Apple	Carbohydrates, unsaturated fats
Banana	Protein, carbohydrates, fats (saturated and unsaturated), iron, magnesium, manganese, phosphorus, potassium, vitamins B1, B2 and B6, niacin (amino acid)
Fig	Protein, carbohydrates, calcium, iron, manganese, phosphorus, potassium, vitamins B1, B2 and B6, niacin
Grape	Protein, carbohydrates, fats (saturated and unsaturated), iron, manganese, potassium, vitamins B1, B2 and B6
Orange	Protein, calcium, manganese, phosphorus, vitamins A, B12 and C, amino acids
Pear	Carbohydrates, fats, iron, phosphorus, vitamin B2
Plum	Protein, vitamins A, B12 and C, niacin
Papaya	High amounts of the enzyme papain

Table 8 Nutrient content of some commonly fed vegetables

Vegetable	Nutrient content
Beetroot	Vitamin A
Broccoli	Protein, phosphorus, potassium, vitamins B2, B6 and C
Capsicum	Vitamin A
Carrot	Carbohydrates, potassium, vitamins A and B6
Celery	Potassium
Cobcorn	Protein, carbohydrates, fats, iron, magnesium, manganese, phosphorus, vitamins B1, B2 and B6, niacin, trace elements
Endive	Vitamin C, thiamine, carotene

Lettuce	Calcium (especially in Iceberg lettuce)
Peas	Protein, carbohydrates, fats, iron, magnesium, manganese, phosphorus, vitamins B1, B2 and B6, niacin
Spinach	Iron, manganese, vitamins B2 and C
Sugar beet	Calcium, iron, vitamins A, B2 and C

Table 9 Some well-tried flowers, weeds, berries, branches and herbs

Flowers	Alyssum, antirrhinum, bedding begonia, buddleia, broccoli, clematis, elder, feverfew, forget-me-not, fruit tree blossom, fuchsia, lavatera (mallow), marigold, nasturtium, pansy, parsnip, rose, wallflower, wild honeysuckle (not garden evergreen), wild rose
Weeds	Buttercup, chickweed, groundsel, nettle (rich in calcium, iron, protein, sodium), plantain, *Poa annua* grass, seeding grasses, shepherd's purse
Dandelion	Vitamins A and B2, calcium, iron
Berries	Alder, elder, hawthorn, rosehip
Branches	Apple, birch, elder, hazel, pear, plum, willow
Herbs	Chives (internal cleanser), fennel (aids digestion), garlic (anti-bacterial), mustard (tonic, disinfectant), thyme (antiseptic)

Sprouting seeds

Fairly recently I acquired a three-tier sprouter. It is very easy to operate, taking only 30 seconds a day to tend. Sprouted seeds are popular with most birds and, importantly, sprouting increases the nutritional value of the seeds; in particular it aids the absorption of vitamin A. This is significant because there is some doubt, even if sufficient vitamin A is provided, whether the birds can utilize it fully. I sprout many seeds, but mainly cress, alfalfa, lentils and mung beans.

Some specific supplements

I prefer to supplement the diets with scientifically tested and balanced vitamins, minerals and amino acids. I use those from the Nekton range – usually S, but also MSA (calcium/phosphorus/D3) before breeding starts

DIET AND FEEDING

and Vetark's Nutribal and Ace High. (I still use Abidec drops for small babies.) These two ranges are specially prepared for birds. General-purpose supplements, such as SA 37, which I give to my dogs and have given to birds, I now believe to contain too great a proportion of bulking agent to allow birds to gain enough benefit. Some proprietary sources of supplements are given below.

Table 10 A selection of supplements

Supplement	Proprietary name	Source	Form
Vitamin A	Spiralina	Healthfood shops	Powder (seaweed product)
Vitamin B	Cytacon	Chemists	Syrup
Vitamin D	Collocal D	Veterinary surgeries, chemists	Liquid
Vitamin E	Vitamin E	Healthfood shops	Crushable pills
Enzymes	Multi-enzymes	Healthfood shops	Powder, capsules

It is impossible to know how much of the above to give, and what if any will be the benefit, because, as we have now learned, these things have to be given in balance. I mention just a few that I have used; there may be occasion for using one or other temporarily to buy time, but not on a regular basis.

Probiotics

Probiotics are preparations containing beneficial bacteria, primarily *Lactobacillus* plus *Streptococcus' Enterococcus* and also yeast. These are all lactic-acid-producing, non-pathogenic micro-organisms which have a major effect on birds' health, convalescence and breeding. The gastrointestinal tracts of birds maintain a delicate balance between 'good' and potentially harmful bacteria. The latter can cause disease if the body's natural defences are disturbed, triggered most often by stress, which results in changes in the conditions of the gut. Illness or the use of antibiotics will also disturb its condition. Multiplication of the toxin-producing bacteria can have a number of serious results. The cells of the beneficial bacteria must be:

(1) Present in large enough numbers to colonize the gut.
(2) Able to tolerate a wide range of pH (acidity/alkalinity).
(3) Grow at the same rate as their competitors.

Disturbances to the gut flora lead to poor digestion and consequent reduction in the absorption of nutrients, which compromises or weakens the bird. You might choose to flood the gut with these non-pathogenic bacteria which then produce the acidic conditions that are inhospitable to pathogens such as *Escherichia coli*. It is probably not necessary for this treatment to be ongoing because the bird can establish or re-establish its own natural bacterial flora when conditions in the gastro-intestinal tract have been made suitable by the introduction of the right organisms.

Probiotics can be used for the following purposes:

(1) Prevention of disease by routinely flooding the gut from time to time with non-pathogenic bacteria.
(2) Stabilization of the gut at times of stress, e.g. during travel, bullying, pairing, weaning, breeding.
(3) Initial introduction of beneficial flora to the virtually sterile gut of a hatching chick that has to be hand-reared, thus giving it a good start in life (or to combat the stress of change if a chick has to come in from the nest for hand-rearing).
(4) Balancing the gut flora after treatment with antibiotics or after illness.
(5) As a safer alternative for antibiotics in the treatment of many conditions affecting the gut. They cannot be used to treat clinical illness, although they are a very useful support during treatment.

Some complete off-the-shelf lory diets from around the world

Various proprietary brands of complete lory diets are available in different countries.

Table 11 A selection of complete off-the-shelf lory diets from around the world

Country	Proprietary Diet
Australia	Elliott's Wild Bird Nectar and Dry Food Mix
Germany	Nekton-Lori, Biotropic, Bio-Nektar
Holland	Lorinectar, Cedelory
New Zealand	Nekton-Lori
UK	Nekton-Lori, Aves Lorinectar (for adults), Loristart (for hand-rearing), Birdquest (both nectar and dry mix), Cedelory (for adults and hand-rearing), Aviplus
USA	Lories' Orchard, New Avico (both nectar and dry mix), Lories' Delight

Water

Public concern over the quality of drinking water has never been higher. Aviculturists also need to be vigilant. Some years ago I lost eight birds within a single month. I explored every possible avenue to no avail, before engaging the services of a 'public analyst for water' who solved the problem.

There are many sources of contamination. Domestic, industrial and agricultural waste are a few obvious ones. Chemicals are often added to water during treatment and some react with each other. There can be recontamination or leaks in the pipes before they reach our homes. Hundreds of chemicals, including some of those passed back into the water cycle by humans after medical treatment, are safely dissolved. There are a number, however, that are worrying and the amounts in the water are variable. Aluminium, lead, cadmium, copper, mercury, iron and zinc, trihalomethanes, nitrates, pesticides and herbicides are only safe when sufficiently diluted. Water that is 'unsafe' will be revealed by its effects, first on fish, then birds, babies and the elderly.

The main contaminants can be divided into four groups:

(1) Suspended solids.
(2) Dissolved metals and minerals.
(3) Synthetic organics.
(4) Microbes – this group includes parasites, bacteria and viruses.

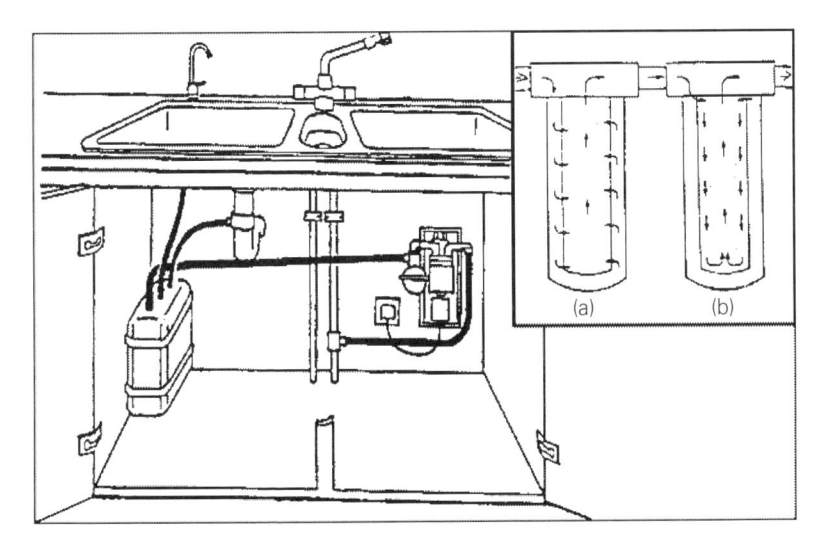

Fig. 14 This filtration unit has been specifically chosen to combine two filters: (a) For metals; (b) For bacteria.

My problem had been very worn iron mains pipes. I should have guessed by the colour – tan – of the inside of my normally white kettle. The bacteria count was also high. I may have worsened this situation by using an urn to boil up the lories' water, believing this would kill any bacteria. In practice quite the reverse happened: bacteria attached to particles of metal multiply faster in the time it takes to sufficiently cool the huge amount of water needed.

The solution is to filter but you first need to know what you want to filter out. I was advised by Hydropure of Cambridge to have a double cartridge, the first filtering against metals and other particles, and the second containing an ultraviolet light to kill the microbes. This water is then piped through a separate tap and is now drunk by us as well as the lories. These cartridges are changed at regular intervals.

8 Sexing

Visual sexing

A few species of lory are dimorphic, i.e. males and females can be recognized by differences in feathering. (Where this occurs it will be specified in the individual species sections.) Most, however, are monomorphic, i.e. the sexes cannot be distinguished visually. Nevertheless many people are able to sex birds correctly by differences in the beak and skull, or in behaviour and stance (males have a more upright posture than hens, which tend to crouch), etc. Certainly if you keep, or have kept, several of a species, or if you can see a number together, you will be right most of the time; but it is still 'best guess' because there are always 'borderline cases' which catch out even the most practised eye.

Surgical sexing

The advent of surgical sexing almost 20 years ago was one of the greatest boons to aviculture. It can be practised on birds from the age of about 12 weeks and identifies the sex both positively and immediately. It has the added advantage of enabling the condition of the gonads to be assessed at the same time, which indicates whether the bird is of breeding age, or likely to breed. A good veterinary surgeon can also judge, with the laparoscope, the condition of other organs, e.g. the air sacs (detecting, for instance, the presence of aspergillosis which shows up as a blue/green coating). It is best to have a split ring put on the bird at the same time, so that it will not have to undergo the operation again. Rings can either be put on different legs (e.g. right for cock, left for hen) or be of different colours (e.g. black for cock, gold for hen). The veterinary surgeon should issue a certificate with the bird's individual ring number. This can be passed with the bird like a passport if it is later sold. Alternatively, if the bird is already wearing a closed ring, the number can be noted and certificated by the vet in the same way.

A disadvantage of this method of sexing is the need to anaethetize the bird. This involves some risk, particularly if the bird is already under stress. To this you must also take into account the experience of the practitioner and his or her standards of hygiene. I like to have a couple of stitches put in the incision after the operation to avoid the possibility of disease entering. This method means the bird should be starved for 12 hours, or overnight, to be sure its crop is empty; this avoids any chance of food entering the lungs, which can have disastrous consequences.

The first time I had birds sexed with general anaesthetic, I found it traumatic to watch and stressful for the birds, which flailed around and took a long time to regain full consciousness. Birds can be put in a sort of straitjacket to protect them during this 'recovery' period – this was offered to me on another occasion – but I felt that would also be stressful. Gas-and-air on the other hand, particularly if the operation is done at home, offers little stress, or so I believe. (Catching up and travel always involves stress but this can be minimized by good conditions of transport, see Fig. 11, p. 46). Within seconds of being returned to a clean cage after surgical sexing, the birds should be back on the perch and eating.

Chromosomal sexing

This is also known as genetic sexing, blood-feather sexing, or karyotyping and has been available in the USA, where it is said to be 100 per cent reliable, for some 10 years. It can be done from about 4 weeks of age. The results take just over 3 weeks to come through. It involves taking a growing blood feather and sending it, by courier, because time is important, in a carrier medium to a laboratory where a cell culture is grown from the pulp of the feather shaft. A first wing or tail feather can be taken from a chick. A feather can be pulled with just a moment's pain from any adult; the replacement feather, which will grow in about 3 weeks, is then pulled and used. In the UK there were great hopes for this method when it arrived about six years ago, but unfortunately it did not prove reliable, although it is still practised in Germany.

DNA sexing

DNA sexing (see Fig. 15) was developed in the USA, using a DNA probe (a chemical molecule) in 1990 and is now available in the UK. Time is not of the essence and samples can be sent by ordinary postal service from anywhere in the world once you have obtained the kit. The test can be done at any age – my youngest were done at 10 days – and the results will be returned in usually just over 2 weeks. Taking the sample involves cutting a toenail and collecting a drop of blood in a capillary tube. This is placed in a tube of fluid, shaken well, and sent together with the forms giving ring number or other identification. The preserved DNA sample is digested with what are known as 'restriction enzymes', which chop the DNA into pieces. The treated DNA is then placed on agarose gel by

SEXING

Clip the nail about a third of the way up from the tip → **Collect a drop of blood in the capillary tube** → **Put the tube in the vial of fluid and shake until the blood comes out** → **Label the tube and send by ordinary mail**

NO COURIERS NEEDED

Extract the DNA

Digest the DNA with restriction enzymes

DNA fragments spread out on agarose gel by electrophoresis

After denaturing, single strands of DNA are transferred to a nylon membrane (Southern Blot)

Hybridization solution plus radioactive probe fixes the DNA and marks the target portions

THE RESULT — ♀ ♂ — Z / W

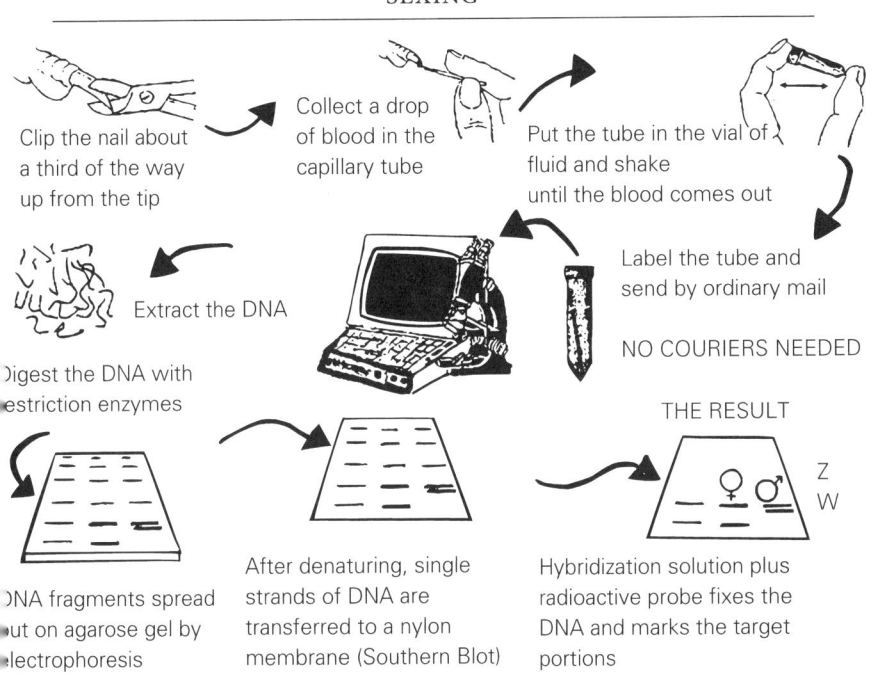

Fig. 15 DNA sex determination.

electrophoresis (through which an electric current is passed; this moves the segments according to their weight). Once the segments have been spread out, the DNA probe is used in the same way as a stain to identify the sequence it recognizes – in this case the ZZ chromosome of the cock or the WZ of the hen, which gives a clear distinction between the sexes.

On my first attempt at taking a sample, I found that the blood clotted in the capillary tubes while it was being collected. (The birds were three 10-day-old chicks that had been removed from the aviary for hand-rearing during renovations; the presence of veterinary assistance had given me the opportunity to test the method.) Warming the capillary tubes, I eventually found, prevented this. Bleeding is a concern, particularly with tiny chicks, and I would not take blood from such young birds again. They did become stressed because it took some time to stem the bleeding completely. Several times I thought it had stopped but, when they moved, it began again, despite the use of a silver nitrate stick and medicated powder. Afterwards probiotics were added to their feed and all was well by next morning. I feel quite confident with older birds in the future.

9 Breeding

Preparing to breed

The first consideration is to have a compatible pair of birds, of breeding age, which has been allowed enough time to settle together (see Chapter 6). Bear in mind that, if one bird is older, the breeding age of the younger will be brought forward by at least a year. Let us assume that the perches are secure, ready for a successful mating, and that ponds have fresh water so that the nest can be kept at the required humidity. Let us further assume that worming and de-lousing (if appropriate) have already been carried out in preparation. Let us even further assume that the birds appear, both in feather and behaviour, to be in breeding condition.

The next consideration is a good, balanced diet. With other types of birds we might expect to increase the vitamin E and calcium content of the feed prior to the breeding season. However, as there is no set season with lories, the best option might be to:

(1) Offer a good diet throughout the year.
(2) Increase vitamin E when you expect breeding might occur.
(3) Boost calcium periodically (e.g. with ColloCal D, from veterinary surgeons, or with Nekton MSA).

The onset of breeding can usually be detected not only by condition but by behaviour, in the form of increased 'showing off'. This is a good indication that mating and laying could ensue.

Mating displays

Displays include flashing eyes, clicking sounds, running back and forth on the perch puffed up, flapping the wings while standing very tall, arching the neck and hissing, and slow deliberate goose-steps along the perch, interspersed with billing, cooing and preening. This foreplay can go on for as long as two minutes. Copulation usually follows and may last up to one minute. The cock will circle round the hen with outspread wings, constantly jerking his head up and down. The female may do the same but, more usually, she will crouch, tail bent upwards. They may chase each other around, hissing and cheeping, before embracing, puffing out their feathers and preening, with pupils constantly dilating. This display is followed by deliberate slow mounting and copulation, which can be lengthy and may be accompanied by whimpering. Once copulation is over, there is more extensive mutual and self-preening.

If nothing happens

If no mating is observed and the pair sits at opposite ends of a perch or, e.g., some fighting over food occurs, etc., or mating is observed but no eggs are laid (in which instance we might assume that one or both birds are too young, eggs are being eaten or there is a more serious problem), action is called for. I would suggest trying to stimulate their interest by:

(1) Altering the position of the nest-box.
(2) Adding another nest-box of different dimensions with a different nest-hole.
(3) Changing the substrate and adding an extra chewing block.
(4) Removing the cock to a cage for a while (after a week or so, if all else fails).
(5) Surgically sexing the birds. If you have bought them on hearsay, this operation will not only conclusively prove the birds' sex and tell you a lot about their condition, but may also stimulate reproduction.
(6) Moving the pair to a different aviary. (This has proved successful for me, even at this late stage.)
(7) Changing partners.

Bear in mind that it is prudent never to have pairs of the same genus in adjoining aviaries.

Eggs and natural incubation

Incubation will not usually start until after the second egg is laid; indeed it may start a day or two later. I count the days from the laying of the second egg.

Egg-breaking and eating Sometimes a particular pair are known to break or eat eggs, in which case, as soon as the first egg is laid, it should be taken and kept in a cool place and a substitute china one put in the nest.

Turn the real egg, which should be marked with an 'X' and 'O' for the date and '1st', once daily. When the second egg, which should be marked '2nd', is laid, a second china one should be placed in the nest; both marked eggs should then be disinfected and placed in an incubator.

Non-sitting This occurs most commonly with birds which are laying for the first or second time. They exhibit the following behaviours:

(1) Failure to sit for a number of days.
(2) Sitting for some days then abandoning the nest.
(3) Coming off the eggs at the slightest excuse and leaving them unattended too long.

If potentially viable chicks are not to be lost, incubation or fostering may be necessary, although I feel that the parents should be allowed the opportunity to do the job themselves first.

An alternative is to put the real eggs in the incubator and watch the parents' behaviour with china eggs. Very often, by the end of the incubation period, by which time the damage would have been done to the real eggs, birds will be sitting tightly. At this point, the china eggs should be exchanged for the real eggs (which should be well rubbed in the nest material) when the chicks can be heard. There is a risk that the parents will fail to hatch the eggs (which would have almost certainly hatched in the incubator) but I give them the benefit of the doubt first time. My favourite method of switching a chick in its rubbed egg shell with a china one will probably *not* work with first-time birds.

One of my Moluccan hens (*Eos b. bornea*) simply would not sit at all for her first three clutches. There were no options except to foster, or incubate and hand-rear. It caused the cock, who was older, much consternation. Gradually, over a couple of years, the hen sat for longer periods and she has now become a model parent. One of my pairs of Black-capped Lories (*L. l. erythrothorax*) ate their chicks for the same number of clutches. By the fourth clutch I was beginning to despair, but allowed them to keep only one real egg and one china one (the other egg was fostered). We also kept extremely quiet in the aviary for several days around hatching time. The aviary may have become a bit dirty but it was worth it. They reared the one chick and, subsequently, have managed two. Who is to say that birds in the wild do not go through this learning process too?

Candling Candling the eggs is essential if you wish to monitor their progress. I do this at 10 days, when, even in bad light, I can tell without question whether or not eggs are fertile. If one is not, I replace it with a china one. The hen then becomes accustomed to two eggs. I can then check other nests and work out which other hen could have just *one* fertile egg, due to hatch at about the same time, and give her the fertile egg; in this way the original hen is given an opportunity to lay again sooner, in the hope that the next eggs will be fertile.

Fostering Choice of foster parent is made on the grounds of the hen being a reliable rearer. Thus, if it is important for a particular hen to produce an additional clutch, you need have no qualms about removing an egg.

Egg-binding may be a problem and this is dealt with in Chapter 14.

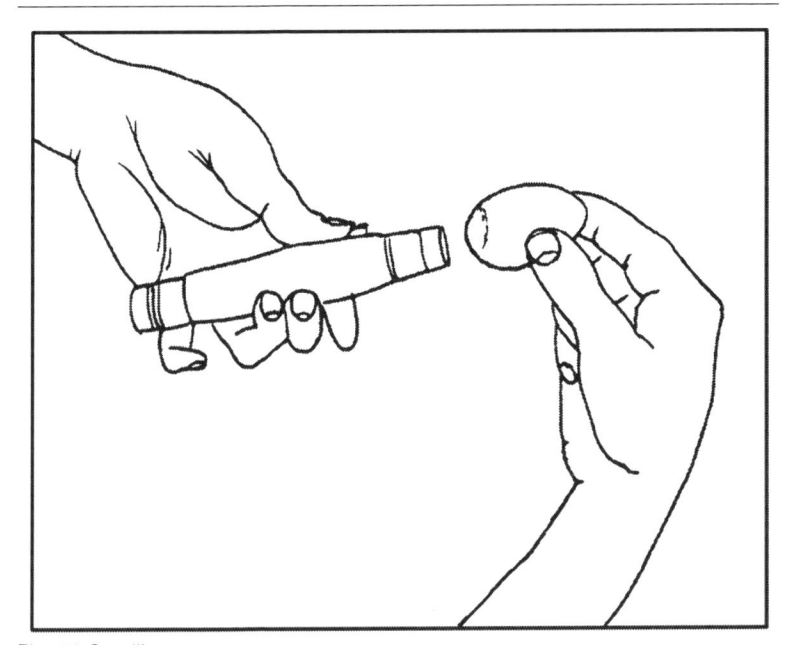

Fig. 16 Candling an egg.

Chicks

The parent's food consumption will probably go down for a day or two about the time that the chicks hatch. Sometimes chicks can be heard quite soon; at others not for a long while. Most of our birds come out of their nests when we do the twice-daily nectar rounds and, because the nests are positioned by the door, it is easy and quick to check a particular nest at that time. If the hen does not come off the nest, I do not disturb her. After about day 2, she will usually do so for a few moments. Around this time the food consumption will start to increase, or preferences for particular food items will develop. In any event, sponge is offered at one nectar feed and the usual bread at the other. Chicks appear to have almost nothing in their crops during this time but grow well.

When the hen comes off the nest again, I start very quick inspections; this has never worried the hens because they are used to it routinely. For the first couple of weeks the nest may need no attention. After that it may need topping up with clean substrate (with some of the old on top to maintain the right smell). After a few weeks a total clean-out will be necessary fairly frequently. I have three small honey buckets for this purpose: one for the dirty nesting, one containing fresh nesting, and one with tissue and plastic mesh in which to put the chicks. They all hang over one arm, leaving the other free.

Weak chicks Early-morning inspections seem particularly important. From time to time I have found one or two very cold, white chicks, too weak even to stand up. There is no way such chicks can be fed. You may well be in time and their swift removal to a heated brooder and, in due course, a drop or two of honey-water will do the trick. It is difficult to know whether then to return the chicks to the nest. I have done so but I think it is risky and usually prefer to keep them in for hand-rearing. Great care should be taken not to give such chilled chicks too much food; this is a shock to the system and can, in itself, kill.

Disappearing chicks This phenomenon is often associated with young parents and it is the newly hatched chick that disappears or is chewed; I believe it is the result of the adults being in too much of a hurry. Sometimes there is something amiss, e.g. the adults are not getting sufficient food. I had a case of a thoroughly reliable pair of Edwards (*Trichoglossus haematodus capistratus*) that, in error, gained access to the vitamin E intended for those pairs which had not started to lay by mid-season. At 4 weeks they just attacked and chewed up the baby. This was human error – but a salutary lesson to label the aviaries and not trust to memory.

Abandoned chicks Shortage of food, or something wrong with a chick, may cause it to be abandoned. The first sign may often be that one chick is being well cared for and another is not. The neglected chick will then lag further and further behind. If you cannot see anything obviously wrong, e.g. a broken leg, you may decide to bring the abandoned one in for hand-rearing or for supplementary feeding.

Supplementary feeding You can arrange to do this at the twice-daily feeds and leave the parents to do the rest. This worked out quite well in the case of some of my Black Lories (*Chalcopsitta a. atra*). I took the feeding tray into the aviary at 8.00am and 4.00pm. While the parents went out into the flight, I put the chicks on the tray and fed, cleaned and returned them all within a couple of minutes; although my activities were viewed through the pop-hole by the adults, all was harmonious. For this to be successful, your birds need to be accustomed to inspections.

Weight checks It can be useful to weigh chicks for a number of reasons:
(1) It helps the aviculturist get the feel of growth patterns.
(2) Comparative performances of different pairs can be gauged.
(3) Growth rates of siblings can be compared.
(4) Weight gains between parent-reared and hand-reared chicks can be compared.
(5) Early indications of potential ailments or disease can be recognized.

There is such individual variation between both individuals and cocks and hens, that I do not weigh religiously now unless I have a particular reason for doing so. Colour, demeanour, behaviour and crop performance tell me far more. One summer I had two chicks of different species, both with abnormally tiny crops. There was no way they could match their siblings' intake or growth. One came in for hand-rearing and was given extra feeds and the other received supplementary feeding in the nest. Our concern was to get them to independence when they could feed *ad lib*. A graph on either of these pairs of young would have merely been frightening; it took about 6 months to level out but their weight is now indistinguishable from that of other chicks and they can only be recognized by their coloured rings. Of course you will only know what is an average weight for your birds if you have weighed enough chicks at various ages and of different species, and have kept records for reference.

Fig. 17 For weighing chicks, choose scales that weigh to the nearest gram. The tray has sides for safety and is lined with plastic mesh (Netlon).

Cold-weather chicks A number of lories breed in the winter. The parents have an inbuilt clock that is no respecter of season and, regardless, they will tight-brood for only about 10 days. With regular winter-breeders you can buy yourself more time by:

(1) Placing the nest in the house.
(2) Heating the house.
(3) Providing below-nest heating (see Fig. 6, p. 30) for delicate species.
(4) Bringing chicks in at about 9 days for hand-rearing.

Feather-plucking This is an all-too-common occurrence with many species. No one is yet sure why some individuals pluck themselves and/or their young, but it is a major reason for chicks having to be hand-reared. Certain species always seem to do it and you eventually learn how long you can safely leave the young with the parents. Two rules apply:

(1) Take the chicks sooner rather than later; once the wing tips have been damaged, they will never fly.
(2) If circumstances make hand-rearing such birds impossible, and you have a pair who pluck their young, place them elsewhere. There are plenty of people who do not mind hand-rearing chicks.

Fledging

Vigilance is needed at this time. The birds may all fledge successfully but a number of things can be done to obviate any problems.

(1) Note before dusk whether chicks have returned to the nest. They probably will not do so and should therefore be shut in for a few nights at this stage.
(2) Place extra pots of nectar and pieces of fruit near the nest and perches.
(3) Introduce extra perching, particularly leafy branches, at the far end of their aviary until they have completely mastered the art of flying.
(4) Usually, about a couple of weeks after fledging, the chicks will become independent. It can be dangerous to leave them any longer with the parents because one, usually the cock, may turn on a youngster and kill it. On the other hand the only way I can stop one pair of mine constantly laying is to leave the fledged young with them for some months. In this particular instance the young are quite safe, but only experience with the individual birds can tell you this.
(5) The time to separate the young must be judged individually. When the time comes, they can be placed in an aviary of their own, or in a group of birds of about the same age in an aviary new to all of them. I keep a couple of big aviaries especially for this purpose because I think this adolescent time of socializing is very important psychologically. Plenty of toys should be available.
(6) The time comes when a pecking order develops among the young birds, usually in late Autumn, if it is a mixed sex group, or the following Spring, if it is a single-sex group. This is the time to move them on to a new home or new mates.

10 Incubation

Reasons to incubate

There are many good reasons to incubate:
(1) Death or illness of a parent bird.
(2) Failure of young parent birds to sit, or to sit tightly enough.
(3) As a precaution when laying occurs in freezing conditions.
(4) After a hen has been egg-bound and brought in to lay.
(5) If you are expecting a disturbance, e.g. bonfire night, next-door's party.
(6) Pulling (removing eggs for fostering or artificial rearing) in order to gain extra clutches, e.g. in the case of rare blood-lines.
(7) For the handler to gain experience of the subject.
(8) Comparison.

Choice and management of incubators and hatchers

Incubators can be home-made, very sophisticated and expensive, or somewhere inbetween. The bottom line is that you understand your equipment and can trust it dependably to produce chicks. Size, price and ease of cleaning are considerations. One thing is certain: no serious aviculturist can afford to be without one. The most advanced and currently popular are those with a fan to move air and automatic turning (which is said to be more accurate). I use the old-fashioned, still-air type. I have two which run the whole time so they are ready whenever needed. They are the small, basic, manual-turning Brinsea models, which are not expensive to purchase (or run). I can thus afford two and a spare for the price of one sophisticated model, and I have always found them to be very reliable. Of the two, one runs as an incubator at 37.4°C (99.32°F) and the other as a hatcher at 36.5°C (97.7°F). Constant opening is to be avoided as it alters temperature and humidity. Choose a model with a good viewing window. The room in which these appliances are housed should stay at a fairly constant temperature for success. If it is too damp a de-humidifier can be used. Once, while my home was being renovated, my incubators had to be housed where there was excessive damp; my lory eggs, hitherto successful, failed to hatch but my Hawaiian Geese had their best season

– which taught me a valuable lesson. I have used other incubators – ones that fluctuated regularly in temperature, ones that were reliable most of the time but then surged, and others that were, for me, too technical, with too much that could go wrong. I found the last type required me to give more of my attention to the science of their management than to my birds. I realize many people would enjoy this challenge but I prefer to keep things simple. Whatever your preference, the yardstick is: will it regularly produce viable chicks?

Requirements of the egg

Temperature Eggs must be kept at an accurate constant temperature, with minimal or no variation. Electronic thermometers are said to be the most accurate but all thermometers vary. I use the maximum/minimum type and suggest placing two in each incubator, in different positions. Several times a year I run checks by inserting a control thermometer.

Humidity The level of humidity is important because a steady rate of water evaporation should take place from the egg into the atmosphere. This ensures that the air sac is the correct size just before hatching. A wet-bulb thermometer is the most accurate means of measuring humidity (but remember to keep the wick germ-free). Alternatively a hygrometer or humidity dial can be placed in the incubator or hatcher.

Turning With an automatic-turning incubator the grid must be set for the particular size of eggs to be incubated. The eggs must be moved to a hatcher at the appropriate time, or the incubator must be taken off its rotating base.
  Manual turning should be done as quickly as possible to maintain heat. Eggs should be turned in alternate directions through 180° to avoid 'winding up' the coil (chalaza) in the egg. An odd number of turns (e.g. 3, 5 or 7 per day) will ensure that the egg does not lie on the same side every night (when it is left for longer).

Water Use either distilled or filtered water to maintain humidity. It should be at a suitable temperature and should contain a solution which will inhibit the growth of micro-organisms.

Hygiene Each egg should be cleaned before it is placed in the incubator and the incubator should be cleaned after each batch of eggs and after each hatch.

Powercuts To safeguard against these I use an inverter attached to a

12-volt battery and this will hold the temperature for a couple of hours. You need to know the total wattage of the appliances you wish to attach to the inverter. The more you add the less time it will operate for, and some appliances may overload it completely. With one small incubator, one small hatcher and one small brooder the temperature will be maintained for 2 hours. Two of these appliances can be run for about 4 hours and one for almost 6 hours. To my cost I have learned that you need to run the inverter through a surge-breaker plug. Lastly, a simple alarm attached to the above will alert you to any cuts which occur at night.

Growth within the egg

The ideal weight loss from an egg during the period of incubation is about 14 per cent. On approximately the following days you should see:

Day 7	Tiny red circle of minute veins (if you have good eyes).
Day 12	Network of veins visible down one side of the egg.
Day 16	The whole egg covered with a mesh of veins.
Day 21	The available air space solidly filled.
Day 24–25	Air space has increased and hatching should be imminent.

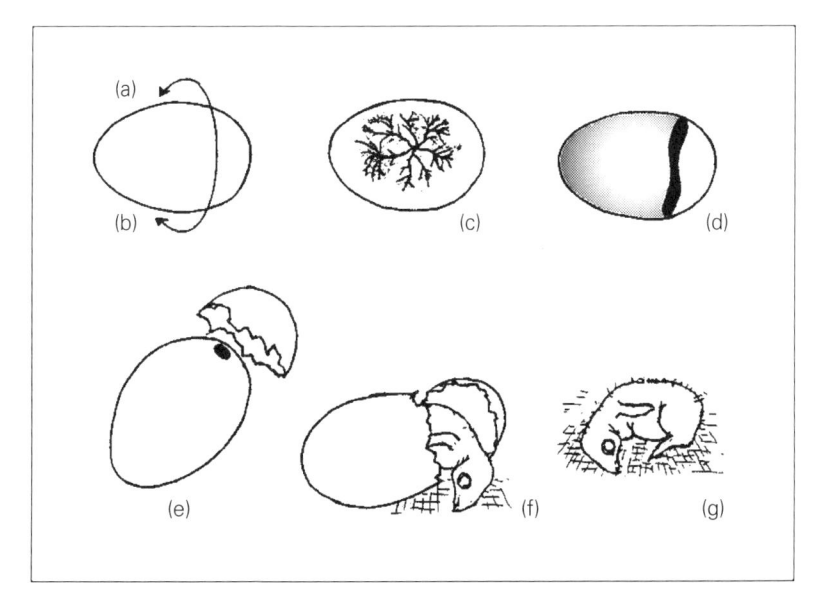

Fig. 18 Stages in the development of the egg: (a) and (b) Alternate directions for rotating the egg. (c) Growth within the egg at about 10 days (as seen with a candler). (d) Growth within the egg at 23–25 days (as seen with a candler). (e) Capping. (f) Emerging chick. (g) Newly hatched chick.

At this point the beak may be seen trying to break into the air space. If nothing further has occurred in, e.g., 24 hours or so, intervention *may* be called for but is *not* recommended unless you have experience. It is better to find someone who, in the event of an emergency, will come and assist you. You will learn much from this. (On rare occasions the beak may be seen breaking through the blunt end; this can result in the chick drowning.) Occasionally the beak comes through the membrane but can get no further, either because the air space is too large or because the chick is too exhausted. If, after 12 hours, there is no further progress, intervention may save the situation; otherwise the chick may run out of oxygen. Check the state and colour of the veining before proceeding further.

If the atmosphere in the incubator has been too dry the weight loss from the egg will have been too rapid. This can result in the air space becoming too large and the membrane too dry, necessitating assistance. Conversely, if it is too humid, there will have been insufficient weight loss, the air space will be too small, and the chick will not be able to reach it. It will therefore pip below it and probably drown. It is not feasible to adjust the humidity in the incubator for the sake of one particular egg and thus jeopardize the others. I run my incubator in an average-to-dry state and the hatcher at maximum humidity.

Candling, capping and china eggs

Candling This should be done at approximately 2-day intervals to:
(1) Monitor growth in the egg.
(2) Assess fertility or non-fertility.
(3) Detect any dead embryos, these should be removed from the incubator as soon as possible to avoid possible contamination of other eggs.
(4) Note when hatching is imminent so that eggs can be removed to the hatcher.
(5) Discover whether there is a problem with hatching. It may be time to think about intervention or taking up an experienced friend's offer of help.

Capping Make a collection of 'caps' from infertile eggs. You can prise them open (by pin-pricking all the way round first), then, after emptying the contents, thoroughly sterilize them. After thorough drying they can be stored for emergencies (see p. 77). This collection should consist of different sizes of egg, varying in shape from tips to three-quarter egg shells (see Fig. 18).

China eggs I keep these in two sizes and store a few of each in a pot in the incubator so that they are warm for emergencies.

Intervention

'Assistance box' Be prepared for emergencies with a box of essential 'tools'. These should include:
> Small tray (such as a seed-container with sides in which layers of warmed tissue can be inserted)
> Sterilized needle
> Tweezers
> Caps of various sizes
> Small pot for boiled water
> Fine paint-brush
> Spray for warm water
> Sticky tape

Assisting the hatch More than one drop of blood spilled can mean disaster, so work slowly using your candler and the 'assistance box'. With a sterilized needle make a tiny hole in the air-sac space near the chick's beak. Check the condition of the membrane and veins: they should not be bright red but dry out and appear slightly brown at hatching. If the hole is not big enough, carefully remove one small piece of shell at a time with the tweezers. Return the egg to the warm base between each move. If the membrane is dry or tight it may have to be opened right at the point where the beak has been pushing in vain for some time. This is enough for now; place either a tiny square of sticky tape or a cap over the hole, spray one side of the egg with water and return it to the hatcher.

In a couple of hours the procedure can be repeated, possibly removing another piece of shell and another tiny piece of membrane so that the beak and cere show. At any hint of blood, stop. At this stage, if you can, dampen the membrane, avoiding the beak and nostrils. An hour or three later, hatching may be successful but, if not, remove more shell and, if possible, release a little membrane; it may be tight or stuck, so work away carefully with your paint brush. If the chick's head is through and it appears lethargic, a drop of water may revitalize it. Simply tickling the side of the beak with the paint brush should encourage the swallowing action. At this point the temptation is to go too fast. The chick will come to no harm in the short term, as long as it receives a drop of water every few hours to combat dehydration and the membrane is dampened periodically. If you go too fast now you may find the yolk is not all absorbed. I have left chicks happily overnight in this state and resumed loosening the membrane from the chick's body in the morning with no ill effect, whereas I have lost them by going too fast. If I need to work on one egg in a hatcher containing others, I quickly spray the upper side of the other eggs with some cooled boiled water before shutting the lid.

Most hatchers or incubators have a mesh grid on which the eggs are positioned and I once found a chick with its leg stuck. Since then I have

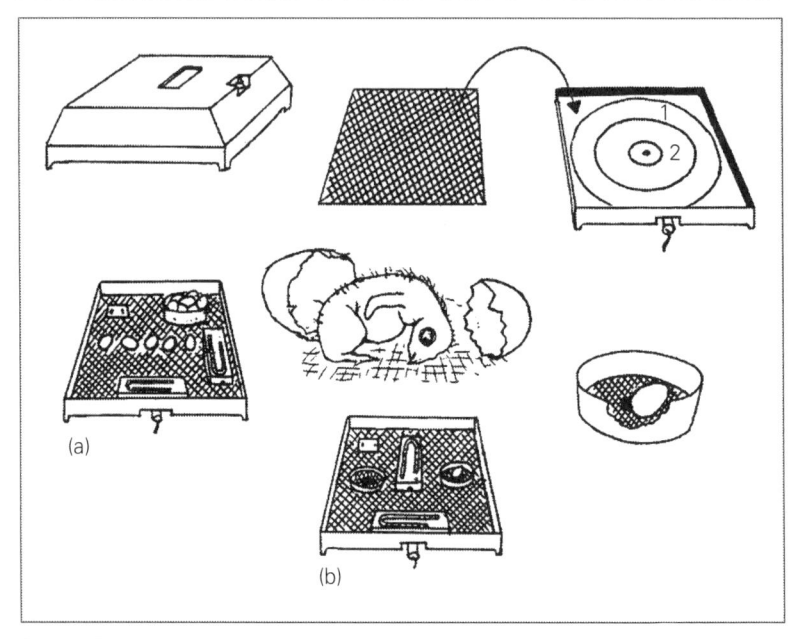

Fig. 19 The incubator/hatcher has two channels (marked 1 and 2) in its base for water: (a) Contains little or no water, two maximum/minimum thermometers, a humidity dial and a pot of standby china eggs. (b) Contains the maximum amount of water (pots of water can be inserted if more is required) and hatching pots with plastic mesh in the base above the hole.

always put hatching chicks on netlon in a hatching pot. This has the advantage of:

(1) Keeping the chick safe.
(2) Allowing the chick some foothold, so that its legs do not splay.
(3) Containing the chick in one readily visible position.
(4) Avoiding contamination of the rest of the grid.

Hatching

I move chicks to the hatcher when their beaks are just pushing the membrane, or when I calculate that hatch day is imminent. This calculation is based on my records and observations via the candler.

Once the chick has hatched, by whatever method, it can safely be left in the hatching pot unless it is to go under an experienced hen. If this is the case, now is the time to move it, complete with egg shell, which should be rubbed in the nest substrate. Position it in the place of one of the two china eggs, or beside an already hatched chick which is not too different

INCUBATION

in age. If, however, the newly hatched chick is staying in, it should be transferred after some 12 hours to a brooder kept at about 36.5°C (97.7°F). Move it in a padded rearing pot with tissue covered by the plastic mesh (Netlon) at the bottom. This will:

(1) Provide a foothold.
(2) Protect the feet from any ill effects of the tissue.
(3) Keep the chick and its feet dry.
(4) Enable the state of the droppings to be checked between feeds (the plastic mesh and tissue should be changed at this time).

Now is the time for the first tiny feed. Nothing is required other than a warmed bent spoon. Care, now and at all stages of hand-feeding, is required in order to avoid damaging the sides of the beak. This may lead to candidiasis at a later date. Refer to Chapter 7 for suggested hand-rearing diets.

You should aim to reduce the temperature (36.5°C/97.7°F) a degree at a time so that chick will be feathered by the time room temperature is reached. The chick can then be removed before fledging from a warm brooder to a cooler one (if younger chicks are now around) and from there to a fledging cage. To the cool brooder and the fledging cage, introduce a fledging perch (see Fig. 8, p. 34) to encourage perching. Other perches should be included in this cage and the addition of an open-fronted nest, which I find chicks love experimenting with, will accustom them to use a nest before they are removed to an aviary.

11 Hand-rearing

Reasons for hand-rearing

(1) *Poor parenting.* Perhaps the chick is being left too long and becoming chilled, or not being fed properly, or even being attacked.
(2) *Death of a parent.* The remaining bird will sometimes rear the chick or sometimes not, or will rear it only for a short while, so close observation is required.
(3) *To obtain multiple clutches.* In the case of rare birds or blood-lines, this may be desirable.
(4) *Better nourishment.* Inspection may show that the chicks are constantly not being adequately fed, despite plenty of food being available. First try supplying additional types of food but, if a short time later, the chicks are not being adequately fed, it may be necessary to remove them because they may die.
(5) *To observe, learn about and compare clutches.*

Consider keeping common species when starting with lories, and always keep several. Thus there is less chance of an endangered specimen being lost because of inexperience. I aim to have in a batch of hand- and parent-reared young in my adolescents' flight which can only be distinguished by their temporary coloured rings.

Brooders

Types As with incubators, the type of brooder is relatively unimportant as long as it fulfils some provisos:
(1) It should be reliable with minimal fluctuations in temperature.
(2) There should be a facility for circulating fresh air. (Forced air dries the skin.)
(3) It should be possible to increase the humidity if required. (This may only be possible with a brooder which does not allow adequate ventilation.)
(4) The heat source should come from the back or side.

Currently none of those available in the UK has a suitable heat source.

HAND-REARING

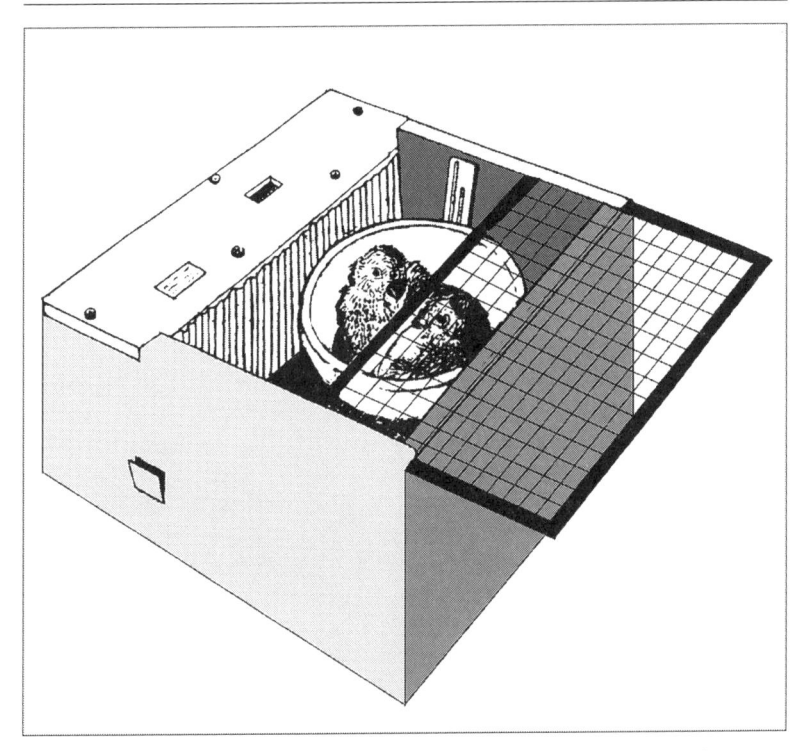

Fig. 20 Chicks in a brooder. The heat comes from the back and there are adjustable ventilation laps at the side. The lid can be of mesh or Perspex, or both. There is a maximum/minimum thermometer and, for added protection, a grid between the chicks and the heat source.

I have adapted a small hospital cage, which, when laid on its back (see Fig. 20), has the heat source at the back. By placing their pot next to but not against the heat source, chicks can decide whether to stay close to or away from the heat. With top or bottom heat they have no choice.

Make some provision, even if it is only a towel, to keep the brooder dark. This is important when bringing in slightly older chicks which will be distressed in full light. With two brooders, you can run one at a higher temperature than the other. The hotter one can be used for young chicks and the cooler for birds which are about to be transferred to the fledging cage.

Temperature The heat source in my brooder is two light bulbs. From experience I know that, if one blows, the other burns more brightly and somewhere near the required heat is maintained. As a precaution I change the bulbs each month, keeping the old ones for house use. A maximum/minimum thermometer is kept in the brooder and thus I know that this simple appliance maintains a constant temperature, and is easily regulated. The temperature of the room housing the brooder is best kept as even as possible and should never drop below 15.5°C (60°F). Controlling heat in the summer has been a problem but the insertion of a roof window has helped to overcome this.

Fig. 21 Chick with a full crop. Support the chick by encircling it with the thumb and forefinger. Slide a finger under its feet when transporting it back to the brooder after feeding.

Ventilation My brooder has ventilation holes each side which can be open or closed and, because of their position, the chicks get no draught. The old Perspex front is now the lid, so fresh air can be drawn from above and we have made a wire grid which slides in under this for added two-way protection.

Humidity I have never needed to increase this. On the only occasion I found a chick panting (I had introduced it from the aviaries and the temperature of the brooder was too high for it) I simply cooled the brooder a little and gave the chick a drink of water so that it would not dehydrate. If necessary, a pot of water with a fungal growth inhibitor added, and a mesh cover, could be placed in the brooder.

Rearing formulas

The water with which you make the formula is important; filtered water is ideal, or bottled water. Tap water can be dangerous. In the UK the electrolyte Lactated Ringers (or Paedialyte in the USA) can be used for the first few feeds, plus a special paediatric probiotic, e.g. Avipro Paediatric (UK). Chicks could also be started off with boiled rice water. Although I have not used it at this stage, I have used it for chicks brought in with upsets of one kind or another because it is easy to digest.

The formula which I currently use is given on pp. 54–5. Although weight gains of birds on this formula do not quite match that of parent-reared chicks until around fledging, the feathering is now, in nearly all cases, just as good. For several years I used a proprietary brand of rearing food with fairly good results; weight gains matched those of parent-reared chicks although feathering did not. Suddenly, however, the chicks stopped doing well on it; they showed variations in feather colour suggesting liver damage and I lost one or two. I believe there had been some small change in the overall nutrient balance, or perhaps it was just in my batch. A friend had mentioned a similar experience the previous year on this formula, but at that time I was still satisfied with it. Previously I had fed Heinz Bone and Beef Broth, Heinz Pure Fruit, Farex and, once a day, Abidec drops; the formula was made very weak to begin with and, later, adult nectar was added gradually. Prior to that I had added Casilan to increase the protein, but chicks made extremely poor growth compared with parent-reared ones and most died, usually at about 1 month old. I found it interesting that of three birds that I bought over the years from a breeder who also used Casilan, but in smaller amounts than I did, all died before maturity. We now know that, whereas it is thought safe for adult birds, it is lethal to youngsters and, for this reason I believe that it is best avoided altogether.

A rearing formula has to satisfy the chicks but it must not be too rich or it will cause problems later, with either the liver or the feathers. Sometimes, for example, we see Blue-streaked Lories that are a brick colour instead of bright red; this happened with a pair of mine which was never quite right. This colour change, I feel, makes its own statement about the diet, of the parents and the chicks. Hand-rearing is a commitment but it should be kept straightforward and should occupy no more time than is necessary to do the job well (see also Table 12).

Feed will be absorbed by the chick more quickly early in the day than later on. For this reason the intervals between morning feeds should be

Table 12 Hand-rearing regimen

Day (hatching)	Week	Food temp. °C (°F)	Number of feeds per day	Interval (hours)	Feeding times
1	–	36.1 (97)	Nothing for 12 hrs, then 2-hourly	2	2-hourly
2	–	35.6 (96)	7	3	6am, 9am, 12 noon, 3pm, 6pm, 9pm, 12 midnight
4	–	35.0 (95)	6	3–3½	7am, 10am, 1.30pm, 4pm, 7.30pm, 11pm
8	1	34.4 (94)	5	3–4½	7.30am, 10.30am, 2pm, 6.30pm, 11pm
14	2	32.2 (90)	4	4–6	7.30am, 11.30am 4.30pm, 10.30pm
21	3	29.4 (85)	4	4–6	7.30am, 11.30am, 4.30pm, 10.30pm
28	4	26.7 (80)	4	4–6	7.30am, 11.30am, 4.30pm, 10.30pm
35	5	23.9 (75)	4	4–6	7.30am, 11.30am, 4.30pm, 10.30pm
42	6	21.1 (70)	4	4–6	7.30am, 11.30am, 4.30pm, 10.30pm
49	7	18.3 (65)	4	4–6	7.30am, 11.30am, 4.30pm, 10.30pm
56	8	15.6 (60)	3	4–7½	8am, 12 noon, 7.30pm
63	9	12.8 (55)	3	4–7½	8am, 12 noon, 7.30pm
70	10	10.0 (50)	2	8½	8am, 4.30pm

shorter than those of evening feeds. I feel the relatively long night-time rest is beneficial to the system of even quite young chicks.

Management

It has been said that hand-reared chicks will not make breeding birds. I have not found this to be the case and believe it is much more to do with the management during hand-rearing. Whenever possible, rear more than one chick at a time and, however much you are tempted, do not spend too much time encouraging a bond between yourself and the chick.

Generally speaking chicks in a brooder should be touching each other – not panting or shivering. They should be a good pink colour – not white and certainly not deep pink/purple. Healthy chicks appear cheerful and may or may not be vocal. They need not all be the same size. A tiny chick will stay relatively warmer in the presence of older ones and cope happily with slightly less heat. After the age of, e.g., one week, you need not worry unduly about larger chicks treading on a smaller one. Provided that the smaller one is strong and standing well, it will struggle to get in the middle where it is warmer. Alternatively, if a chick is really tiny and the others are several weeks old, but not ready to be moved to a cooler brooder, it can be placed in a tiny pot with a china egg on which to rest its neck; this should be placed right next to the heat and the older chicks should be moved away from it. In a few days the tiny one may well be strong enough to join the older ones. You could also select the smallest of the larger chicks to move in with the tiny one for company.

Feeding Despite a comfortable ambient temperature it may be a good idea to hang a lamp above your feeding table so tiny chicks do not chill while feeding.

The tiniest chick will feed well from a warmed, bent spoon but take care not to damage the soft sides of the beak, thus increasing the chance of candidiasis. The formula should be maintained at 40°C (104°F). Stir it before feeding and note the temperature (stirring is essential if the formula has been warmed in a microwave oven, because of hot spots) or test it on the lip (I am told it is possible to spread candidiasis to the chicks in this way) or on the inside of the elbow or use a thermometer. If food is too hot chicks may get burned; at worst this will cause irreparable damage to the crop or, at best, it will put them off feeding. If food is too cold they just will not accept it and will thus go short. I prepare two trays: a seed tray lined with Netlon and with sides 3.75cm (1½in) high to protect chicks from falls, and a tray bearing a tin or bottle of prepared formula, a bent spoon, two small pots for the food and two jugs (one of hot, boiled and filtered water and the other of cold, boiled and filtered water). This enables me to top up the formula with dry mix and water as

LORIES AND LORIKEETS

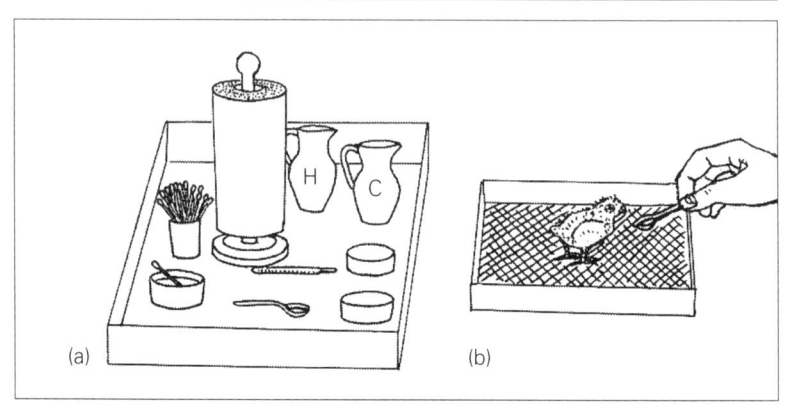

Fig. 22 Hand-rearing utensils: (a) Tray containing two jugs for hot boiled water and cooled boiled water, a roll of kitchen towel, cottonwool buds, a pot with water and a cottonwool bud for cleaning, two food-pots (in case food needs cooling) and, important where several chicks are to be fed, a bent spoon and a thermometer with which to check the temperature of the food. (b) Plant tray with low sides and plastic mesh on the base to provide purchase for the birds' feet.

necessary to gain the right temperature. I mix up a fresh amount for each chick, tipping unused formula into the second pot, for later addition to the nectar of adult lories.

Cleanliness Also in the tray is a roll of kitchen towel for mopping up spills and some cottonwool buds and a pot of warm water for cleaning each chick before it is placed in a prepared clean tub after the feed. Some people wrap up chicks in tissue or towel but, as many chicks prefer to be fed while standing with their wings outstretched, I allow them to do this. When I have wrapped them in towel the chicks have still become sticky, and I have still had to clean food off with cottonwool buds, as well as having towels to wash. Everything is washed after each feed and, once a day, cleaned more thoroughly in Milton solution. As the chicks get bigger, faeces will be sprayed onto the sides of the pots and even the inside of the brooder. As a precaution, I always wash my hands with Hibiscrub or Phisohex before handling chicks or eggs.

Base Netlon is a rigid plastic mesh and makes an ideal base because it:
(1) Enables even the tiniest chick to stand without splaying its legs.
(2) Keeps the chicks clean because faeces drop through it.
(3) Keeps the chicks, especially their feet, dry.
(4) Allows droppings to be clearly monitored through it.

At all stages during rearing, from the hatching tub, to the rearing tubs (the sizes of which are increased with age), to the cage, and when they are being weighed or fed, my chicks stand on Netlon. It can be bought from garden centres, in rolls or by the meter, and cut to size. I buy the smallest gauge. It is easily washed after each feed and lasts for years. The pots in the brooder are lined with tissue beneath plastic mesh (Netlon); for larger chicks, shavings are put beneath both. (Chicks that stand directly on shavings are at some risk of ingesting it and faeces from the shavings tend to adhere to the skin.) If they stand on tissue, their feet may become irritated and bleed, thus allowing the entry of infection. If they stand on, e.g., old handkerchief or sheet, there is a risk of a thread tightening on a leg; I have seen this necessitate the intervention of a vet.

The crop Each bird's crop should be monitored before every feed. If the crop is not empty, on no account feed more. It could be that:

(1) Too much was given at the previous feed.
(2) Insufficient time has elapsed since the last feed.

Fig. 23 Spoon-feeding, showing the bent spoon and the ring made by the thumb and forefinger to secure the chick while not pressing on the crop. The plastic mesh in the tray prevents the chick sliding about or splaying its legs.

(3) The temperature of the brooder has dropped, chilling the chick and slowing digestion.
(4) The chick is unwell, in which case other symptoms will soon become apparent.

In each case water, as specified on p. 85, should be given – just ½–3 teaspoonfuls depending on the chick's size. This should help dilute and disperse the food and prevent dehydration in the interim.

Occasionally I have brought in from the aviaries a chick with an impacted crop, in which case I just feed honey-water and massage the crop gently until the food has all dispersed, ideally within 24 hours.

When chicks first come in and join the others, it can be hard to judge how much food to give, and any change can be upsetting. In such an instance food may be found in the crop at the second or third feed. It is best to play safe and give water and/or honey-water, in place of the normal ration for a chick of that size, until it has settled.

Faeces Pay attention to the nature of the faeces. You can tell so much from them and thus avoid problems if you act quickly. Any change in colour or consistency should be noted. Chicks freshly in from the aviaries invariably pass faeces of a worrying blackish colour with all sorts of bits but, if all is well, they will return to what is normal for a hand-reared chick within about 36 hours.

Late chicks Bringing in chicks after about 4 weeks can be stressful for them and you. Out of fear and what appears to me to be resentment they may bite, refuse to eat, cower and growl. It helps to keep them in as dark a place as possible but it is worrying because they must have fluid. Usually, within a day, they will be eating well. Affection lavished on them at this time only makes matters worse. I have found that letting them stand in a tray watching another chick can help, or I may try to feed them first and, if they refuse, try again after the last chick has been fed. The other chicks communicating with me, I feel sure, is picked up by the new one and gradually inspires confidence. There are not always problems. I have had chicks come in and take to hand-rearing right away, in which case, for their own good, they have to be restrained.

Probiotics and chicks

I had not used probiotics when hand-rearing until fairly recently, when I decided to hand-rear two clutches from the egg, giving probiotics to one but not the other. Little difference was noted although probiotics may well act as a safeguard against trouble, or an aid with less than strong chicks. At a different time parent-reared clutches from these two pairs were weighed for comparison. There were only slight variations: all the hand-reared ones were just a little lighter but, by fledging time, they were within the range of normal. The hand-reared ones were considerably lighter on the then current formula compared with young from these pairs when fed on my old proprietary formula. Their feathering, however, was infinitely better. You can so often tell a hand-reared specimen by its lack of feather gloss. I now feel this is mainly to do with the formula, although management, in particular of feather cleanliness and whether there is enough fresh air in the brooder, also come into it.

Three older chicks were subjected to an unforseen move and this caused stress which resulted in stomach upset in the form of green droppings. I reduced their feed to honey-water with electrolytes and probiotic for a couple of days, then alternated this with normal formula for another 3 days, by which time they had recovered. Similarly, in the case of three 10-day-old chicks which appeared stressed and miserable after having their nails clipped for DNA sexing, I just added probiotic to the normal formula for one day. A few years ago many chicks would have been treated with a broad-spectrum antibiotic. Now we realize the potential hazards of such treatment, probiotics can be seen as a safer and more beneficial option. Naturally there are occasions when they will not be suitable.

Weighing

Choose scales that are graduated to the nearest gram, possibly ones that will also read in ounces. Weighing should be performed at the same time every day, or every 2 days, as preferred, and prior to the feed. If you wish, you can then weigh after the feed in order to determine how much has been consumed. Weight will be lost in various circumstances:

(1) At the approach of weaning.
(2) When a chick has just been brought in from the nest.
(3) If the diet is inadequate in composition or quantity.
(4) If the temperature is wrong causing lack of appetite or digestion.
(5) During illness.

Weighing is a guide, but there is a wide variation from the average between both individuals and sexes. Chicks that start growing slowly can catch up later and vice versa (see Fig. 24). Nevertheless weight records, when viewed in conjunction with appearance, colour, demeanour, appetite, droppings and temperature, help to build a picture of a bird's condition and can give an early warning.

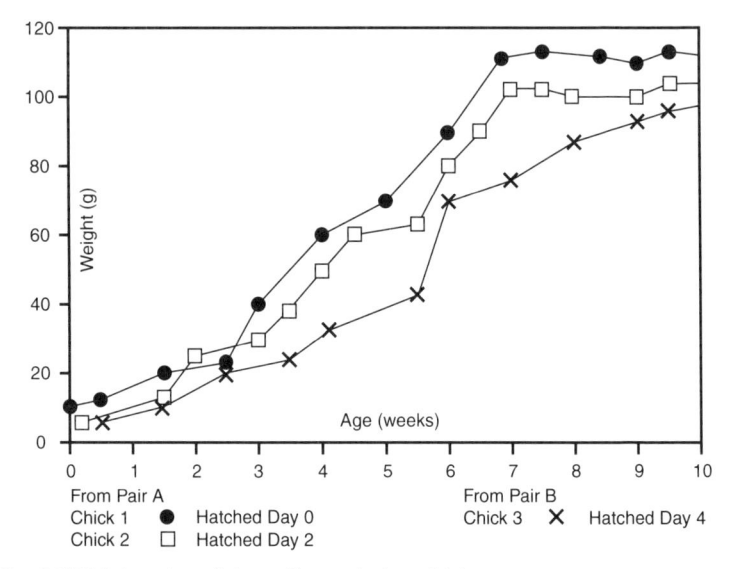

Fig. 24 Weight gains of three *Eos reticulata* chicks.

Records

Records can be kept in various ways. I put a sticky notelet onto the brooder for each chick and these can be changed or updated as required. Details are transferred to a logbook each night and, once a year, the relevant material is transferred to studbooks. The logbook helps you compare, over the years, how you dealt with situations, problems and treatment, what worked and what did not, alterations to feed, weights, fledging times – and much more.

Ringing

Ringing (or banding) is increasingly accepted by serious aviculturists as essential for identifying birds and closed rings are proof of captive breeding. The age at which rings are applied varies slightly and this will affect the size of ring selected. In this book it is assumed that close ringing will normally take place between days 10–15. In the UK there has seemed relatively little information on this subject as far as lories are concerned and the sizes hitherto quoted for the various species has varied enormously. This has led to confusion and maybe even some reluctance to ring chicks. I have collected data concerning the sizes recommended for the various species in the UK, Europe and in the USA, and details are given for each species in Part II. The UK ring manufacturer J & E Bandings can now provide all types of ring for all species of lory. Application techniques are shown in Fig. 25. The right size of closed ring is important. If it is too small it will eventually restrict the blood supply to the foot. If it is too large it can fall off or get caught, e.g. on wire. If it is too wide, dirt can get trapped and rubbed into the skin (I know of one bird which lost a leg in this way).

Split rings can be applied at any age for identification purposes, e.g. after sexing, males and females can be ringed on different legs or with different coloured rings. These rings can be removed fairly easily. The 'Swiss Institute' rings have tangential pins which afford better security.

Coloured plastic rings are useful for identifying chicks at a glance. Make sure that they do not become tight as the bird grows. They can easily be removed at any stage.

Transport

If chicks are accustomed to being transported from a young age they will not find it stressful but any change or move will prove stressful to older chicks. While they are being moved a suitable temperature must be maintained. For short journeys a polystyrene box containing a warm hot-water-bottle covered with mesh, so that the chicks do not come in direct contact with it, can be used. In emergencies I have also used a tiny open-fronted box secured next to my body. Portable brooders can now be bought or your own brooder can be used in your car with the aid of an inverter, a 12-volt battery and a lead attached to the cigarette lighter. This is the method I use most frequently. While the car is moving, the appliance is kept at the correct temperature. When the car is stationary, the inverter switches to battery mode and the chicks can be safely left for a couple of hours; alternatively the brooder can be disconnected and plugged into a socket at your destination.

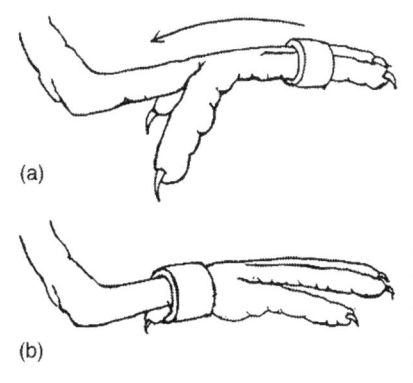

Fig. 25 Ringing methods: (a) Two toes forward (preferred). (b) Three toes forward (useful if, for example, a hind toe has grown too long but will necessitate using a larger ring).

12 Studbooks

In the UK the Lory Group now works in close association with the Parrot Society and the International Loriinae Society and runs studbooks for most species of lory, based on those which the ILS set up in the USA. Similar studbooks are now in operation in most European countries and this greatly facilitates the exchange of birds and the setting up of breeding pairs. Most zoos around the world participate in studbooks. Meetings organized like those in the UK, by *Lory Journal International*, now also occur in Europe. Such groups are vital not only for the furthering of knowledge, the social aspect and the maintaining of studbooks, but also to ensure that aviculture presents a strong, united voice.

In Germany there are strict regulations concerning the registration of all bird-keepers. Despite this, the Government there recently attempted to ban the keeping of birds. This failed because the German avicultural community is so strong and well organized. Protectionists are currently using the umbrella of the European Community to pass similar legislation, which would then come into effect throughout Europe. We in the UK, along with bird societies from other European countries, should give support to a national governing body (the National Council for Aviculture in the UK) which could represent us in Europe with one voice.

Certain species once considered common are now declining. It is therefore vital to breed not only rare birds but also those species which are now considered common, but which tomorrow might be extinct. The Mitchell's Lorikeet (*Trichoglossus haematodus mitchelli*) is a case in point. Once common, there are now only a few left in captivity and, in the wild, it has been extirpated over much of its range. The remaining captive stock will become inbred or crossbred and, if kept in a few large colonies, vulnerable to disease. (I recently heard of one breeder, who holds several pairs, in whose aviaries French moult had broken out, depleting the viable stock further.) It would be far better to spread the few remaining pairs among several breeders in the studbooks and to pair the remaining progeny via this route. In this way the same opportunity of restocking wild populations may occur for this species as it did for the Ultramarine Lorikeet (*Vini ultramarina*).

The Chattering, Yellow-backed and Blue-streaked Lorries are now low in numbers in the wild. Thankfully many zoos are running related projects, participating in studbooks and working closely with aviculturists.

Project LORY STUD BOOK

Species	GORGEOUS LORY A.N. OTHER		Name/Institution	FRED SMITH. TEL. 0440-123456					
Date Begun	JAN '92		Date of Yearly Update	JAN '93	Participant Number: 5				
Studbook #	Leg Band #	Sex	Sire Studbook #	Dam Studbook #	Date of Hatch	Date of Arrival	Owner	Source	Date Relocated	To Whom Relocated	Date of Death	Remarks
016		M	W			1986	F.SMITH	IMP				
017		F	W			1986	"	"				
018		M	W			1988		P.HAY		10.91		
019		M	W			1988	"	D.GREEN				1 FOOT
020		F	W			1989	"	K.DAY				
021	FS.43.78	M	016	017	1.7.90				4.91	N.PEW		
022	FS.43.79	F	016	017	3.7.90				4.91	B.BATT		
023	FS.43.92	F	019	020	1.4.91				11.91	P.ZEK		
024	FS.43.94	F	019	020	3.4.91						9.91	
025	FS.43.103	M	016	017	3.8.91							RETAINED.
026	FS.43.104	F	016	017	5.8.91							RETAINED.

Leave shaded areas blank. These will be completed by the stud book keeper and the information sent you.

Fig. 26 Project lory studbook.

Our aim for all species should be a viable captive population of pure stock. We should also be prepared to do an apprenticeship with easier, more plentiful birds. Studbooks are the only way to safeguard the future of many species in captivity but, to be effective, everyone must participate. There appear to be three reasons for non-participation:

(1) *Security* Many people believe, mistakenly, that participation will jeopardize the security of their stock. So far in the UK there has been no evidence to substantiate this belief and full studbooks have been up and running for almost 3 years.
(2) *Pride* Lorriculturists would have to show that not all their results are enviable.
(3) *Laziness* Once set up, studbooks take but a few minutes a year to update. If they appear difficult in the first instance, there are always people on hand to help – through the various specialist lory groups, parrot societies and zoos – and these can be traced, in many countries, through bird magazines.

As certain birds become scarce, they will increasingly become available *only* through studbooks. There are some interesting and exciting programmes and opportunities lying ahead of us, including the possibility of obtaining other members of the Loriinae not presently in captivity. It goes without saying that studbook participants will be given first preference. In 1994 five pairs of *Charmosyna josefinae sepikiana* were offered to the UK from the Continent. I hold that studbook and naturally offered the pairs to breeders who were specializing in that species and were known to me as such through their participation in the studbook. I seriously urge everyone who considers themselves to be a bird-lover to participate in studbooks – for the good of the birds.

13 Conservation

> Most accessible forest in the North Moluccas will have been selectively logged by the end of the decade; much has already gone. A pair of *Lorius garrulus* were observed investigating a potential nest site in a logged forest at the top of a broken palm. Their preferred site being in main trunks at about 20–25m in trees 30–35m tall.
> [Frank Lambert, 1993]

There is grave concern for many species of Loriinae, particularly those confined to islands. The situation in the wild becomes more serious with each new day. We must face the fact that, if we want lories in the future, we need to do something now; in 20 years it will be too late. If we do not take this responsibility seriously we will have a heavy burden of conscience. Aviculture is not conservation but it can be a tool of conservation. It has been said: 'If we are not part of the solution, then we are part of the problem'.

> As man continues to allow wanton destruction of our natural resources, such as the rain forests, and continues to inhabit the lands without regard to the continuation and survival of our feathered jewels, we, the members of the International Loriinae Society, are faced with the tremendous task of trying to conserve and protect all Loriinae species in the wild and capitalizing on the captive species throughout the world. We must all continue to do our part in educating and assisting new lory owners. Let us continue to share our knowledge, experiences, both successful and not so successful, and promote the keeping of Loriinae in captivity. We should make a concerted effort to keep accurate records of all birds in our collections, and keep track of all offspring by providing permanent identification bands as well as genetic history and husbandry techniques when we sell a bird. We must continue to fund much needed field conservation work to determine how many Loriinae species are left in the wild, solicit and fund detailed avian research in diseases affecting Loriinae, and conduct specific workshops and educational seminars regarding all species of lories and lorikeets.
> [Phyllis Martin President of the ILS. From the opening speech at the 1st International Loriinae Conference, June 1993, Walsrode, Germany.]

Some species poised on the verge of extinction

Mitchell's Lorikeet (*Trichoglossus haematodus mitchelli*) Human population explosions in Bali and Lombok, with all the attendant pressures that people put on land, plus huge logging contracts taken out and speedily implemented by the Japanese, has led to the deforestation of the majority of the Mitchell's Lorikeet's habitat. This occurred before the outside world realized what was happening.

Through being on the ILS sub-committee for conservation with reference to the Mitchell's Lorikeet, my enquiries for specimens from various quarters to make up pairs have shown that the captive population is now too low to be considered viable. To make matters worse one adult cock that was put with a new mate in 1994 has unfortunately died. Possibly one of the biggest collections of this species in Europe had an outbreak of French moult, reducing the numbers even further. It was hoped that, through the captive population, pairs might one day be returned to the wild, via e.g. Bali Drive-in Zoo. With training given to keepers in the hope that after relevant advice had been given, some young from these pairs might eventually be released in suitable reserves and protected areas. Unfortunately this seems to have been an indictment on aviculture, at least as it once was, because, through lack of coordination, record-keeping and foresight, we let the destiny of this little bird slip through our fingers and all but disappear for ever. Today I sincerely believe that the majority of aviculturists adopt a more responsible attitude.

Red and Blue Lory (*Eos histrio*) There are three subspecies of the Red and Blue Lory. *E. h. histrio* and *E. h. challengeri* are thought to be probably extinct. *E. h. talautensis* is found in the Talaud Islands northeast of the Sangihe Islands, including Karakelong, Salebabu and Kabaruang. There has been some recent fieldwork on the taxon. The population of this bird is declining and estimates indicate that there are fewer than 2000 birds and that the species will probably be extinct within 20 years.

This subspecies was considered fairly common in 1978 (White & Bruce, 1986), but it was observed that these birds seem 'to have suffered tremendously from an anti-locust spraying campaign in the 1970s' (Rozendaal, letter to T. Inskipp, March 1987). During 1992/93, TRAFFIC (see also p. 100) Southeast Asia uncovered a worrying trade in this bird which, until the previous year, had been primarily threatened by loss of habitat on the tiny group of islands. TRAFFIC estimates that possibly as much as 33 per cent of the population has been removed from the Talaud Islands. (Most of the birds to have arrived recently in captivity are this subspecies.) The islanders recognize that the capture of these lories, mostly in protected forest, is illegal and that the bird has been trapped to a point where it is now no longer worth the effort to catch further specimens.

TRAFFIC Bulletin Vol. 13, No. 3 states: 'Support is needed for Indonesian authorities to complete an assessment of the status of all populations'.

There are currently about 50 specimens in Europe which have arrived via South Africa, as well as others around the world. Hopefully the progeny of these will, in part at any rate, be put to good use one day. There may, however, be much to learn about this species which is relatively new to aviculture. In the summer of 1995 York University is taking part in an expedition to the Talaud and Sangihe Islands on behalf of the Red and Blue spp., and it is hoped that Frank Lambert of the IUCN will go later in the year.

Two species reprieved by recent research

Blue-streaked Lory (*Eos reticulata*) Many zoos are currently taking part in a specialist breeding programme for this species (and *Lorius garrulus*). Recent field research on Tanimbar, however, shows that the Blue-streaked Lory in not in as dire a state as thought.

Violet-necked Lory (*Eos squamata*) Recent fieldwork in the North Moluccas (see p. 105) shows that *Eos squamata* is represented there by two endemic subspecies, *E. s. riciniata* and *E. s. obiensis*, but it was found that these lories were being traded in relatively low numbers. *E. s. squamata* is the less vulnerable because it is found in all types of habitat, including coastal coconut groves, mangrove and scrubby, secondary growth. None is as scarce as previously thought, including *E. s. obiensis*, which was once thought to be rare.

Who is helping lories?

CITES (Convention on International Trade in Endangered Species)
In 1976 CITES set up a system of Appendices. Its representatives state:

> An endangered species is any beleaguered bird, plant or animal for which the survival stakes have become desperately high, for which losing the next game could mean being toppled out of existence.

For all species on Appendix 1 trade was and still is banned. Species listed on Appendix 2 can be traded as long as certain controls are applied. All lories are still currently on Appendix 2 (and I think a number should now be transferred to Appendix 1).

A problem occurred at the eighth meeting in 1992, in Japan, when it was decided that the listing criteria should be reviewed. The impulse for change came not from conservationists or government agencies but from traders. The new criteria are likely to cause trouble in the future. An

Appendix 1 listing will now be justified only if a species has:

(1) A very small population (as low as 250–2500) adult birds.
(2) A range restricted to less than 100km^2 (38 sq. miles).
(3) A less restricted range of 500km^2 (193 sq. miles) with mixed threats.
(4) A marked decline of more than 50 per cent in 5 years or 2 generations.

These figures will be endlessly quoted by trade lobbies as scientific. How can it be acceptable to trade in a species with a stable population as low as 251? The demands for research will fall on conservation bodies and are likely to prove expensive and, in many cases, impossible to meet.

Sadly, CITES appears to have failed to meet its goals for a variety of reasons:

(1) Certain countries ignore its rules.
(2) Trade is meant to be strictly controlled by agreed quotas but failure to control it is hardly surprising when it is considered that there are 13 000 islands.
(3) The less trade that is done with the West, the more traders turn towards the increasingly interested East.
(4) Many instances are known where birds of an endangered species have been caught to fill the quota of a fairly similar but more common species!
(5) There is no central collation of information and no way to check the level of international trade in any current year, and the reports sent to the CITES secretariat are always several years late.
(6) Birds which die after capture are discounted for the purpose of trade statistics.

TRAFFIC (Trade Records Analysis of Flora and Fauna in Commerce) 17 million hectares (65 640 sq. miles) of rainforest are being destroyed every year. TRAFFIC, which is concerned with the wise use of natural resources, ensures reporting on illegal and unsustainable trade in endangered wildlife. It receives support from the National Westminster Bank via the World Wide Fund for Nature (WWF). This sponsorship of WWF is to the tune of £3 million for 3 years, has been renewed for a further 3 years, and is the largest conservation sponsorship in the UK.

IUCN (International Union for the Conservation of Nature) The function of this organization is to act as a catalyst. The IUCN builds partnerships between governments and environmental groups in order to carry out conservation projects. It has standing commissions covering species' survival plans, national parks, environmental planning and law, education and ecology.

Birdlife International (formerly International Council for Bird Preservation – ICBP) The various conservation programmes are based on field research designed to identify the threats to birds and their habitats. Each programme demonstrates that natural habitats can be managed for birds and other wildlife with positive benefits for people too.

Birdlife Indonesia This organization now has new offices and a staff of 10 and, with several projects in hand, is working with governments to set up National Parks and Nature Reserves for parrots and other birds endemic to Indonesia. Mining, as well as logging and trapping, is a major concern and threat throughout the region.

If we act now, then in 20–30 years there will be protected areas which are well established and secure.

South Pacific species There is a conservation programme for threatened South Pacific species operating in the area, so it is to be hoped that forests will be better preserved in future. One species for which there is special concern is the Red-throated Lory (*Charmosyna amabilis*) of Fiji.

Some points to consider: Captive breeding is the most controversial conservation practice.

Captive breeding programmes are only encouraged where it is considered that they can benefit conservation of the taxon in question and if concurrent recovery programmes are also initiated.

The vulnerability of small populations has been consistently underestimated. This has erroneously shifted the timing of the establishment of captive populations to the last moment, when the crisis is enormous and when extinction is probable. It would be better done while the wild population is still in its thousands.

Last-minute intervention, when a population is known to have decreased radically, increases the risk of losing a significant part of the genetic diversity of a taxon and may even lead to its extinction. This is particularly true if such action involves experimenting with the management, in any form, of the last few survivors of a species.

Properly structured captive breeding programmes, with the potential to restock or reintroduce to the wild, have stimulated the protection of remaining wild populations or restoration of their habitat (Durrell *et al.*, 1987)

Collectors of rare birds have often used captive breeding programmes as an excuse for their activities but there is no evidence to suggest that this has boosted trade in a species.

The existence of a number of cryptic, presently untreatable diseases has been a strong argument against captive breeding in multi-species facilities, such as zoos.

It is hoped that advancement in the recognition and, therefore, treatment of diseases will become possible.

Genetic diversity in the gene pool of a healthy population ensures the survival of the taxon during an epidemic, since not all individuals succumb to a single disease outbreak. However, in a small inbred population, the chances of a larger percentage of the population, or indeed the whole taxon, succumbing to a single disease outbreak is much higher because of the increased genetic uniformity.

Captive populations should be seen more as an insurance against the failure of other conservation efforts.

Because of the risk of disease, reintroduction or restocking from captivity needs extreme caution.

Captive breeding programmes should not be carried out in isolation but should be part of an overall conservation strategy that includes field conservation; they should be managed in a coordinated way and aimed primarily at those species already identified as having decreased in number:

Eos cyanogenia
Eos histrio talautensis
Eos reticulata
Lorius domicellus
Lorius garrulus flavopalliatus
Lorius garrulus morotaianus
Trichoglossus haematodus mitchelli
Vini peruviana

RARE After its success with parrots in the Caribbean, RARE is beginning to utilize the same conservation programme with some of the Pacific nations (primarily I believe Samoa). Paul Butler, Conservation Officer, is again at the helm.

Avicultural input

International Loriinae Society (ILS) The impetus for the Captive Breeding Studbooks came from the ILS. The Conservation Chairman, Jan van Oosten says:

> We need to know the situation on every species of lory. If we are serious with our birds we have no choice but to join the Stud Book System and systematically ring our birds. We also need to broaden the base of the captive gene pool worldwide through the exchange of wild-caught birds.

ILS is currently funding fieldwork, and possibly an *in situ* breeding programme, in the Soloman Islands and the Province of New Britain in Papua New Guinea. Some work is already under way.

ILS raises money through the sale of limited edition prints. The auction of an original of one of these prints, at the 2nd International Parrot Convention in Tenerife, raised $5000. A donation was then made towards 'The Goffin/Blue-streak Project'. Another original was auctioned in September 1994 at the 3rd Convention in Tenerife. Another donation will go towards the $28000 needed for 'The *Histrio* Project', to be led by Frank Lambert, hopefully in late 1995. Stop press, May 1995: the Loro Parque Foundation is to fund half the total cost of 'The *Histrio* Project'.

UK Lory Group This has been up and running for four years. Four or five meetings are held annually, to which all who are interested in lories are welcome. It is not a splinter group and there is no subscription, committee, etc. A nominal entrance fee is charged to cover running expenses. Meetings are held all over the UK and are partly social, to encourage new members, although the Group also tries to invite first-class speakers from around the world. The Group is serious about lories, and studbook participation features largely in its activities; in this respect, it is now happily, and gratefully, partly funded by the UK Parrot Society who print our newsletter. A 'For sale and wanted' list is published six times a year; this keeps members in touch with each other and helps pairing lories.

Currently the Group has raised funds from raffles and meetings for York University Red and Blue Project. We will be contributing to the IUCN *Histrio* Project. In 1994 we made a donation to 'The Friends of the Sepik'.

Lory Journal International This, the only specialist journal on lories is now in its fourth year. It is very informative and beautifully presented, with subscribers from 19 different countries, many of whom are contributors. It has become a forum for making friends and exchanging knowledge and birds, through its columns, its agents and its editor, Jos Hubers.

Private aviculturists and zoos
(1) Purple-capped Lory (*Lorius domicellus*) An international stud book has been set up to promote the exchange of knowledge and pairing of unrelated Purple-capped Lories, and to make long-term plans for at least partial relocation of this species to the wild, after all relevant advice has been taken from conservation bodies and local governments.
(2) Blue-streaked Lory (*Eos reticulata*) A zoo specialist breeding programme has been set up for the Blue-streaked Lory, although the most current fieldwork on Tanimbar suggest that the situation may not be as dire as originally thought.
(3) Chattering Lory (*Lorius garrulus*) A breeding programme similar to that for *Eos reticulata* has been set up for the Chattering Lory spp. In this case the findings of the IUCN project in the North Moluccas found that this species is seriously threatened.
(4) Rosenberg's Lorikeet (*Trichoglossus haematodus rosenbergii*) For several years, to my knowledge, a single Rosenberg's Lorikeet sat here on its own in the UK. When the occasion arose, the owner generously let it

go to Holland to make up a pair there. Happily, plans are now afoot for the import to the UK, from Holland, of a young bird from this pairing and an unrelated mate.
(5) Weber's Lorikeet (*Trichoglossus haematodus weberii*) A similar tale can be told of the Weber's Lorikeet, but unfortunately so far these have proved hard to breed.
(6) Sepik Lorikeet (*Charmosyna josefinae sepikiana*) The Sepik Lorikeet has so far proved very hard to maintain in good health in the UK (probably due to the administration of antibiotics in quarantine leading to irreparable internal damage – certainly almost all in the last shipment have died (see also Chapter 15). Recently, as holder of the UK Studbook, I received an offer from abroad of several pairs; naturally they have all found homes amongst Studbook participants.

Cooperation between zoos and private aviculturists is now occurring frequently, possibly because of the increased awareness that has come about since Studbook participation and the inception of the Zoo Tag Group, whereby, among other things, species at risk have been identified. Recently, through the UK Lory Group Newsletter, a zoo was supplied with a specimen identified previously as one needing assistance. The zoo in turn supplied a private aviculturist specializing in another species, about which little is yet known in captivity, with their last remaining youngster in order to make a pair.

Some inspiring conservation examples

Currumbin, Australia This sanctuary was founded in 1946 by Alex Griffiths who was feeding the region's lories in a bid to rescue his exhibition 'Red Charm' gladioli from their attacks. Today the sanctuary includes 1250 native Australian birds (not including the free-flying birdlife). He has increased his land and gifted a piece to the National Trust of Queensland, thus ensuring its safety for the future. The birds are still the major draw but there is now a wider selection of flora and fauna as well. Currumbin plays a vital role in the mission to preserve the country's heritage by its operation as an Australian flora and fauna sanctuary. Wild birds and animals can be brought to the on-site hospital. Through interpretive graphics, the sanctuary hopes to educate the public about the importance of conserving and protecting the unique Australian species. The sanctuary's bird-breeding programme is impressive and includes various owls, fig parrots, the Forest Kingfisher and Spotless Crake (for which it boasts a world-first breeding award). Finches, including the now endangered Gouldian Finch, are being bred. (Let the plight of this bird in captivity be a lesson to us all in deviating too far from natural methods of rearing.) There is now a conference centre at Currumbin, and the sanctuary has increased its annual number of visitors from 1229 to 450 000. Is this not a role model?

The French Polynesia/Zoological Society of San Diego Ultramarine Project The Ultramarine Lorikeet (*Vini ultramarina*) is one of the least known and most threatened of all the island lory species. Known only from the Marquesas Archipelago, it is a lory of special concern to the Marquesan islanders as well as the Office of Environment for French Polynesia. Its distribution once included Nuka Hiva, Ua Pou, Hiva Oa and Ua Huka, but it has become extinct on all the islands except Ua Huka. A special expedition in November 1991, co-sponsored by the Office of the Environment (French Polynesia) and the Zoological Society of San Diego (ZSSD) found no lories on the former three islands and between 1000 and 1500 on Ua Huka. Although this population is fiercely protected by the Ua Hukan islanders, its future is of much concern because of the proposed construction of a wharf. Large cargo ships docking may result in rat invasions and industrial, agricultural and urban development. Such factors, in addition to cats, a large goat population, the possible presence of avian malaria and the introduction of the Common Mynah and Great Horned Owl, have led to the extinction of the Ultramarine Lorikeet on all the other islands.

The IUCN and Captive Breeding Specialist Group (CBSG) Parrot Action Plan for *Vini ultramarina*, ZSSD undertook the first step of an experimental translocation of this lory species from Ua Huka to Fatu Hiva. This decision was based on the prehistoric evidence of the presence of this lory in Fatu Hiva, the island has many of the plant species known to be food for this lory and is unspoilt, with few of the negative features of Ua Huka. Ten days were spent mist-netting the Ultramarines. Seven were caught and kept for 6 days before being transferred by boat to Fatu Hiva. The inhabitants of the island were encouraged to visit the birds before their release, which took place at first light on the appointed day. The lories immediately began to feed on coconut flowers. The birds will be monitored in the future by an employee of the Rural Economy Service who will make field observations. This translocation programme will continue on an annual basis to provide enough founder birds to establish this species on Fatu Hiva. This translocation project is just one component of a comprehensive joint conservation programme between the Government of French Polynesia and ZSSD, which includes field research, continuous monitoring of endangered bird populations, translocations and captive rearing.

IUCN – Species Survival Commission, trade specialist group project in the North Moluccas Between October 1991 and February 1992 Frank Lambert was part of the team involved in field surveys on the status of parrots in the North Moluccas. These were conducted on

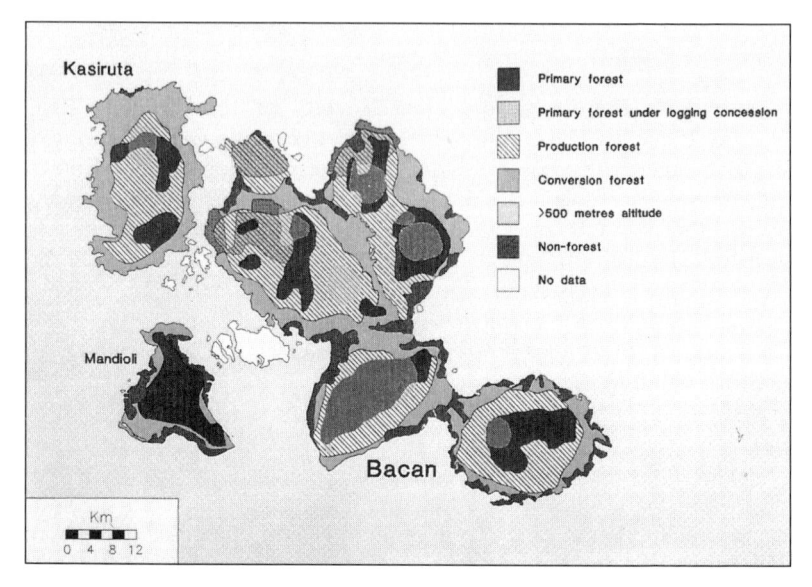

Present land use and forest status on Bacan

Halmahera, Bacan (Batjan) and Obi, with the principle focus being on three significantly traded species, two of which were the Chattering Lory (*Lorius garrulus* spp.) and Violet-necked Lory (*Eos squamata* spp.). The maximum and minimum population densities were established at each of 18 sites. *L. garrulus* was found to prefer hilly, forested areas to at least 1300m (1417 yd). *E. squamata* frequented all habitat types, being commoner in disturbed habitats. As well as the surveys, trappers and traders were interviewed and markets visited (including some mainland ones). Minimum populations were set against estimated captures. This indicated over-exploitation of *L. garrulus*.

The primary objective was to assess the biological status of the lory species. *L. garrulus* is represented on Obi and Bacan by the yellow-backed Lory (*L. g. flavopalliatus*) which is a very important species both in domestic (it is a favoured pet bird) and in international trade. This lory was reported as very common in 1946. However, by 1985, it was rarely encountered and considered scarce.

E. squamata is represented in the North Moluccas by two endemic sub-species *E. s. riciniata* and *E. s. obiensis* but these lories, it was found, were being traded in relatively low numbers. *E. s. squamata* is less threatened because it occurs in all types of habitat, including coastal coconut groves, mangrove, and scrubby secondary growth.

Current levels of exploitation suggest that 15–20 per cent of *L. garrulus* and 25+ per cent of *E. squamata* die prior to shipment! There is a discrepancy between permits issued and lories caught. Here the current

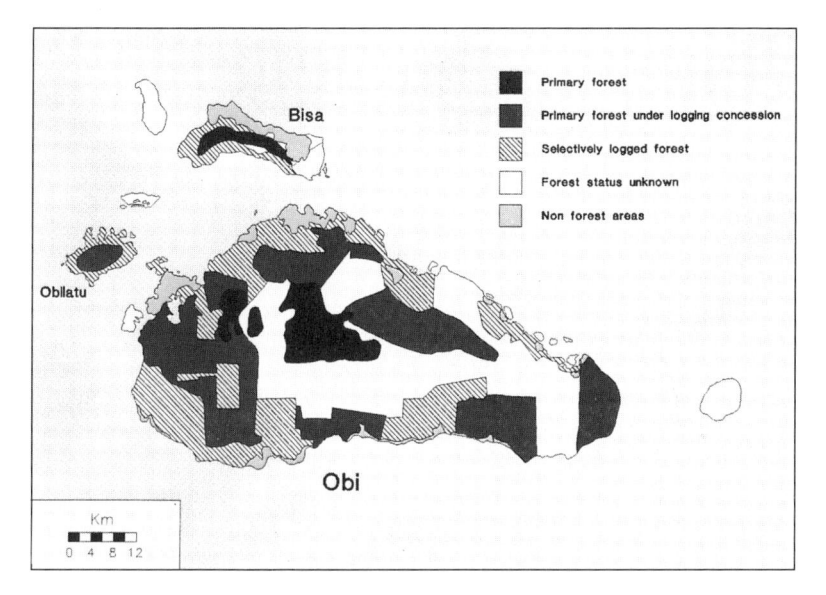

Present land use and forest status on Obi

levels of exploitation suggest that *L. garrulus* trappers maybe removing 10 per cent of the world population of this species. *E. squamata* trade levels are probably low in relation to the estimated population size, but both should be treated as vulnerable.

Frank Lambert suggests that, in the long term, one option might be to switch from catching adults to harvesting eggs and nestlings. The training and management necessitated would require time and considerable funding, and trappers would need some incentive and compensation. An active law and strict policing are required to see that quotas are not exceeded.

Most accessible forest in the North Moluccas will have been logged by the end of the decade.
Obviously trade should, where possible, be supplied by aviculturists.

14 First aid

Develop a working relationship with your veterinary surgeon. It is important to choose an avian specialist but probably almost equally important to choose one who has time for you and your birds and has their interests well and truly at heart. The Association of Avian Veterinarians now has members in most countries of the world and, as a group, runs active meetings in the USA, Europe and Australia, with the aim of educating and interesting veterinary surgeons in birds.

You should feel able to speak to your veterinary surgeon about your birds and to trust his or her judgement. Ideally a partnership should be formed between the two of you making it a two-way exchange of information, so that, at the onset of anything untoward, appropriate advice can be sought and a solution worked out jointly.

Prevention

Accidents and illness can stress and debilitate birds quickly. Because of their rapid metabolic rate, a very short period without sustenance will probably have seriously adverse affects. Stress, losing the will to eat and live, and chilling can prove fatal quite quickly. A working knowledge of basic first aid is therefore vital for bird-keepers.

We all know what a difference a doctor with a good bedside manner makes and it is the same with birds. We need to feel confident and relaxed in dealing with a bird, and to carry out any necessary treatment quickly and with minimal disturbance. If we give up, or leave things too long, birds very often fade and die quite quickly. I have sensed this on many occasions with all sorts of creatures. On the other hand, when I have forced myself to do the mental fighting for a very sick bird, I have often been amazed at how it has rallied. Of course it goes without saying that this will not work on all occasions, a lot depends on whether the bird's 'number is up', but I feel it does no harm to bear this in mind and to give it a try on every occasion, even if I do lose some battles.

It is usually less stressful, less time-consuming, easier and cheaper to prevent disease than it is to attempt late in the day to cure disease.

Observation

As prevention is better than cure, there is no substitute for observation so note the following.

Appearance, condition and demeanour

(1) How does the bird look?
(2) Is there any weight loss?
(3) Are the eyes open and bright or more oval and sleepy?

Appetite and faeces Loss of appetite and changes in the colour or consistency of the faeces indicates that something is wrong. Greener faeces may indicate a gut upset and reddish-brown or yellow faeces suggest liver or kidney problems.

Breathing Laboured or wheezy breathing, coupled with tail-bobbing, indicates a respiratory problem.

Vomiting and/or regurgitation This may be seen in a variety of conditions.

Cuts and injuries This suggests bullying or incompatibility. The dominant bird may chase the other, or prevent it feeding.

Anything unusual Any abnormal changes in behaviour or appearance should be regarded as a warning sign.

Routine care

Making sure that your birds are adequately provided for, and following a regular routine day care, will help them stay healthy.

Adequate nourishment and clean water These must both be available at all times.

A draught-proof shelter and a thick, dry nest Cold will very often be tolerated, whereas draughts, lack of shelter or a wet nest will quickly result at best in a chill.

Adequate exercise The ability to fly and exercise promotes metabolism and health. Overfeeding and under-exercise are almost as bad for birds as underfeeding. I once lost a hen and was shocked when the post-mortem result showed the problem to be nothing more than over-indulgence. Certain species seem to suffer more than others in this respect. In particular

I find that Black-capped Lories (*Lorius lory*), if given the opportunity, will spend as little time as possible exercising and much time eating, and thus they need protecting from themselves. *The term malnutrition applies as much to over-feeding as it does to under-feeding.*

Clean air Dust, pollutants and the use of electrical appliances all upset the natural electrical balance of the environment by producing more positive than negative ions. In a bird-room the natural replenishment of ions from the outside atmosphere is not as rapid as usual. An ionizer will produce a stream of negative ions which will help to freshen and purify the bird-room air. They can help to remove dust particles, bacteria, fungal spores and viruses. The risk of spreading air-borne diseases, including fungal ones, is thus minimized and the health of the birds is improved.

Regular attention to beaks and nails Both beaks and nails sometimes grow too long. To trim, the bird should be held in a towel (see Fig. 28).

(1) *Beaks* Overgrown beaks can be filed down. Little and reasonably often is the best course if you have such a bird and the condition

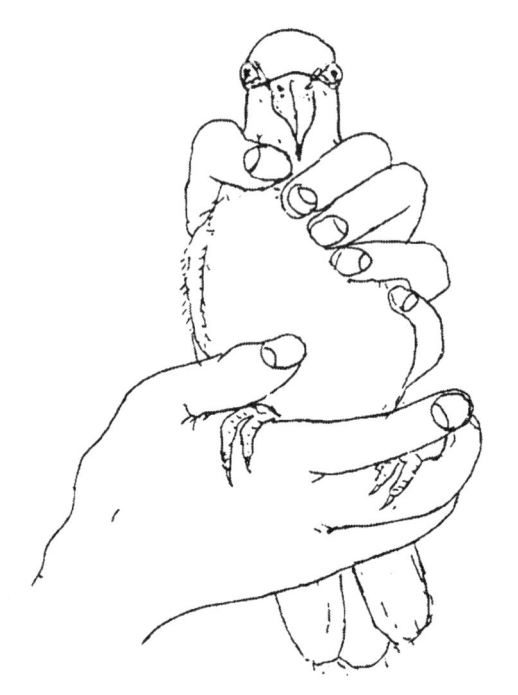

Fig. 28 How to hold and support a bird securely. Normally a towel would be used but for reasons of clarity this is not shown.

Fig. 29 (opposite) Nail clipping is best done with two people. Normally a towel would be used but for reasons of clarity this is not shown.

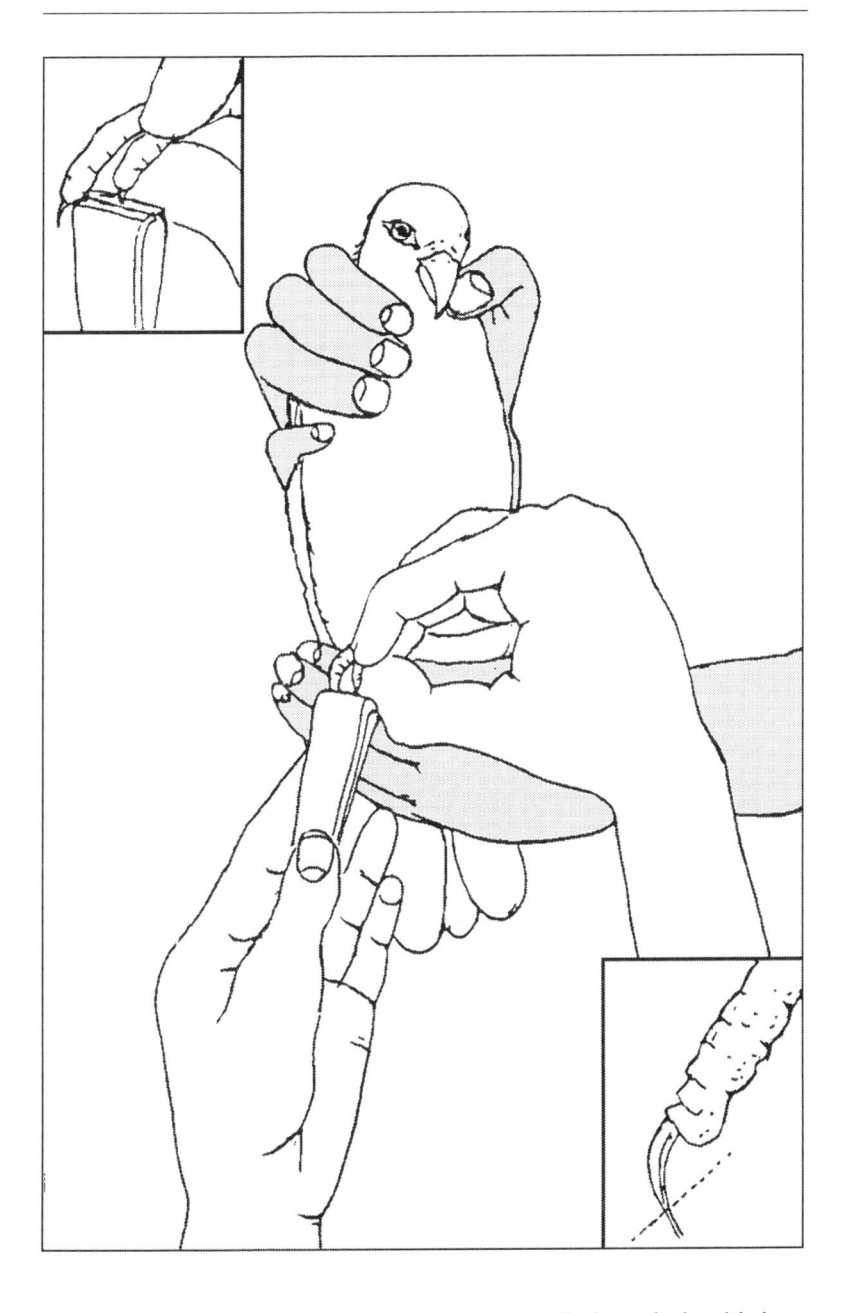

is mild. If it is more severe, beaks are usually best dealt with by a veterinary surgeon, who may use an electric drill with a sanding wheel for very precise trimming.

(2) *Nails* These usually wear down naturally during exercise and play. It is sad (and bad management) to lose a bird caught by its nail on the flight netting or nest ladder. I once acquired a pet lory (to save it from such a fate) whose nails had grown into several loops. I did not feel competent to clip them in the normal way (see Fig. 29), with human (or dog) nail clippers but chose to have a veterinary surgeon do them while the bird was under anaesthetic being sexed. When clipping nails in the routine way you may go too far and hit the quick; bleeding can be arrested by pushing the nail into a bar of soap, white pepper or wound powder, or by using a silver-nitrate stick or styptic pencil. Battery-powered hot-wire cauterizers are available but I prefer to avoid them because I feel they may cause pain.

Quarantine All birds should be quarantined on arrival, for several weeks where possible.

Regular cleansing and disinfecting This is essential for the birds' well-being.

(1) *Hands* Before touching eggs, feeding chicks, dealing with food-pots, or after handling sick birds, always wash your hands. Use, e.g., Amprotect Hand Rinse, Hibiscrub or Phisohex.

(2) *Food-pots and chicks' utensils* As well as being routinely cleaned, e.g. with Ark-Klens, these should be soaked regularly in Tamodine E, Vanodine V18, or the virucidal agent, Vircon S. (Beware of soaking metal pots longer than the recommended time.) These products kill bacteria and are highly effective against avian viruses and fungi, e.g. *Aspergillosis*, and are non-toxic.

(3) *Incubators* These are prone to bacterial contamination but this can be inhibited by using a product, e.g. Ark-Klens, in the incubator water or in the wet-bulb thermometer reservoir.

(4) *Hospital cages and incubators* Both should be disinfected after use. I clean them regularly with Milton or Ark-Klens, followed by Tamodine E, after which they are thoroughly rinsed.

(5) *Aviary walls and floors* After the routine cleansing described above, these can be sprayed with a small backpack sprayer containing Tamodine E, Vanodine V18, or Virkon S. Note that detergents and disinfectants should not be mixed together, as they may have conflicting actions.

(6) *Eggs* Prior to incubation all eggs should be wiped with, e.g. Amprotect, which leaves a bactericidal coating on the egg.

(7) *Nest-boxes* These should be cleaned as in (2), then air-dried and sprayed against mite, before being left to dry thoroughly.

Stress Avoid stress wherever possible as it is an underlying cause of many diseases, and leads to a weakening of the immune system.

Probiotics Regular (and specific) application of probiotics can prevent bacterial infection. In the past, aviculturists may have routinely reached for antibiotics. Now we believe that, in most cases, it is just as beneficial and less harmful, to reach for probiotics.

Medicine cupboard

It is advisable to have a few items on hand in the medicine cupboard.

Table 13 Recommended items for the medicine cupboard

Cleansers/Disinfectants	Amprotect Hand Rinse; Ark-Klens; chlorhexidine solution (Hibiscrub, Phisohex); Milton; Vanodine 18; Vircon S
Utensils	Cottonwool buds for cleaning-up jobs; scales; bag for weighing birds, chicks and hatching equipment (see also Chapter 7), adhesive bandage; Micropore tape; plastic mesh (Netlon) and kitchen towel; padded catching nets (two sizes are useful); place for intensive care heat or hospital cage (see Heat and Fluid Therapy below); syringes, bent spoon and eye-dropper for administering medicines; tweezers and needle; scissors, nail clippers
For sampling	Bacteriological swabs with transport medium; box suitable for sending a carcase for post mortem; DNA sexing/blood-testing kit (ask your vet to demonstrate); faecal sampling kit (which can be sent to a pathology laboratory)
Medicines (non-veterinary)	Eucalyptus (for inhalation); probiotics*, Rid-Mite Spray; 'scaly' cream; silver nitrate sticks (styptic pencil)
*Medicines (veterinary)***	Anti-bacterials/antibiotics; electrolytes (for dehydration); nystatin (for candidiasis); wound powder or spray (for cuts); ophthalmic/antibiotic cream (for swollen eyes); wormer (levamisole [Panacur or Nilverm] plus niclosamide [Yomesan or Droncit] for tapeworm)

*Many probiotics, e.g. Avipro, contain electrolytes, which further assist in balancing the gut flora after illness, stress, and as a support through medication, particularly antibiotic treatment. There is a paediatric version, Avipro Paediatric, for hand-rearing from the egg.
** These may be obtained from your veterinary surgeon as appropriate. Keep a list of approximate weights of your birds to assist with calculating dosage.

Heat and fluid therapy (HFT)

A very important aspect of nursing is the intensive unit for care of the critically sick bird. Birds which are ill should be isolated in a warm/hot cage. An important aspect of this care is the use of probiotics.

Heat can be provided by using a special hospital cage or by converting an ordinary cage with the aid of an infra-red heater (see Fig. 30); in emergency a simple fan-heater will do an excellent job. The heat should come

Fig. 30 Treatment of a sick bird showing the two options: a cage and lamp or a hospital cage. If the bird is unable to perch, perches should be removed and a half-log placed on the floor. It is essential to choose a hospital cage in which the heat source is at the back or side.

from the back or side, and I place a half-log on the floor so that the bird can perch beside the heat or move away from it. A towel draped over the cage will give the bird privacy and help to reduce the stress caused by being in a small cage. This gives some comfort, particularly to nervous birds. The heat should be maintained at 28–30°C (83–87°F). Kitchen towel on the base will allow examination of faeces and some Netlon above this will keep the bird's feet dry. At least some hand-feeding will probably be necessary. Fresh glucose/honey-water (frequently changed) should be put in an accessible position, as well as a piece of favourite fruit (nibbling this is a good indication of returning good health). At this point a probiotic and electrolytes should be offered in nectar or water.

Accidents

In the case of all accidents swiftly apply heat and fluid therapy. It is surprising how often even a wild-caught bird, if really sick, will allow itself to be hand-fed. I am quite happy eventually to be bitten as this is often the first sign that things are taking a turn for the better. The following are some of the commoner accidents and the action which should be taken.

Bites and cuts When bleeding has ceased these will need thorough cleansing and the application of wound powder.

Broken wing A veterinarian should be consulted. If there is to be a delay, the wing may be strapped up gently in the normal position, using adhesive bandage; the bird should be kept in a warm cage with a lamp, a perch right on the ground and a nearby nectar pot. I have known wings heal quite well in time, provided that the strapping stays in place but is not too tight. I have, over the years, acquired two birds with drooped wings that have not healed correctly. Neither could fly but they were quite happy using running poles that reached the full length of the aviary. You must guard against two things with these birds: falling and putting on weight through lack of flying.

Broken leg Until a veterinarian can be seen, making a splint to support the leg in its normal position may be helpful. The bird will go into shock so it must be kept warm and not allowed to dehydrate.

Broken and lost toes Recently I lost a young Musschenbroek's Lorikeet (*Neopsiltacus m. musschenbroeki*) whose parent had bitten off its leg a week or so after fledging. I found it too late in the morning. A young yellow-backed Lory (*Lorius garrulus flavopalliatus*), on whose foot someone had inadvertently shut a door, was found 3 hours later, still hanging, but having all but bitten the two toes off. I treated him for shock and stress in the normal way, and cleaned the wound. He stood with his eyes shut on the log in the hospital cage on his good leg. He was hand-fed and moved to a cooler cage within a couple of days. In two weeks the toes dropped off. Within about six weeks, he was managing well on the stump. The practice of using old sheets and handkerchiefs to line chicks' pots in the brooder is dangerous because thread from these can easily tighten round a leg. Netlon is far safer and more hygienic (see p. 81).

Night fright Sudden disturbance may cause a bird to fly headlong into the netting or wall, resulting in death from a broken neck, or perhaps haemorrhaging from the beak. Most commonly, birds are merely shocked and benefit from HFT.

Chill Draughts, or being soaked for some reason, are the most common cause of chills. A newly fledged bird may not be able to find its way back to the nest, or it may escape from the aviary and be forced to spend a wet night out in the open (see Fig. 31). Steady birds appreciate a hairdryer or fan-heater. The treatment is as above but should be administered quickly to prevent the development of pneumonia. Inhalation of eucalyptus may alleviate suffering here, as with all diseases of the upper respiratory track. Steam from a boiling kettle can be directed into the cage through a sieve lined with a eucalyptus-soaked towel. A more sophisticated form of this (nebulization) is now being used by some veterinary surgeons as a means of supplying medication.

Preparing to visit the veterinary surgeon

The patient should be transported in a cage or box, protected from draughts. Ideally a perch should be fixed in the transport box. Details, or examples, of food should also be taken, together with samples of droppings or vomit, as well as relevant details of the bird's history: any recent changes in diet, additives, breeding, death of mates, changes of partners, other illnesses, medication, etc.

Euthanasia

Sooner or later this fact has to be faced. It is not an option to leave a bird to suffer and do nothing. I can only recommend discussing this with your veterinary surgeon.

Post-mortem examination

This should be carried out as soon after death as possible. You should have the name of you local MAFF Veterinary Investigation Centre, or a pathology laboratory as supplied by your veterinary surgeon to hand. If you use a laboratory regularly, it will probably have supplied you with the forms which need to be filled in and sent with the body. Give all relevant details, including the name of your veterinary surgeon (not forgetting to notify him/her). Dampen the body, but do not remove any secretions (which can be wrapped separately if found elsewhere or inadvertently removed) and wrap it in newspaper; then carefully secure it in polythene bags and put it in a box. This should be labelled 'Pathological Specimen' and sent to the pathology laboratory as soon as possible. If death occurs after post-office hours, keep the body in the fridge (not freezer) overnight.

Do not forget: Post mortem can help protect the remaining birds.

Fig. 31 Catching escapees. Put the escapee's mate in a cage in the escapee's aviary or, in the case of a range of aviaries, in the walkway. Place fruit and nectar on the open door as well as on the mate's cage. If the bird has not been caught before nightfall, shut the door but leave food outside and resume the procedure in the morning.

15 Diseases of lories and lorikeets

Co-written with
Peter Scott MSc., BVSc., MRCVS, MIBiol., ACOArb.

Ascites

In the UK we lost many Mount Goliath Lorikeets (Stella's) (*Charmosyna papou goliathina*) through the 'light beak syndrome' that many aviculturists have come to dread. The signs can occur over a few hours or increase insidiously over weeks or years. First the beak becomes pale and then the feet. The stomach appears swollen as though the bird is about to lay (this can happen to either sex), breathing may be shallow and fast, and droppings, which in this species may appear thick and pasty if the diet does not suit, may adhere to the tail. Such a bird is normally no use for breeding, and will most probably die in due course. We believe that Stella's Lorikeets in general have a low tolerance to antibiotics and it is possible that these last shipments of them into the UK received too many antibiotics either in their country of origin or at the importers. To date I have not heard of any evidence of this among captive-bred birds. If only mild cases, i.e. orange beak, are evidenced, altering the diet to a much lighter, less rich one can be helpful. Ascites can also be a sign of polyomavirus.

Aspergillosis

This is one of the most serious fungal diseases. It usually affects the respiratory system and spreads best in warm, humid, unhygienic and usually overcrowded conditions, particularly in the presence of rotting vegetation, wood, etc. It can be suspected by failure to thrive, puffed-out chest with some attempt to vomit, and laboured breathing. In a living bird it is a very difficult diagnosis to confirm but a veterinary surgeon can sometimes do so by taking and culturing a swab from the trachea. It may also be seen during endoscopy (perhaps for surgical sexing): in infected birds the air sacs appear to have a blue-green coating.

Candidiasis

Caused by the yeast *Candida albicans*, this is often present if the hygiene is poor or if the bird is deficient in vitamin A, or it has been subjected to antibiotics. Cottage-cheese-like growths in the beak are the commonest sign but often these will spread down the oesophagus (gullet) and into the crop, where you may feel a thickened wall. For this reason local treatment, such as Daktarin gel, often fails to work, whereas the condition usually responds well to the administration of a course of nystatin (which is not actually absorbed by the body so is very safe). Bad cases may need a further course after a rest period to clear it up altogether. Other drugs, such as ketoconazole, have been used, but this needs the utmost care as it is potentially toxic. A newer, related drug, itraconazole, is proving useful and safer for the resistant cases.

Coccidiosis

This dangerous gut parasite may be a problem in some aviaries, especially where floors become damp and harbour the cysts.

Dietary imbalances

These occur for various reasons: possibly not enough food has been given, or not the required food; maybe the food has not been eaten, or possibly a mate has been defending a food-pot and starving its partner. Common deficiencies and their consequences are:

(1) *Calcium* The quality of bone, shell and feather and the muscle tone activity of the oviduct is reduced (see p. 120, Egg binding).
(2) *Vitamin A* This increases susceptibility to infection. It is very important in the maintenance of healthy surfaces in the mouth, lungs and even kidney. Candida and other ailments creep in in the wake of a vitamin A deficiency.
(3) *Vitamin B* The nervous system is affected by this deficiency and the symptoms might be loss of coordination.
(4) *Vitamin D* This will lead to rickets or splay legs in chicks (administer Calcium and Vitamin D3).

Ataxia (Drunkenness)

After the third outbreak of ataxia I took photographs which are very dramatic. All three cases were among subspecies of *Lorius lory*. This, strangely, has largely been the case among other breeders. The bird appears to be 'blind drunk' and, lying on its back, it seems to be dead but for its eyes blinking. While it is ataxic, the bird should be laid on its side in a cage with a lamp not too near. In due course it will attempt to stand and perch, and then various falls will occur, so keep the perch no more than 2.5cm (1in) off the ground. When the bird is almost 'sober', offer some honey/glucose-water off a spoon. Even wild birds take it gratefully at this stage. Withhold normal nectar for a day or so, avoid giving any food containing lactose.

Lories do not produce the enzyme lactase and therefore cannot digest lactose properly (it is present in all milk products to some extent). The birds who suffer from this have a low tolerance to lactose. Over about 3 hours gradually reduce the heat and, the next day, the bird should be fit to return to its aviary.

Egg-binding

Noticing this early enough can save both hen and egg. The causes of egg-binding are:

(1) Lack of calcium; prevention is better than cure. Providing regular calcium is not only essential for the egg but also for uterine muscle.
(2) Breeding too young – first-time layers which have been fed well may have begun to breed too young.
(3) Breeding at too great an age.
(4) Lack of, or inability to, exercise.
(5) Sudden drop in temperature.

Immediate application of heat at around 29.4–32°C (85–90°F) can save the situation. If the hen is brought into a hospital cage, she may well be saved, but the egg will be lost unless it is fostered or incubated. Early application of heat from a lamp when trouble is only mildly suspected, directly by the hen's nest and perch, may help her muscles to relax sufficiently, whereupon she should return to her nest to lay. Keep watch. One winter a Red-collared Lorikeet (*Trichoglossus haematodus rubritorquis*) laid a double-yolked egg of 10gm (⅜oz) (her normal is 7gm 1¼oz).

Some years ago, by non-intervention, I lost a Goldie's Lorikeet (*T. goldiei*) when the only other double-yolked egg I have had became stuck. Alternatively if you have ready prepared a clip-on form of additional heat (see Fig. 6, p. 30) this could now be applied. I have this appliance in position for the Red-Collared Lorikeet for when she next prepares to lay.

If the situation seems to be advanced and veterinary assistance is sought in time, an injection of calcium and hormones will assist most cases of uterine non-contraction. On no account try to remove the egg yourself. I personally believe inserting KY Jelly in the vent is too intrusive and dangerous. Even handling an egg-bound hen carries a risk.

Enteritis

This is not a diagnosis, it is a sign or symptom of disease. The word means 'inflammation of the intestine'. Unusually green droppings are the first sign and the bird may also appear depressed, fluffed and lacking in appetite. The complaint may be caused by poor hygiene, chilling, irritants, contamination of food, or stress. Often these problems will cause an imbalance, perhaps food moving too quickly through the gut, and the proliferation of *Escherischia* (*E. coli*) in the gut. It may be the result of infection, e.g. *Salmonella*, or part of another disease. Specks of blood may be present. A very acute necrotic enteritis has been described, probably caused by *Clostridium* spp.; birds may show tarry faeces or simply be found dead. Dehydration is to be avoided. The usual heat and fluid therapy is to be recommended. Probiotics, with or without antibiotics/antibacterials (depending on your vet's advice), are the normal course of action. Most cases recover if treated in time.

Eye infections (discharges, swellings)

This may occur because of draught, dust, grit, a knock or coming into contact with undiluted disinfectant, etc. The eye should be washed out with warm, boiled water or Optrex. This is best done with a dropper or lint gauze; the fibres from cottonwool may cause further irritation. Then administer a course of Ophthalmic or antibiotic ointment, using the fingers to hold the lids apart and 'pouch' the lower lid. Swollen eyes can be a symptom of various diseases.

Feather conditions

Feather-plucking There are two types of feather-plucking:
(1) Self- or mate-plucking by adults.
(2) Plucking of chicks by parent birds.

These may both be due to a deficiency, boredom, stress or some other unknown factor. It appears to occur more with some species than others. Those prone to it need attention in the form of protecting adults from cold and bringing in chicks for hand-rearing before permanent damage is done to their flying ability.

French moult This disease most usually affects young birds just before or after leaving the nest; then, for no apparent reason, the tail, flight and sometimes some of the body feathers just drop off. Examination will reveal that the feathers appear to have been strangulated, after which the feather falls off. There is no known cure. These birds can live for some while, but become what is known as 'crawlers' or 'creepers' because of their inability to fly; they need to be protected against falling. Occasionally you hear of an outbreak among adults. Recently, sadly, I heard this had occurred in Europe among a collection of a few of the remaining breeding pairs of Mitchell's Lorikeets (*Trichoglossus haematodus mitchelli*), reducing the gene pool of this highly endangered species even further.

Psittacine Beak and Feather Disease (PBFD) This viral disease, the scourge of certain other types of parrot-like birds is not unknown among lories. Signs most usually occur between the ages of 5–12 weeks; the feathers (often containing a blood-streak) become pinched off and drop out; later the beak may become mealy and parts crumble, leading to deformities of the beak. Australian studies report that it is common in wild lorikeets, although up to 40 per cent are said to recover in a couple of moults. Recovery is not normally a feature of this disease and the newer polymerase chain reaction (PCR) tests may show whether this is a different but related virus (as is seen in lovebirds).

Evidence of the virus can be found in crop-washes and feather dust. There has been a major breakthrough at the College of Veterinary Medicine, Georgia University, USA, by the team which includes Dr Branson Ritchie. They have developed a very sensitive (PCR) test for blood samples, which is far more accurate than feather biopsy in detecting the presence of the virus; it can even detect carriers. At the moment no cure is known, but research into a possible viral vaccine is being carried out in the USA, and in Australia led by Dr David Pass at Murdoch University.

Some years ago some chicks of mine were diagnosed as PBFD-positive at post mortem. This gave me an enormous shock and days of disinfecting work. I was advised that it could have been spread from one chick to another during routine nest inspections, when all chicks are put into a bucket during topping up of substrate. Six chicks were brought in at that time for hand-rearing because I thought they were being plucked but, within a day or so, five of them died after becoming quite naked. I was advised that adults were unlikely to catch this, but that it could be spread from chick to chick, or from an infected parent to chicks via the eggs. I was told not to hand-rear at all and to observe strict hygiene during subsequent nests involving the three pairs. In due course two pairs appeared to be cleared of suspicion after the chicks had been parent-reared to independence. The third pair plucked their young so badly that the chicks died without the intervention of hand-rearing – suspicion naturally still pointed at them. I had kept the sixth remaining chick as a control bird because I thought it might be a carrier; he, in due course, grew an immaculate set of new feathers. In 1994, Vetgen Europe made the University of Georgia tests available in Europe which, for me, was a great step forward. Blood was collected from these three birds and all have tested negative for the virus.

Colour changes Yellow feathering is fairly often seen when it should be green or, occasionally, red or brick-pink sometimes replaces bright red feathering. These colour changes are often due to a vitamin or mineral deficiency. A change of diet may reverse the situation. Sometimes, however, changes may be due to PBFD or polyomavirus, so testing should be carried out before birds are lost.

Fits and concussion

These could be the result of inhaling certain poisons, or from a blow to the head. Depending on the severity; the bird may recover or remain paralysed. It may only be on post mortem that an area of bleeding in the brain is found to be the cause of death or paralysis. Deficiency of vitamins B and E can be another cause of fits and the symptoms can resemble ataxia (see p. 119); however, it will be progressive unless the vitamin is administered. This is naturally where to start treatment.

Frostbite

Most lories roost in their nest-boxes, or at least in their shelter. If the perches provided are of reasonable dimensions, the toes should not hang down so that they are not covered by feathers and frostbite should not occur. If a bird does suffer from frostbite, the toes will eventually turn black and drop off.

Impacted crop

This can happen to any lory but is most likely with chicks. If a chick does suffer from impacted crop, bring it in and feed dilute honey-water or water with probiotics/electrolytes and massage the crop gently, several times, maybe for hours. I have known the impaction take over 24 hours to disperse. It is possible to use a crop needle to extract fluid but this is risky and delicate to perform. If no improvement is seen, or if you suspect that a foreign body is lodged in the crop, seek a veterinary surgeon's advice.

Lice and mites

I treat all birds annually (or more often if I see evidence of these external parasites) with Rid-mite or a pyrethrum-based preparation, taking care to spray or dust against the lie of the feathers at the back of the neck, under the wings and the vent area, and to avoid the eyes and nostrils. Red mite are best seen in the dark, when they come out of crevices and appear on perches and feathers as red dots. Being blood-suckers, they can be debilitating in sufficient numbers.

Pneumonia

This infection of the lungs can be caused by a number of bacteria and viruses and its acute nature gives almost no time for treatment. If it is suspected early, the usual isolation and heat and fluid therapy (HFT), accompanied by the administration of antibiotics, should be tried, once a veterinary surgeon has been contacted.

Time is of the essence. There will be apathy and raspy, jerking breathing, accompanied by tail-bobbing.

Poisons

Contaminated seed Soaking, rinsing or sprouting seed has been recommended. This in itself can be dangerous because bacteria and fungus grow quickly in the water. Adding Milton or Tamodine E to the sprouting water inhibits this. Thorough rinsing is vital.

Mould or fungus This grows on stored foodstuffs, e.g. soya flour, and, because it is not visible, may not detected for some while.

Lead and zinc The galvanizing on new aviary netting is a source of these two metals. This netting can be treated by scrubbing with vinegar before putting the birds in the aviary.

Affected birds are difficult to treat, particularly in the case of zinc poisoning. If lead poisoning is detected right away, the administration of Calcium EDTA by a veterinary surgeon may help. This binds any lead in the body and increases the rate of its excretion. Antibiotics may be recommended and the administration of copious amounts of fluid should help.

Pesticides and fumes Agricultural sprays, exhaust and paint fumes and burning non-stick pans are all noxious and can kill birds, depending on the amount.

Encourage the bird to drink well. Avoidance is really the only course here.

Water Problems may arise, depending on the source of the water (see p. 63).

Psittacosis (Ornithosis)

The causative organism is *Chlamydia psittaci*. Typical symptoms are those of pneumonia or liver damage, i.e. discoloured faeces and any urates taking on a yellow colour. In severe infections there may be drowsiness, diarrhoea, nasal discharge and pneumonia itself. Detection depends on laboratory testing; there are now very sensitive tests which look for the chlamydia in faeces. It is frequently harboured and excreted by apparently healthy birds, and stress of any kind can precipitate an outbreak. It is transmissible to human beings and produces severe influenza-like symptoms, which last 3–4 weeks; it can cause death in the elderly. Specific antibiotic treatment, usually with doxycycline or enrofloxacin lasts 30–45 days and must cover all birds on the premises where there has been an outbreak. Repeat tests are carried out a month after the treatment has finished. Quaternary ammonium compounds (e.g. Ark-Klens) are recommended as cleanser/disinfectants to remove and kill psittacosis.

Ring injuries

Rings may become too tight and cause circulatory problems, even cutting off the blood supply and causing the leg to wither in severe cases. In the case of very wide rings, dirt can get trapped underneath. Plastic rings can be fairly easily removed. Metal types require much more care. This is best performed by an avian veterinary surgeon who will have specific ring-removing tools and may administer an anaesthetic.

Scaly leg and face

This is caused by *Cnemidocoptes* sp., a mange mite, burrowing under the skin, and can be controlled by rubbing 'scaly cream' under and against the lie of the raised scales. Treatment with Ivomec is now also extremely effective. Consult your veterinary surgeon.

Sinusitis

Symptoms include swellings above and below the eye. It is commonly associated with lack of Vitamin A. The 'pus' that collects is thick and stringy. One of my lories was treated with three different antibiotics over a period and all were resisted, despite intramuscular injections to speed absorption. Draining and flushing the sinuses can be, and was, done by a veterinary surgeon. This is not, however, always successful and the sinuses may refill. In the end, I lost the bird. I believe that the large amount of handling necessary caused it too much stress.

Trichomoniasis

This flagellate protozoan disease is now encountered among lories although it is more commonly found among pigeons, where it is known as 'canker'. In the early stages vomiting may be observed or a tendency to vomit, as in regurgitation of food for young or a partner. Later a bulging crop will appear, together with loss of weight. A freshly collected crop sample, examined microscopically, will show whether the flagellates are present. (This must be done within minutes, so don't post samples!) In the UK, the usual treatment is metronidazole (Flagyl S) although Emtryl has also been used; both have shown toxic effects in very small finches. Ronidazole (Ronidizal) is used in Europe, where it is also routinely used as a preventative.

Worms

I do not worm all my birds regularly, with the exception of the Musschenbroek's Lorikeets (*Neopsilttacus m. musschenbroeki*) which are given a broad-spectrum anthelmithic, such as Panacur or Nilverm, once a year. Advice on the correct dosage should be sought from a veterinary surgeon. It is helpful if you know the approximate weight of the bird (see the individual species) or its weight can be determined by securing the bird in a substantial and secured hessian bag and using kitchen scales. Any bird whose condition gives cause for concern may also be wormed and it may be worthwhile asking your veterinary surgeon to examine a faecal smear. It was by doing this that I discovered the presence of worms and larvae (other than tapeworms) in my Musschenbroek's Lorikeets (*N. m. moschenbroekii*), shortly after their arrival in the UK almost 10 years ago. At that time the chicks were constantly dying with their crops full of regurgitated larvae. I worm any new arrivals against tapeworms. This used to be particularly vital with wild-caught birds. The day after administering Yomesan or Droncit fragments of tapeworm, often in abundance, could be seen on the paper which had been placed for the purpose below the inside flights (the birds having been shut in overnight for this reason). While still maintaining this practice, I should add that I have not seen any tapeworms for a long while now.

Yersiniosis (Pseudotuberculosis)

Although not a form of tuberculosis, this disease is so called because the white spots on the spleen and liver revealed at post mortem resemble those of tuberculosis. I have lost three birds over the years with this condition. Two were just found dead with no warning; I had a day's notice with the third, long enough to note that she had passed a little blood on the paper. I sent this to the laboratory with the body, separately packed. Post mortem identified yersiniosis, with abscesses on the liver and spleen, and I was advised to keep the birds away from soil and check for mice. Neither of these recommendations applied and I was mystified until I learned it could be spread by wild birds, particularly starlings, of which we had flocks around the aviaries. We moved the ponds (and perches) under cover and my pheasants were no longer thrown free-range food but supplied with 'peck-on-demand' feeders; these baffled the starlings who have thankfully moved away, no doubt for easier pickings.

PART II Genera and species

16 Classification

Class   Aves   (Birds)
Order   Psittaciformes   (Parrots)
Family   Psittacidae   (Parrots and Parrot-like Birds)
Subfamily Loriinae   (Lories and Lorikeets)

The subfamily Loriinae is currently divided into 11 genera, 55 species, and 59 subspecies.

The genera of Loriinae

Genus	Species	Sub-species
Chalcopsitta	4	6
Charmosyna	14	12
Eos	6	7
Glossopsitta	3	0
Lorius	8	9
Neopsittacus	2	3
Oreopsittacus	1	2
Phigys	1	0
Pseudeos	1	0
Trichoglossus	10	20
Vini	5	0
11	55	59

How to interpret the following chapters

Each chapter is devoted to one genus of lory and opens with a breakdown of that genus into species and subspecies. The species and subspecies (with the exception of the nominate and certain lesser known species) are then treated in alphabetical order.

Availability in aviculture

* = Available in aviculture
** = Readily available in aviculture
† = Available in Australian aviculture

No asterisk is given if the species is not available.

In each species section the following details, as supplied by Birdlife International, and where available, will be found.

Where birds are dimorphic, this will be stated at the beginning of the **Description**.

Distinguishing features These state points that should help differentiate the bird being described from those most similar to it.

Range
Is = Island species
M = Mainland species

Population trend
I = Increase
S = Stable

Plate 1 Fairy Lorikeet (*Charmosyna pulchella pulchella*)

Plate 2 Rothschild's Fairy Lorikeet (*Charmosyna pulchella rothschildi*)

Plate 3 Mount Goliath (Stella's) Lorikeet (melanistic) (*Charmosyna papou goliathina*)

Plate 4 Mount Goliath (Stella's) Lorikeet (*Charmosyna papou goliathina*)

Plate 5 Red-spotted Lorikeet (*Charmosyna rubronotata rubronotata*)

Plate 6 Red-flanked Lorikeet (*Charmosyna placentis*)

Plate 7 Black-winged Lory (*Eos cyanogenia*)

Plate 8 Dusky (yellow) Lory (*Pseudeos fuscata*)

Plate 9 Dusky (orange) Lory (*Pseudeos fuscata*)

Plate 10 Blue-streaked Lory (*Eos reticulata*)

Plate 11 Purple-capped Lory (*Lorius domicellus*)

Plate 12 Jobi Lory (*Lorius lory jobiensis*)

Plate 13 Black-capped Lory (*Lorius lory lory*)

Plate 14 Erythro Black-capped Lory (*Lorius lo erythrothorax*)

Plate 15 Chattering Lory (*Lorius garrulus garrulus*)

Plate 16 Yellow-backed Lory (*Lorius garrulus flavopalliatus*)

Plate 17 Yellow-bibbed Lory (*Lorius chlorocercus*)

Plate 18 Sepik (Josephine's) Lorikeet (*Charmosyna josefinae sepikiana*)

Plate 19 Cardinal Lory (*Chalcopsitta cardinalis*)

Plate 20 Talaut Red and Blue Lory (*Eos histrio talautensis*)

Plate 21 Weber's Lorikeet (*Trichoglossus haematodus weberi*)

Plate 22 Buru Red Lory (*Eos bornea cyanothus*)

Plate 23 Red Lory (*Eos bornea bornea*)

Plate 24 Violet-necked Lory (*Eos squamata squamata*)

Plate 25 Obi Lory (*Eos squamata obiensis*)

Plate 26 Duivenbode's Lory (*Chalcopsitta duivenbodei duivenbodei*)

Plate 27 Rajah Lory (*Chalcopsitta atra insignis*)

Plate 28 Yellow-streaked Lory (*Chalcopsitta sintillata sintillata*)

Plate 29 Black Lory (*Chalcopsitta atra atra*)

Plate 30 Swainson's Lorikeet (*Trichoglossus haematodus moluccanus*)

Plate 31 Red-collared Lorikeet (*Trichoglossus haematodus rubritorquis*)

Plate 32 Edward's Lorikeet (*Trichoglossus haematodus capistratus*)

Plate 33 Green-naped Lorikeet (*Trichoglossus haematodus haematodus*)

Plate 34 Coconut Lorikeet (*Trichoglossus haematodus massena*)

Plate 35 Forsten's Lorikeet (*Trichoglossus haematodus forsteni*)

Plate 36 Mitchell's Lorikeet (*Trichoglossus haematodus mitchellii*)

Plate 37 Rosenberg's Lorikeet (*Trichoglossus haematodus rosenbergii*)

Plate 38 Goldie's Lorikeet (*Trichoglossus goldiei*)

Plate 39 Ornate Lorikeet (*Trichoglossus ornatus*)

Plate 40 Striated Lorikeet (*Charmosyna multistriata*)

Plate 41 Yellow and Green Lorikeet (*Trichoglossus flavoviridis flavoviridis*)

Plate 42 Perfect Lory (*Trichoglossus euteles*)

Plate 43 Scaly-breasted Lorikeet (*Trichoglossus chlorolepidotus*)

Plate 44 Meyer's Lorikeet (*Trichoglossus flavoviridis meyeri*)

Plate 45 Musk Lorikeet (*Glossopsitta concina*)

Plate 46 Musschenbroek's Lorikeet (*Neopsittacus musschenbroekii musschenbroekii*)

Plate 47 Iris Lorikeet (*Trichoglossus iris iris*)

Plate 48 Mount Apo Lory (*Trichoglossus johnstoniae*)

Plate 49 Little Lorikeet (*Glossopsitta pulsilla*)

Plate 50 Varied Lorikeet (*Trichoglossus versic*

Plate 51 Pulple-crowned Lorikeet (*Glossopsitta porphyrocephala*)

Lorius l. somu

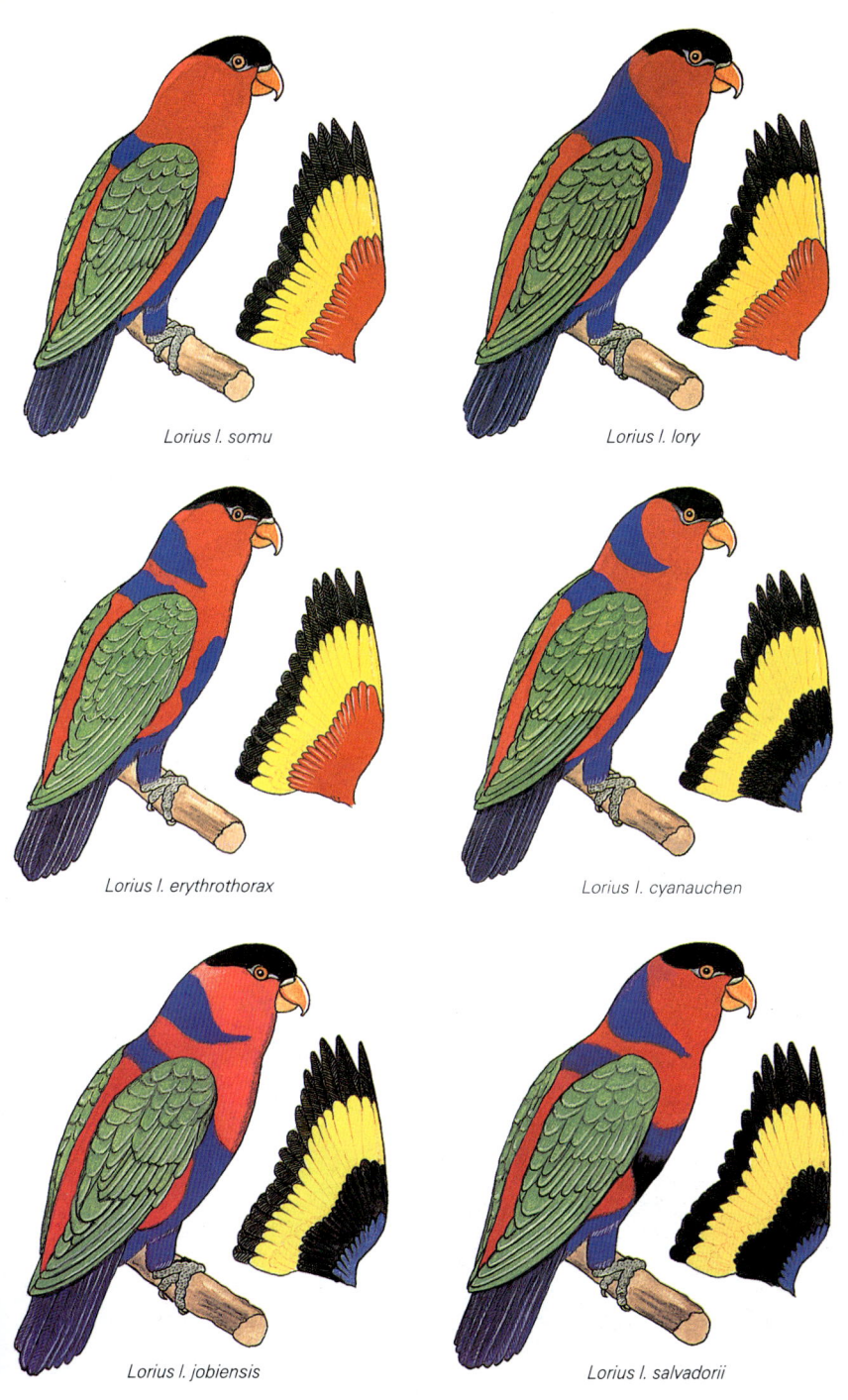

Lorius l. lory

Lorius l. erythrothorax

Lorius l. cyanauchen

Lorius l. jobiensis

Lorius l. salvadorii

Plate 52 Western Black-capped Lories (*Lorius lory*)

Plate 53 Some Rainbow Lorikeets (*Trichoglossus haematodus*)

CLASSIFICATION

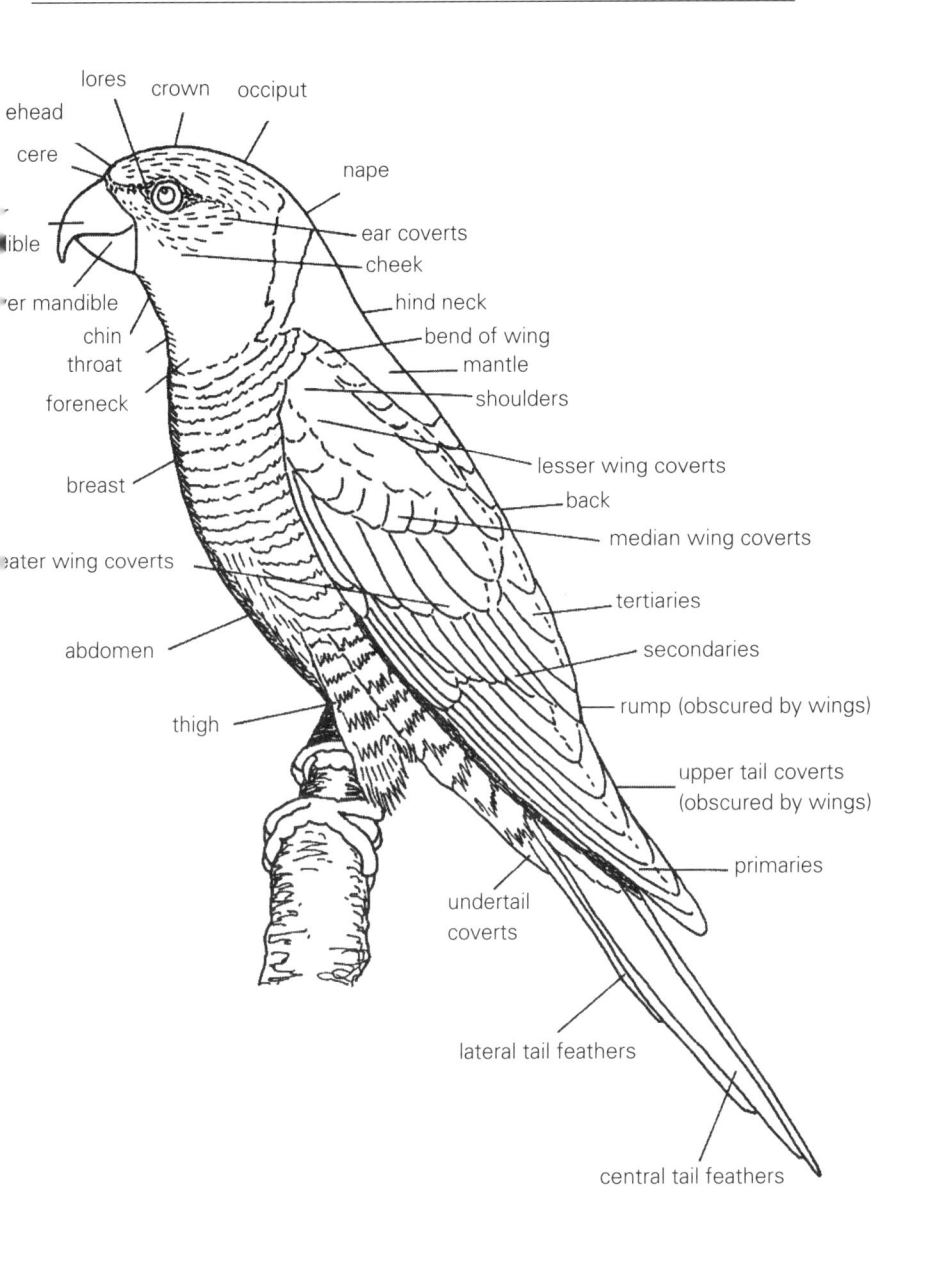

Fig. 32 Topography of a typical lory.

D = Decrease
Ex = Extinct
? = Possibly extinct; insufficient knowledge at this time to be sure.

M-L (Mace-Lande criteria which govern the assignment of threat status:)
S = Safe
C = Critical
E = Endangered
V = Vulnerable
? = Possibly extinct

In the field
C = Recent population census has been undertaken
F = Recent general fieldwork has been undertaken
S = Survey work is needed
R = Relocation

Status
In each species or subspecies section 'Status' is followed by:
a = Known in the wild
b = Known in captivity

Specific threats, where known or suspected, will be listed under 'Status'. Critically endangered = 50 per cent probability of extinction within two generations at best. Endangered = 20 per cent probability of extinction within 20 years.

Nest-boxes The type of nest-box is indicated by the following letters (see Fig. 9, p. 35), and are a guide to what is suitable or preferred:
A = Small
B = Large
C = Large L-shaped
D = Small L-shaped
E = Large slanting
F = Horizontal with half-open front
G = With porch and nesting area
H = Hollow log
I = Rectangular box adapted for extra heat

Ring size The letters denote UK ring sizes. (Continental sizes are measured in millimetres and those for the USA in inches.)

Any subspecies not afforded its own section will be found at the end of the section on the nominate bird. This is because it is not known, nor likely to be known, in aviculture, or because it resembles the nominate bird but for some small exception. Some birds are currently not known in aviculture but there may be a glimmer of hope or, as with *Vini ultramarina*, are of interest for a specific reason, in this instance its relocation to the wild.

My thanks to Richard Grummit and Birdlife International's (formerly International Council for Bird Protection) Parrot Specialist Group for providing this information. Their work in the field and in Cambridge, UK, is of great significance to all bird-lovers.

17 Chalcopsitta

Species	Subspecies	Common name	Availability
atra	atra	Black Lory	*
	bernsteini	Bernstein's Lory	**
	Insignis	Rajah Lory	*
	spectabilis	Handsome Lory	*
cardinalis		Cardinal Lory	*
duivenbodei	duivenbodei	Duivenbode's Lory	*
	syringanuchalis	Lilac-naped Lory	–
sintillata	sintillata	Yellow-streaked Lory	**
	chloroptera (?)	Green-streaked Lory	–
	rubrifrons	Red-streaked Lory	*
4	6	10	

All members of the genus *Chalcopsitta* are large birds, with the characteristic rounded tail of a lory, somewhat longer than in other species. They all have two other distinguishing features:

(1) An area of naked black skin around the eye and lower mandible.
(2) The feathers at the back of the head and neck at times appear as a semi-erectile spiky 'ruff'.

This genus is mainly considered safe currently in its habitat. Its range is wide. The most at risk is the Cardinal Lory (*C. cardinalis*), an island species. Recent fieldwork has been carried out on the taxon. In general the main threats are from loss of habitat and potential trapping.

Black Lory

Chalcopsitta atra atra (Plate 29)

Common names
DUTCH Zwarte lori
GERMAN Schwarzlori
FRENCH Lori noir

Distribution Batanta, Salawati, northwest New Guinea.
Range M/Is. *Population trend* S. *M-L* S. *In the field* F.

Description Apparently entirely black, large and majestic; on closer examination almost iridescent in a good light. Underside of tail red and yellow; slight bluish tinge on the rump; beak, legs and peri-orbital skin (in adults) black; iris variable brown. Monomorphic: in an adult pair the sexual difference seems

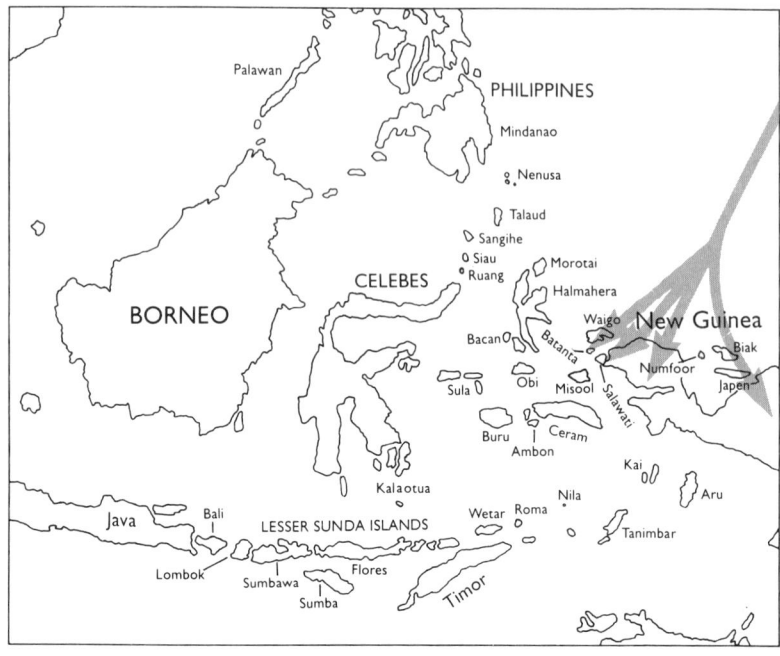

Distribution of the Black Lory

obvious, the cock being more massive in the head and of generally bolder demeanour.

Distinguishing features Almost identical to the Rajah Lory (*C.a. insignis*), but lacking the red, and to Bernstein's Lory (*C.a. bernsteini*), which has red thighs and forehead. (Young Blacks may show some red.)

Status a-b Relatively safe in northwest New Guinea, less so on the islands. It is still threatened by habitat loss, slightly less now from trade. In aviculture, with virtually no imports now, it could become dangerously scarce, as not all pairs settle and reproduce well. This species therefore provides a very worthwhile challenge to aviculturists.

Maturity 3–3½ years.
Length 32cm (12½in).
Weight 200–250g (7–9oz).

Call Variable. These lories can produce a high, piercing call, which fortunately is not sustained for very long. I used to think my two pairs were quiet birds until, after some 10 years, I had sadly to replace a wonderful cock (a bird with whom I felt I was honoured to have a rare spiritual affinity) with a rowdy fellow, who set both pairs off for a while. The calls now come in short intermittent bursts, very often during rain, which seems to give this species more joy than bathing.

Management Hardy. It has a large appetite. Generally wild-caught birds are quite shy. It settles and breeds well in many aviaries.

Nest-box A, C, E, H.
Eggs 2. *Incubation* 25–26 days.
Ring size 7.5–8.5mm (⅜in) 'S–T'.
Fledging About 12 weeks.

Practical experience The Black Lory is one of my favourites. It is something to do with its regal bearing combined with the irresistible devotion showered on me by any young which have to be 'finished off' by hand-rearing. I find it takes all my strength of mind not to lavish too much attention and cuddling on them. It is, however, really vital that we do not do this, and that such hand-rearing should be done in the company of other youngsters. They should be handled as little as possible so that they do not become imprinted on human beings and thus rendered useless for future breeding. This goes for most lories, but most particularly for Blacks. However, even if you do a spectacular job in this respect, I find that, long after weaning is attained, when they are out in an adolescents' flight with a number of other young, they will rush to welcome me, 'ruff' raised, wings outstretched and flapping, calling in a baby fashion solicitously for food.

When rearing I find the parent birds relish all sorts of additional and more solid items of food. Before I adopted this approach I lost one or two chicks because brooding just ceased at about 2 weeks. One or two more I saved on finding them weak and unfed. A few years back I practised supplementary feeding at 8.00 a.m. and 4.00 p.m., in the aviary, speedily returning the chicks to the nest. This slight delay was well tolerated, these being the times at which the lories expected fresh food to arrive. The procedure was watched over by both parent birds from the pop-hole from the flight – a team effort. I was well pleased when the chicks reached independence in this way.

The next round of eggs, however, proved to me that the parent birds had not enjoyed the experience as much as I had. On discovering the eggs (nests are inspected once or twice a week only, unless there are eggs, chicks, or I am training birds to get used to inspections) I was happy. Not so on my next visit as they had disappeared. This had never happened before. The next eggs to be laid were temporarily switched for china ones immediately and, at this point, a variety of additional solid food was supplied. It proved very popular. Under this system the chicks were raised until fully feathered, a big improvement. Then one morning I found the chicks stripped naked. They were very aggressive, actually biting me for a day or so, as by then they were really too old to take for hand-rearing; but eventually it worked well. They had to be hand-reared with much younger chicks, because of their temperature requirements, and now, some months on, they are immaculate once again and it is not apparent that anything untoward ever happened.

Since the introduction of the rowdy cock mentioned above, neither he nor the two-clutch-a-year hen have entered the nest-box. I have changed the nest-box and added different ones and, recently, changed the aviary. If this produces no result I may try a period of separation and reunion. If that fails, I shall have to think again. Is this part of the challenge of lories? The cock of my other pair also died some 5 years ago. When I introduced his replacement, breeding continued twice yearly as though no change had been made!

Subspecies There are four sub-species of *Chalcopsitta atra*:

(1) *C.a. atra* as described above.

(2) *C.a. bernsteini* (Bernstein's Lory) from Irian Jaya and Misool Island.

Few individuals have ever been kept in captivity. It differs from the nominate species in having purplish-red thighs and forehead and a more distinctly bluish rump.

(3) *C.a. insignis* (Rajah Lory), see p. xx.

(4) *C.a. spectabilis* (Handsome Lory), from northwest New Guinea. (Many people now think this is not a distinct subspecies.)

Rajah Lory

Chalcopsitta atra insignis (Plate 27)

Common names
SYNONYM   Red-quilled Lory
DUTCH   Rajahlori
GERMAN   Sammetlori
FRENCH   Lori Rajah

Distribution Northwest New Guinea and Amberpon; also the Onin and Bomberai Peninsulas.
Range M. *Population trend* S. *M-L* S. *In the field* F.

Description Similar to the Black Lory but with fairly extensive red feathering, particularly on the forehead, lores and cheeks and underwing coverts; the colour deepens with age. Varyingly red quills appear through the black plumage; bases of some feathers red on throat and upper chest; quite distinct blue patch on rump; violet on bend of the wing.
Distinguishing features Red colouring distinguishes it from the Black Lory (*C. atra atra*), which lacks all red (except in some young) and from Bernstein's Lory (*C.a. bernsteini*) which is barely known in aviculture and which has red thighs as well as a red forehead.

Status a-b Rajahs are thought to be relatively secure in the wild. Very few have ever been kept and bred in captivity.
Maturity 3–3½ years.
Length 32cm (12½in).
Weight 200–250g (7–9oz).
Call Depending on the individual, but can be loud in bursts.
Management As for Black Lories, at least until further knowledge is gained.
Nest-box A, C, E, H. *Eggs* 2.
Incubation About 25 days.
Ring size 7.5–8.5mm (⅜in) 'S–T'.
Fledging 12 weeks.

Practical experience A small number of Rajahs were imported into Europe in the late 1980s but, to date, little has been heard about them, possibly because this species is late to mature. The two collections in the UK have as yet not bred, although one pair produced fertile eggs that failed to hatch. Rosemary Low (1993) records the management and breeding of two pairs at Palmitos Park, Gran Canaria. This appears to be the same as for other *Chalcopsitta* spp. Rosemary says that Rajahs, unlike Blacks, are impossible to sex. She finds there can be plucking and that chicks apparently have the same attachment to human beings as Blacks. The Palmitos Park Rajahs eat virtually nothing but nectar and, if the chicks are left with the adults, they make relatively poor weight gains.

It would be too easy, and wrong, to assume that, if the adults be persuaded to eat a more varied and solid diet, the weight gains of the chicks might improve. Perhaps the rates at which these chicks grow is slower

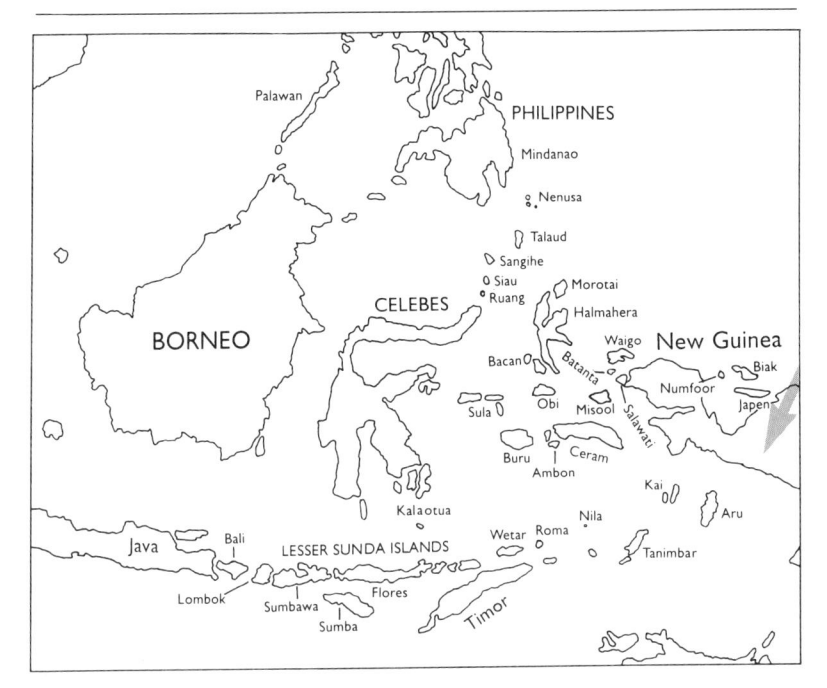

Distribution of the Rajah Lory

and the missing factor is something quite different. (To reinforce my point it might be assumed that the Swainson (*T. h. moluccanus*) and Red-collared (*T.h. rubitorquis*) Lorikeets would be almost identical in all respects. In my experience, however, the two subspecies are quite different in behaviour and management requirements, and not least in the matter of weight gains of chicks.

The pooling of knowledge for this recently introduced species is vital at this stage.

Cardinal Lory

Chalcopsitta cardinalis (Plate 19)

Common names
DUTCH   Kardinal Lori
GERMAN   Kardinallori
FRENCH   Lori Cardinale

Distribution The islands northwest of New Ireland and New Hanover, and the Solomon Islands. The Feni, Nissan and Labongal Group and the islands belonging to Tanga, Lihir and the Tabor archipelago. Recently also found on the Ontong Java atoll of the Solomons. This lory frequents lowland forest up to 830m (2725ft); also coconut plantations. It is abundant and is thought to fly between islands. *Range* Is. *Population trend* S. *M-L* S. *In the field* F.

Description Feathered in varying shades of red, none vibrant; dark, almost rusty chocolate on back and wings; front feathering appears scalloped, having buff edges and giving it a less sleek appearance than most lories. Grey-black peri-orbital skin and ruff-like neck feathers. Like Duivenbode's Lory a neat beard-like

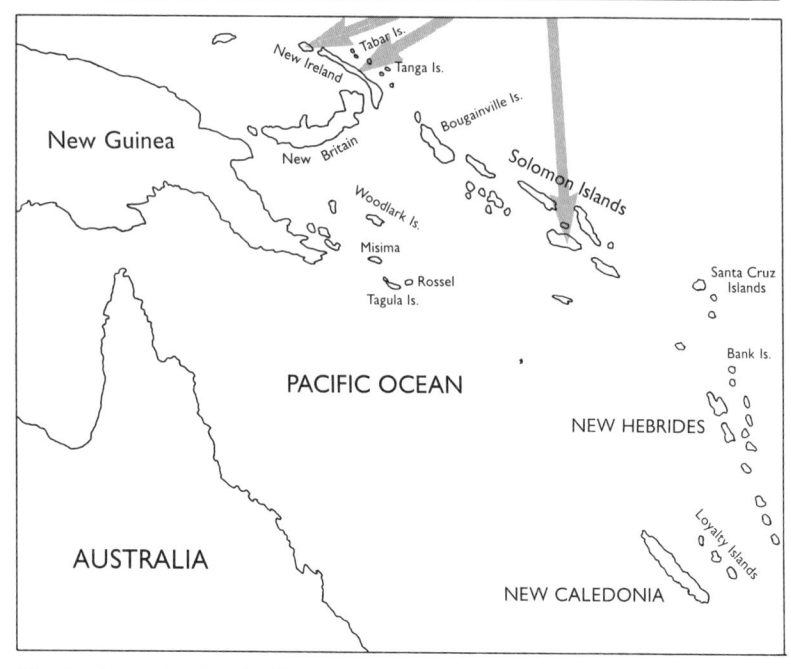

Distribution of the Cardinal Lory

group of darker feathers around the beak, which is orange, darker near the base. Iris dark; legs grey; tail fanned in flight.
Distinguishing features Brick- to rust-red coloration which cannot be confused with any other lory.
Status a-b Currently thought to be common in most parts, but being an island bird (albeit one of several), this *Chalcopsitta* species is the most at risk. Some recent fieldwork has been undertaken on the taxon. Almost unknown in aviculture until 1990, when the Solomon Islands allowed a small consignment to be exported. There are now probably enough specimens to form the basis of a captive population. There are plans for a limited exportation from the Solomons in 1995.
Maturity 3½ years.

Length 31–32cm (12¼–12½in).
Weight 200–250g (7–9oz).
Call Loud, high-pitched shriek, fortunately not long-lasting and mostly when surprised.
Management Hardy. Requires the same management as others in this genus.
Nest-box A, C, E, H.
Eggs 2. *Incubation* 24–25 days.
Ring size 7.5–8.5mm (⅜in) 'S–T'.
Fledging About 10 weeks.

Practical experience Since they became available in 1990 most Cardinals have settled quickly into aviaries and, where age permitted, have commenced breeding (more quickly, I believe than most species). In 1991 I obtained two at weaning from Benaud and Hilda Loman, who lived in Holland and had kept me updated throughout with the birds' progress. My pair consist of one from each of the pairs mentioned below. I find them delightful, hardy, noisy, and very playful. (They spend hours entwined on their swing and branches.) They have large appetites and I find they enjoy a wide range of food.

I keep them in the same manner as other lories, i.e. they have a choice of using their house, which contains their nest-box, or going out in the flight which is 2.74m × 0.9m × 1.8m high (9ft × 3ft × 6ft high). This choice is available all year.

The Lomans (1992) wrote that, after purchasing two pairs from the importers in 1990, they placed them in an inside flight with a fixed temperature of 15°C (59°F). They were fed Aves Lorinectar. Within a year both pairs had laid. The usual 'first offering' problems were encountered: infertile eggs, chipped eggs, disappearing eggs, and eggs of one clutch totally dried out. The first chick was found decapitated, so its sibling was taken for hand-rearing. The other pair reared two themselves. They were easy to hand-rear and, although no difference was found in the weight gains made by the parent-reared and hand-reared specimens, the feathering on the former was found to be superior. The Lomans did find that the adults became very aggressive during egg-laying and rearing.

In January 1994 I was fortunate enough to obtain two black-beaked females from the Philippines. They grew for over a year before I dared to place them with the males. The introduction went smoothly, the birds all having been isolated first. Within a month mating was observed between one pair.

Duivenbode's Lory

Chalcopsitta duivenbodei duivenbodei
(Plate 26)

Common names
ENGLISH   Brown Lory
DUTCH   Duivenbodei Lori
GERMAN   Braunlori
FRENCH   Lori de Duivenbodeii

Distribution Endemic to north New Guinea particularly the Sepik–Ramu regions where it frequents the tops of trees at lower altitudes, up to 180m (600ft) in pairs or small parties, often in the company of other lories. It skirts around forest edges rather than flying through or over trees.
Range M. *Population trend* S. *M-L* S. *In the field* F.

Description Unusual and striking 'bumble-bee' colours; basically olive-brown on wings and back; distinctive yellow forehead and band of yellow spreading from lores and around the lower beak and throat to resemble a well-trimmed beard; bend of wing and underwing, inner thighs and base of some chest feathers yellow; beak and legs black; iris brown; rump violet-blue.
Distinguishing features The yellow Dusky Lory (*Pseudeos fuscata*) is similarly coloured but smaller, with orange beak, brown forehead with yellow crown, and a striped chest.
Status a-b Considered safe, although never abundant; probably safe still in aviculture.
Maturity 3–3½ years.
Length 31cm (12¼in).
Weight 200–250g (7–9oz).
Call Loud two-toned call; also a screech which is not persistent.
Management Fairly hardy, although

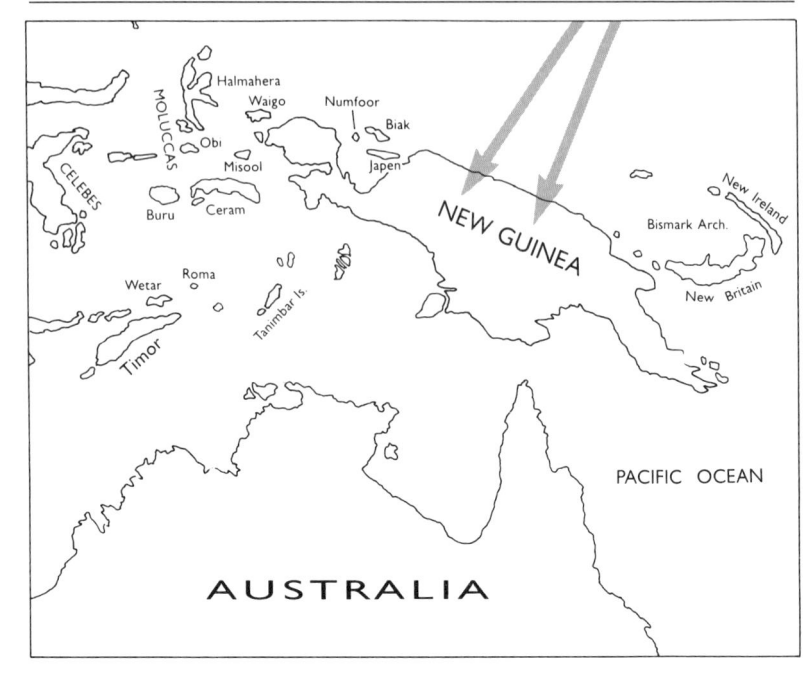

Distribution of Duivenbode's Lory

may be not as robust as others in this genus.
Nest-box A, C, E, H.
Eggs 2. *Incubation* 24–25 days.
Ring size 7.5–8.5mm (⅜in) 'S–T'.
Fledging About 10 weeks.

Practical experience Some people think it possible that, in due course, this lory may be found to be incorrectly placed in the genus *Chalcopsitta*. Mine rush to greet me, wings outstretched, tail fanned, 'ruff' erect, bobbing, lungeing and, in between times, standing tall, arching the neck and hissing. This hissing seems peculiar to Duivenbode's Lory but, in every other respect, their behaviour seems like that of any other member of this genus. It is interesting to note that ornithologists Beehler, Pratt and Zimmerman (1986) consider this large lory less noisy in the field than the Dusky Lory (*Pseudeos fuscata*) and the Green-naped Lorikeet (*Trichoglossus h. haematodus*).

While being fairly hardy to hardy, these lories do not seem as resilient as the others I have discussed in this chapter, particularly the males.

Subspecies There are two subspecies of *Chalcopsitta duivenbodei*:

(1) *C.d. duivenbodei*, as described above.

(2) *C.d. syringanuchah's* (Lilac-naped Lory), from northeast New Guinea. Of doubtful distinction, it is said to have a lilac sheen on the head and back.

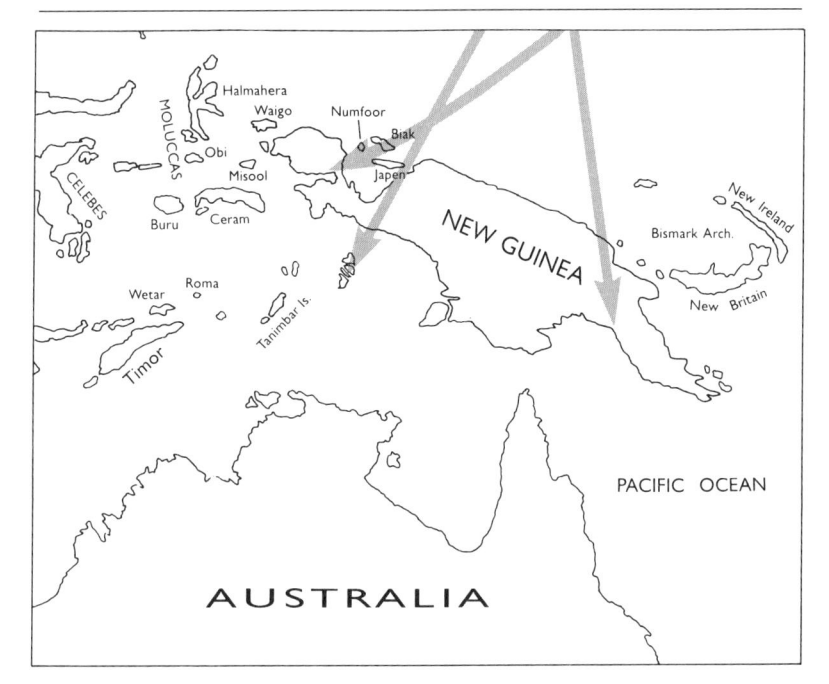

Distribution of the Yellow-streaked Lory

Yellow-streaked Lory

Chalcopsitta sintillata sintillata (Plate 28).

Common names
SYNONYM   Greater Streaked Lory
DUTCH   Orange Geestrepte
GERMAN   Schimmerlori
FRENCH   Lori à front jaune

Distribution Southern New Guinea from Port Moresby area west to Triton Bay and the head of Geelvink Bay; also Aru Islands. The nominate species frequents forest, forest edges, partly cleared areas, coconut plantations and savannah. It is particularly fond of sago palm and schefflera. It is found in flocks where it appears quarrelsome, but is nevertheless seen in the company of Green-naped lorikeets (*Trichoglossus h. haematodus*) and Red-flanked Lorikeets (*Charmosyna p. placentis*).
Range M/Is. Population trend S. M-L S. In the field F.

Description A very beautiful green-backed, green-winged lory. Nape, ear coverts and beak black, as is the peri-orbital skin (in adults); lores, thighs and undertail, underwings and forehead (in adults) red; variable red flecking on throat area; yellow band across underside of flight feathers; front entirely green, heavily streaked with golden yellow; iris brown; characteristic spiky 'ruff' formed by the neck feathers.
Distinguishing features The yellow streaking of the breast distinguishes the nominate subspecies from the Red-streaked Lory (*C.s. rubrifrons*), which

has orange-red streaking, and the Green-streaked Lory (*C.s.chloroptera*) which has green streaking and green underwings.
Status a-b Considered currently safe in both; it has a large natural range.
Maturity 3–3½ years.
Length 30cm (12in).
Weight 200–250g (7–9oz).
Call Medium, with loud outbursts when disturbed.
Management Easy, hardy, free-breeding.
Nest-box A, C, E, H. *Eggs* 2.
Incubation Normally 26 days.
Ring size 7.5–8.5mm (⅜ in) 'S–T'.
Fledging 12 weeks.

Practical experience Some years ago I commissioned an artist friend to 'paint my lories as you see them'. He did several pencil drawings of various species around the edge of the picture and chose a yellow-streaked Lory to paint in colour as the central character. I was not at all surprised with his choice; she was a most beautiful bird (as a lot of people would agree) as she sat unconcernedly in front of him, preening with her 'ruff' erect.

I find these lories hardy and easy to feed, maintain and breed. When this species first arrived in the UK, I was among the first to purchase a 'pair'. This was before surgical sexing really became established. At the dealers I opted for the biggest bird and a much smaller one. After a couple of years, nothing had happened and I had them surgically sexed. The larger bird turned out to be the hen and I was told that the cock was still immature.

By the following year the birds were the same size and, because I had not ringed them, I could hardly tell which was which. The cock must have been quite young when he arrived in the country. From then on four eggs were laid, hatched and the chicks parent-reared every year. There was absolutely no failure of any description – not even one infertile egg. Quite a record!

This went on until the early Spring of 1992 when the hen decided she no longer liked the cock and tried to kill him. I found him lying on the floor, covered with blood, and stupidly thought there must have been some accident. I cleaned him up and kept him in for a couple of days to heal before returning him to the flight. She swooped like a hawk and attacked him right in front of me. I then tried clipping her wing and watched out of sight. She was extremely crafty and would move slowly, wait to corner him and then pounce. I had to separate them.

At this point a second pair had recently started to breed. After much soul-searching I decided to switch the pairs. Psychologically what had gone wrong? To this day I have no idea, so I have learned nothing from the experience. Amazingly, after some weeks, things settled down and both pairs began to breed again.

Getting birds together in the first instance can sometimes be tricky but this sort of occurrence – a case of divorce – is not common among lories. This same pair, who were very gentle with each other and human beings (some Yellow-streaked Lories can be quite aggressive to their keepers when they are rearing chicks) did one other unforgivable thing before their first egg was laid. I had been remiss in not observing the wood-chewing that had taken place. Regretfully, one morning, I found that they had let themselves into the next aviary, killed the resident cock and laid in the nest there. I did learn something from this experience. The occupants of the next aviary were Duivenbode's Lories, (*C.d. duivenbodei*). I had not taken seriously the advice of many years not to keep members of the same genus in adjacent flights. Subsequently I placed *Trichoglossus* and *Pseudeos* spp. on either side and harmony was restored. For me it was a silly way to learn.

Yellow-streaked Lory chicks, if hand-reared, may become imprinted if care is not taken. Chicks at fledging have white eye rings and the forehead is usually black, not red. (If there is any red, it appears, as does the whole bird, to be a duller version of the adult.)

A dealer once gave me the last Yellow-Streaked Lory from a batch in quarantine. We had arranged to meet at the airport because he was going abroad and this was convenient for collecting the boxes of purchased birds and the 'gift'. The content of the 'gift' box was quite a shock – the bird was almost entirely featherless. In due course she (as it was found to be), became quite beautiful but, unfortunately, also totally imprinted on human beings. This was my fault entirely, because of excess pitying attention which I lavished on her in her featherless days.

She also became very fond of her allocated male and all was harmonious until they commenced breeding; then, because of her familiarity with human beings, she became lethal at feeding times and when routine nest inspections were being carried out. Her behaviour must have encouraged the cock because he became just as bad. Wearing gloves was no defence; they would be attacked and shaken to such an extent that they could not be removed without the attached bird coming with them. Ears, nose, bare toes were all fair game.

The feeding problem was overcome by the introduction of revolving feeders and nest inspections were made possible by offering some favoured titbit in the flight and, at great speed, shutting the pop-hole to the house. This is one good lesson on the dangers of imprinting. Another occurred while I was away and someone else was looking after the birds; this pair had young and, although the safety routine mentioned above was in force, the helper received a severe bite, and erroneously thought that nest inspections would be best left until my return. Regretfully it was too late for the chicks, which had been abandoned when their nest became waterlogged.

Subspecies There are three subspecies of *Chalcopsitta sintillata*:

(1) *C. s. sintillata*, as described above.

(2) *C. s. chloroptera* (Green-streaked Lory), from southeast New Guinea, with green streaking and green underwings. (A little red may be present.) There is some doubt whether this is a true subspecies, as opposed to a natural variation as the ranges overlap.

(3) *C. s. rubrifrons* (Red-streaked, Orange-fronted or Carmine-fronted Lory), from the Aru Islands, whose breast streaking is reddish-orange.

18 Charmosyna

Species	Subspecies	English name	Availability
amabilis	–	Red-throated lory	–
diadema	–	New Caledonian Lorikeet	–
josefinae	*josefinae*	Josephine's Lorikeet	*
	cyclopum	Cyclops Lorikeet	–
	sepikiana	Sepik Lorikeet	*
margarethae	–	Duchess Lorikeet	–
meeki	–	Meek's Lorikeet	–
multistriata	–	Striated Lorikeet	*
palmarum	–	Palm Lorikeet	–
papou	*papou*	Papuan Lorikeet	*
	goliathina	Mount Goliath Lorikeet	**
	stellae	Stella's Lorikeet	*
	wahnesi	Gold-banded Lorikeet	–
placentis	*placentis*	Red-flanked Lorikeet	*
	intensior	–	–
	ornata	–	–
	pallidor	Solomon Islands Pleasing Lorikeet	–
	subplacens	–	
pulchella	*pulchella*	Fairy Lorikeet	*
	rothschildi	Rothschild's Fairy Lorikeet	*
rubrigularis	*rubrigularis*	Red-chinned Lorikeet	–
	krakari	–	–
rubronotata	*rubronotata*	Red-spotted Lorikeet	*
	kordoana	–	–
toxopei	–	Blue-fronted Lorikeet	–
wilhelminae	–	Wilhelmina's Lorikeet	–
14	12	26	

Members of this genus are possibly the most beautiful, graceful, delicate and gentle of all lories. Their voice is quiet and melodic. Until the late 1970s they were virtually unknown in captivity.

There have certain features in common:

(1) They are to varying degrees delicate and intolerant of cold and frost. Mount Goliaths (*C.p. goliathina*)

are the hardiest and Sepiks (*C.j. sepikiana*) are able to withstand a few degrees of frost, but the smaller ones really need a constant and fairly high temperature for maintenance of health and breeding.
(2) The majority make their nests very dirty and wet.
(3) In my view they need a different, thinner nectar than other lories. If it is too thick (which is a risk to their health), they flick it around with their beaks, making themselves and their surroundings filthy.
(4) The faeces seem to be squirted further and more horizontally than in other lories, and so perches must be placed further from walls. This behaviour appears to be less pronounced if they are fed a less rich diet. If the lories are fed a normal lory diet, their excreta becomes of a thicker pasty consistency and adheres to walls and netting.
(5) Many will lay eggs and leave them for some days, even burying them for a time before incubation is commenced.
(6) Young leave the nest much smaller than their parents, usually around two-thirds adult size and with short tails. Once fledged the youngsters' size increases quite speedily over a month or so but, in the case of Stella's Lorikeet the tail takes about a year to reach full length.
(7) Most share a love of stripping branches and spreading the sap from under the bark on their feathers.

Those people dedicated to, and specializing in, any of these lorikeets, I am sure will agree that the extra thought and management required is well worth it. *Charmosyna* spp. really are especially delightful birds, as well as being ones that offer a real challenge to the more experienced aviculturist.

Red-throated Lory

Charmosyna amabilis

Common names
ENGLISH	Golden-banded Lory
DUTCH	Roodkin Lori
GERMAN	Rotkinnlori
FRENCH	Loriquet à cou rouge

Distribution Fiji: Viti Levu, Ovalau and Taveuni Islands; in the high canopy of mature forest, where it can be detected by its rapid, fluttering wing beats.
Range Is. *Population trend* S?
M-L V. *In the field* ?

Description Delicate build; mostly green but for the red cheeks, thighs and throat; throat bordered with yellow; undertail and tail tips mustard yellow; beak and legs orange.
Length 18cm (7in).
Call Brief, high-pitched squeak.
Status a Rare. It seems that little more is known of this species than was in Mivart's day (c. 1896) when it was observed in flocks in Taveuni, in the company of Collard Lories (*Phigys solitarius*). The reason for its rarity is at this time unknown. Probable threats seem to be habitat loss and interspecific competition. The Conservation Programme for Threatened South Pacific Species now operates in this area, so it is to be hoped that forests will be better preserved in future.

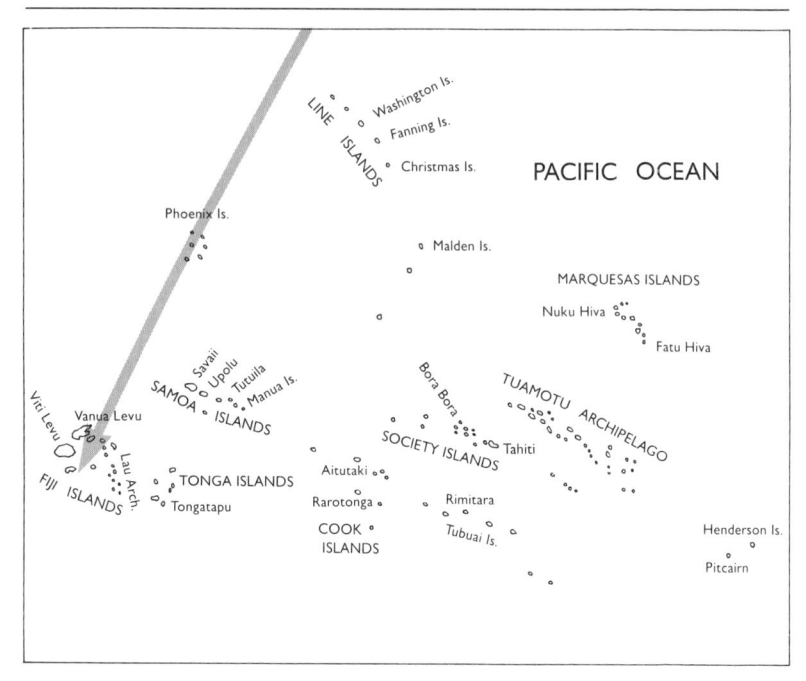

Distribution of the Red-throated Lory

Sepik Lorikeet
(Josephine)
Charmosyna josefinae sepikiana (Plate 18)

Common names

ENGLISH	Josephine's Lorikeet
DUTCH	Josephinelori
GERMAN	Josephinenlori
FRENCH	Loriquet de Josephine

Distribution Central part of western and central New Guinea where it inhabits forest edges, partly cleared areas between 850 and 1200m (2800 and 4000ft). It flies silently and climbs slowly among blossoming trees. Not much has been recorded in the wild because of the density of the terrain around the River Sepik. The region north and west of this is so far uncharted.

Range M. *Population trend* S. M-L S. *In the field* ?

Description Dimorphic. Those in captivity generally red, with mantle and wings green and hind crown and nape black, with some lilac streaking; blue patch on rump; thighs, lower abdomen and flanks black; central tail feathers tipped with yellow; upper base to tail. The hen is similar but with lower back and flanks yellow.

I quote here from Jos Hubers (1993):

From the above description one might assume that the birds we possess are all of the subspecies *C. j. sepikiana*. The birds known in aviculture have a yellow rump. However it is probably not so simple. Studies of skins in the British Natural History Museum showed

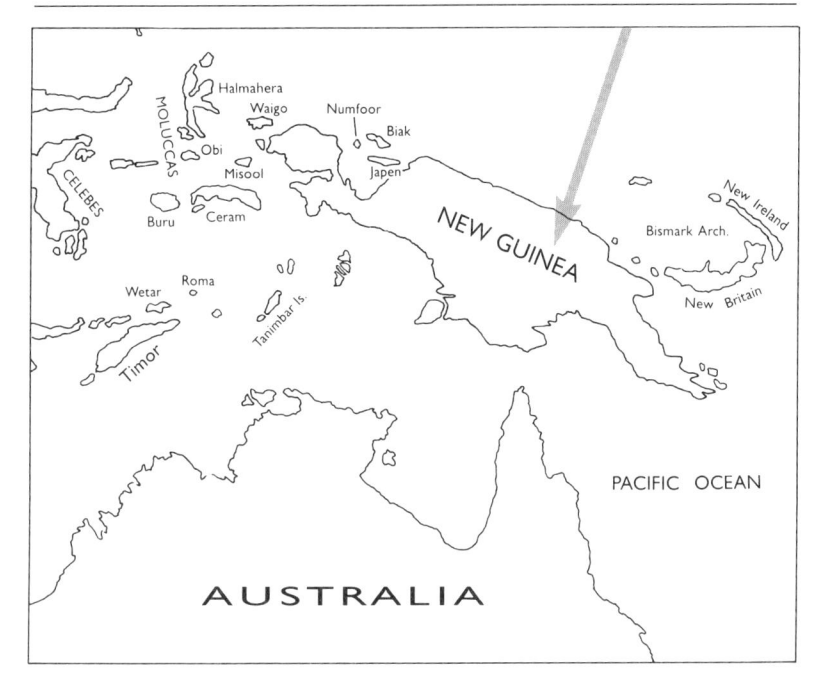

Distribution of the Sepik Lorikeet

that the nominate species cannot be easily distinguished from *C. j. sepikiana*. Most females of the nominate species did not have a green rump, but one which was green-yellow or yellow. The other differences were also not clear. Further studies in other museums will probably clarify the situation.

Distinguishing features Smaller than the *C. papou goliathina* with the upper base of the tail green as opposed to red.
Status a-b Rather common still supposedly in the wild. Not well enough established in captivity, where there are not enough breeding pairs.
Maturity 22–26 months.
Length 24cm (9½in).
Weight 70–80g (2½–2⅞oz).
Call Quiet; repetitive faint squeak.
Management Not totally hardy; can withstand a few degrees of frost.
Nest-box B, F, G, H, I.
Eggs 2.
Incubation About 26–27 days.
Ring size 5.5mm (¼in) 'N'.
Fledging 7–8 weeks.

Practical experience Sepik (Josephine's) Lorikeets were virtually unknown in aviculture till the late 1970s. In common with other *Charmosyna* spp. they cannot take thick nectar, and options for feeding this species appear in Chapter 7. Other than in warm climates it is probably best to house this species in inside flights with a minimum size of 1.8m × 0.9m × 0.9m high (6ft × 3ft × 3ft high), or partly inside and partly outside with additional heating so that the temperature preferably does not fall much below 10°C (50°F).

I have kept two cocks in a planted outside aviary with their house heated only to just above freezing. They have appeared in excellent condition housed like this for the past 3 years. It is possible that aviculturists in the UK are particularly sensitive because the last shipment contained birds, particularly females, that have mostly died from what appears to be a form of ascites (see Chapter 14). In whatever way these lorikeets are housed there must be easy access to the nests, which will need constant refurbishing due to fouling.

About 3 years ago I bought five birds direct from this last UK shipment – three hens and two cocks, or so I believed. However, despite all three hens having bright yellow backs, one moulted out the yellow feathers, thus proving to be a cock. I had heard from Anton Spenkelink in Holland that this happens with Josephine's Lorikeets, but when it came to choosing birds in quarantine, I failed to give it a thought, particularly as none of the birds had dark beaks. With the second 'hen' I had failed to notice that the top of the tail was green and not red. 'She' grew in size and 'her' tail grew in length and almost 2 years later, she became a beautiful little 'stella'. The third and *only* hen died after 2 years of gradual decline from the ascites problem: laboured breathing, sticky appearance, and an enlarged stomach. She had suffered several bouts of candidiasis, possibly because this species seems to have a lower tolerance of antibiotic. It is probable that they receive more of this substance than they can take while in quarantine, in the country of either export or import.

I quote here from Gary Clayton (1993):

January 1992 the hen of Pr No. 2 looks ill, she was fluffed up and vomiting after feeding fresh nectar. She was immediately brought inside and put in a cage with an infra red lamp on her. She was very ill, I rang the vet I use, but he was out of the country. So I was on my own with this sick rare lorikeet. She got worse and worse until it got to the point that I could hardly see her suffer much more, she was unable to stand, unable to perch, there was discharge coming from her nostrils, and her breathing was loud. She was dosed with large amounts of Nystatin and Verkon mixed with the nectar and she was fed off a spoon with this. Four days later she was able to perch, the cock bird was brought in to be with her and the Verkon stopped, but the Nystatin continued for another week. One week after stopping the Nystatin she was back to normal apart from her head being slightly tilted to one side. She was placed with her mate in an indoor cage with nest box attached to the outside. In June it was quite a surprise to find that after all she had gone through she laid 2 eggs three days apart. Both cock and hen shared the incubation and one egg hatched 27 days after the first was laid. The chick was well fed. The only addition to the diet was sponge cake soaked in honey which they relished. When the chick was fully feathered I thought it was a cock, then suddenly it was plucked almost bare apart from its head. It was removed and placed in a heated cage. Some five weeks later it was again fully feathered but this time with yellow on the flanks and lower back. I have got another hen and two more cocks

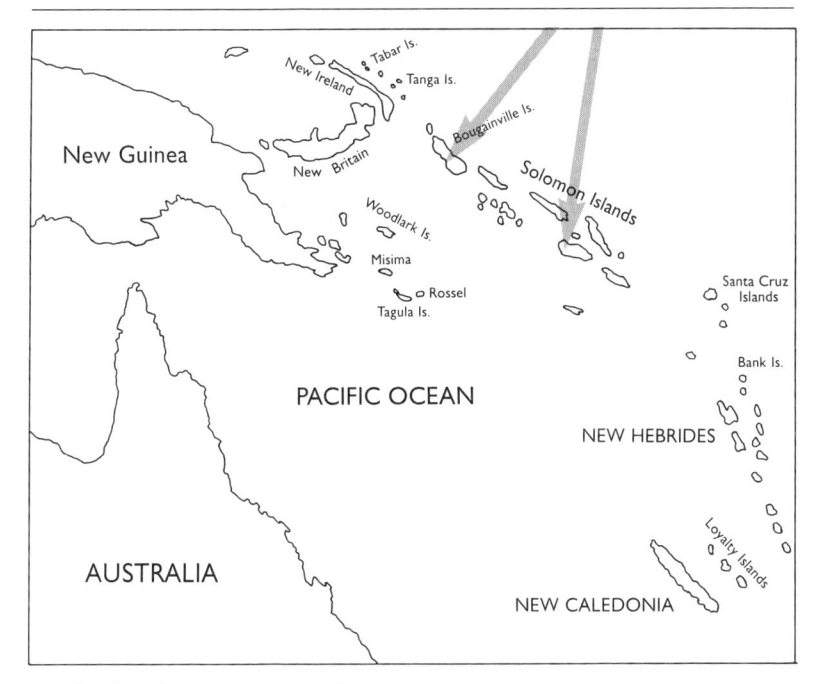

Distribution of The Duchess Lorikeet

although two of them have very light coloured beaks and swollen vents, a condition quite common in *Charmosyna* lorikeets, but little spoken about!

Subspecies There are 3 subspecies of *Charmosyna josefinae*:

(1) *C.j. josefinae* (Josephine's Lorikeet), which has bluer streaks on the crown than *C.j. sepikiana*, and in which the lower back of the female is green.
(2) *C.j. cyclopum* (Cyclops Lorikeet), in which the crown streaking and belly patch are absent.
(3) *C.j. sepikiana*, as described above.

Duchess Lorikeet

Charmosyna margarethae

Common names

SYNONYM	Princess Margaret's Lorikeet
DUTCH	Margaretha's Honingpapegaai
GERMAN	Margarethenlori
FRENCH	Lori de Marguerite

Distribution The Solomon Islands from the coast to 1350m (4400ft) in forests, forest edges, secondary growth and coconut plantations. It is most numerous in the lower hills. On Guadalcanal it is mainly a mountain bird; on Bougainville and other islands it inhabits coastal regions, often in the company of other lories. It is particularly fond of the forest-canopy fruit, especially schefflera.

Range Is. *Population trend* S?
M-L S. *In the field* ?

Description Dimorphic. Mainly red with body feathers edged purple; wings and mantle green; purple-black patch on the crown and abdomen; tail red, tipped yellow; beak and legs orange. The hen has a yellow patch at each side of the rump.
Distinguishing features Yellow breast band bordered by black which extends as a line on the mantle.
Status a-b Considered possibly safe still in its habitat; unknown today in aviculture, although it was once known – there are no records. It is possible that a limited number may become available to aviculture in the future.
Length 20cm (8in).
Call Rapidly repeated squeak, quite unlike the shrill calls of most lories.

Striated Lorikeet

Charmosyna multistriata (Plate 40)

Common names
DUTCH Vcelstrepenlori
GERMAN Vielstrichellori
FRENCH Loriquet multistrie

Distribution West central New Guinea at altitudes between 180 and 1800m (600 and 5900ft) on the southern slopes of the main ranges between the Snow Mountains east of the Upper Fly River. Very little has been recorded about this lorikeet. It has been seen in the company of Red-flanked Lorikeets (*C. placentis*) and Fairy Lorikeets (*C. pulchella*) when trees were in flower.
Range M. *Population trend* S?
M-L S? *In the field?*

Description General plumage green, with hind crown and nape brown; sides of face and entire underside heavily streaked with gold; vent red; beak – one of only two species which have two-tone beaks – the upper mandible grey-blue and lower mandible and tip orange-red; iris red; legs grey. Monomorphic, although the male is said to be more brightly coloured and somewhat larger.
Distinguishing features Similar to Goldie's Lorikeet (*Trichoglossus goldiei*) but with two-tone beak.
Status a-b Possibly scarce in the wild, little as yet is known; rare in aviculture.
Maturity 11–13 months.
Length 18cm (7in).
Weight 40–45g (1⅜–1⅝oz).
Call Quiet; including a long-drawn-out single whistle of changing pitch.
Nest-box 18cm square by 30cm high (7in square by 12in high).
Eggs 2. *Incubation* 25 days.
Ring size 4.2–4.5mm (³⁄₁₆in) 'M'.
Fledging About 7½ weeks.

Practical experience Mr H. J. Michorius of Holland is one of the few breeders of this bird. He says:

My birds are kept in cages measuring 80 by 80 by 120 high cms, provided with a slanting nest log of 18 × 18 × 30 high cms fitted at an angle of 45°. The temperature at the nest site is very humid and is about 17°C. While the male and female of other *Charmosyna* species usually take turns at incubating, in my experience it is only the male that incubates during daytime. Both male and female spend the night together in the nesting log.

He feeds Aves nectar 1 part dry to 5 parts water, 'other' nectar, small pieces of apple, and regularly offers willow branches.

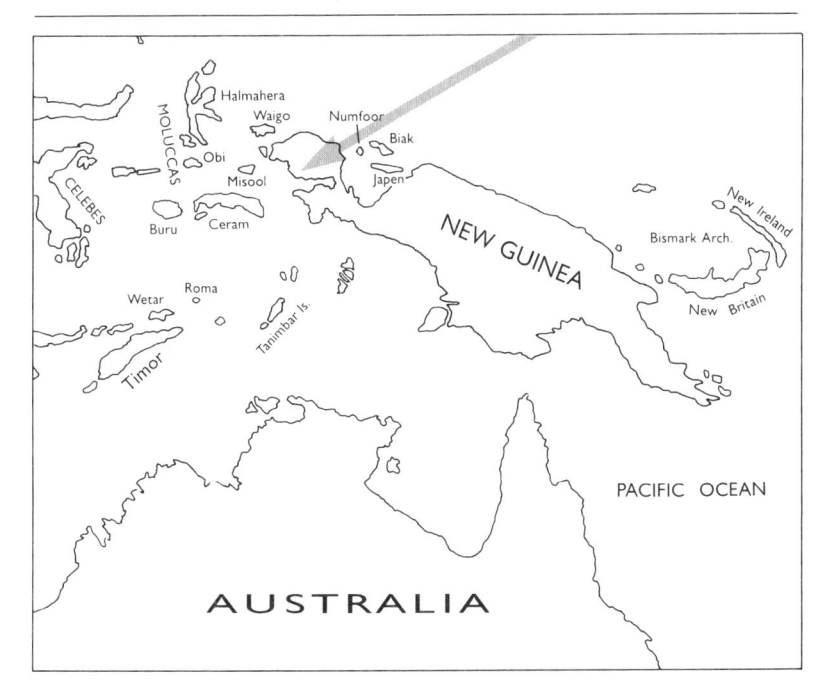

Distribution of the Striated Lorikeet

I hear that currently in the USA many pairs are frustratingly rearing for a period and then abandoning the chicks.

Mount Goliath Lorikeet
(Stella)
Charmosyna papou goliathina (Plates 3 and 4)

Common names

SYNONYM	Long-tailed Lorikeet, Stella's Lorikeet, Papuan Lorikeet
DUTCH	Stellalori
GERMAN	Stella Papualori
FRENCH	Loriquet de Mont Goliath

Distribution The mountains of central New Guinea and the Vogelkop in Irian Jaya, at altitudes mostly about 3000m (9800ft). Sometimes seen in the company of Musschenbroek's Lorikeet (*N.m. muschenbroekii*). It has been observed feeding on fruit, nectar, pollen, seeds, flower parts, insects and larvae. It is conspicuous when flying low, over or through the tops of trees. Its flight is apparently straight but not very fast. In much of its range, its skins and tails are still highly prized by mountain people as head decoration.

Range M. *Population trend* S. *M-L* S. *In the field* ?

Description Dimorphic. Two colour phases: normal red and melanistic (black). Normal colour phase: predominantly red with green wings, mantle and upper tail, and a blue hind crown shading to black; patch of blue

149

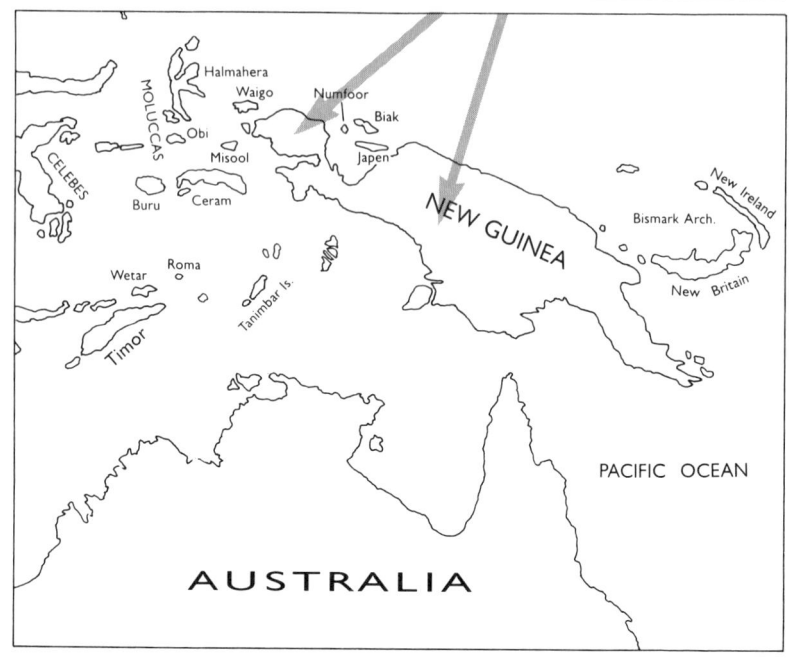

Distribution of the Mount Goliath Lorikeet

on the rump; thighs and lower stomach black; upper tail green, tipped with yellow; underside yellow. The tail comprises 12 feathers; in adults the central two are much longer, tapering, and account for about 20cm (8in) of the bird's total length. Dimorphic: hen has a yellow rump.

Melanistic phase: black with a greenish sheen and distinctive red. The cock has a red rump; some, in my experience, show varying degrees of red on the chest; one in my possession had a complete red band but this appeared to diminish somewhat each year. This is the dominant colour and is important when breeding because colour in this species has been found to be sex-linked (see Table 14, p. 152). Both colour phases should have pink feet and the particularly slender elegant beak should be red. Immatures are distinctly smaller than adults and much duller. The tail does not reach full length until the age of 1–2 years. Dimorphism is not positive until at least the first moult.

Birds are sometimes seen with horn-coloured beaks and pale feet; these are signs of a sick bird. I have one such cock which I acquired with an orange, not red, beak, and from which I bred 2 years ago. His illness arrived without warning. The sudden change in beak colour was the first thing I noticed; then the thick excreta clogging the tail. He was brought in and cleaned up, heat was applied, and he was fed just honey-water, probiotics and electrolytes. In a day or so he seemed quite normal except, to this day, the beak has not returned to orange. (See also Chapter 14.)

Distinguishing features The exceedingly long tail. Red immatures, or those with broken tails, may be confused with the Sepik Lorikeet (*C.j. sepikiana*) but for the upper base of the tail which is green not red.
Status a-b Common still in the wild; relatively well established in aviculture.
Maturity 2 years.
Length 40–42cm (16–16½in).
Weight 92–115g (3½–4 oz).
Call A variety of quiet calls, including a distinctive and melodic warble.
Management Not easy but the easiest of the *Charmosyna* spp. and relatively the hardiest; requires special attention to diet and nests.
Nest-box A, B, E, G, H.
Eggs 2.
Incubation 25–28 days (over 30 have been recorded).
Ring size 5.5mm (¼in) 'N'.
Fledging About 8 weeks.

Practical experience Until recently these lorikeets were very rare in aviculture but at last increasing numbers of breeding pairs are becoming established. There is always a tremendous demand for them in the UK and hens in particular are always in short supply. They should be housed in as large an aviary as possible, firstly because this affords the best view of this truly spectacular bird and secondly because this can be planted safely (see p. 60). It also reduces fouling of the walls; these birds are able to shoot faeces particularly long distances. (Despite this comment, I can only supply regular-sized aviaries to mine.) This species is relatively hardy but should have a draughtproof shelter containing a thick, dry nest-box for roosting. Particular attention must be paid to hygiene with this species. Nests will need constant attention because of fouling, so should be positioned near a door.

It is believed that these lorikeets, in common with other *Charmosyna* spp., need a much thinner nectar than most lories (see p. 56).

The hens have been said to bury their eggs, possibly because the incubation period is long in relation to the size of bird; no doubt some individuals do this, and some lay, then leave the eggs for a few days before commencing incubation. My pairs commence sitting immediately but the eggs take about 28 days to hatch, the same time as they take in my incubator; but I know other pairs which take from 25 to almost 40 days to hatch their eggs. If hand-reared, chicks can feed themselves at about 6 weeks of age.

My first chick was the result of pairing a 2-year-old cock with an older hen. (Birds may take a little longer to breed if both are of the same age.) Hatching and newly hatched chicks make very little or no sound. From about day 12 they start a constant and unique twittering, quite unlike the sounds of other lory chicks. However, they prove just as easy to hand-rear, should the occasion arise. This occasion occurred with one of my eggs which, on day 4, was found to have a nail puncture in the shell. I sealed the shell with nail varnish and put a tiny square of sticky tape over the area; I could not then expect the egg to be turned by the hen without the tape being knocked off. I was amazed to find that:

(1) The egg grew on to prove fertile.
(2) After being returned to the hen, it hatched.

Few people in the UK have so far bred

Table 14 Sex linkage in Stella's Lorikeets

Cock	Hen	Progeny
Black	Black	Black cocks Black hens
Red	Red	Red cocks Red hens
Black	Red	Red/Black cocks Black hens
Red	Black	Red/Black cocks Red hens
Red/Black splits	Black	Black cocks Black hens Red hens
Red/Black splits	Red	Black hens Red cocks Red hens

this lorikeet to the second generation and beyond. (They have simply not been kept for long enough, for one thing.) This is, to many, the mark of an established bird. There was multiple-generation breeding in the first few years of this century in Scotland. This species is therefore a great challenge to aviculturists. Currently, many more pairs are breeding in the UK. Two 2-year-old pairs have both laid their first clutch, and, interestingly, the eggs arrived 6 days apart. The other pair's first egg was dropped from the perch – hopefully this will hot happen again.

Recent studies in Germany suggest that the colour of progeny from matings between red Stellas and black Stellas are sex-linked (see Table 14).

Subspecies There are four sub-species of *Charmosyna papou*:

(1) *C.p. papou* (Papuan Lorikeet) from northwest New Guinea, which is hardly known in captivity. The sexes are monomorphic. Some yellow on the chest and a spot at each side may be evident. There is no melanistic phase.

(2) *C.p. goliathina* as described above.

(3) *C.p. stellae* (Stella's Lorikeet) is similar to *C. p. goliathina* in having a normal red colour phase and a melanistic one, but with orange central tail feathers instead of yellow. This bird comes from southeast New Guinea, an area from which birds are not usually exported.

(4) *C.p. wahnesi* (Gold-banded Lorikeet) from the Huon Peninsula in New Guinea; this bird is not known in aviculture.

Fairy Lorikeet

Charmosyna pulchella pulchella
(Plates 1 and 2)

Common names

SYNONYM	Little Red Lorikeet
DUTCH	Zwartsuitlori
GERMAN	Goldstrichellori
FRENCH	Lori à croupion noir

Distribution Northwest central and southeast New Guinea; in forest edges and lower to mid-regions of the Arfak Mountains and Cyclops Mountains, between 750 and 2300m (2500 and 7500ft); also in secondary growth. It has been observed in the tops of flowering trees in the company of other species of lory. Nesting has been observed in holes in epiphytic moss.

Range M. Population trend S. M-L S In the field ?

Description Mainly red with green

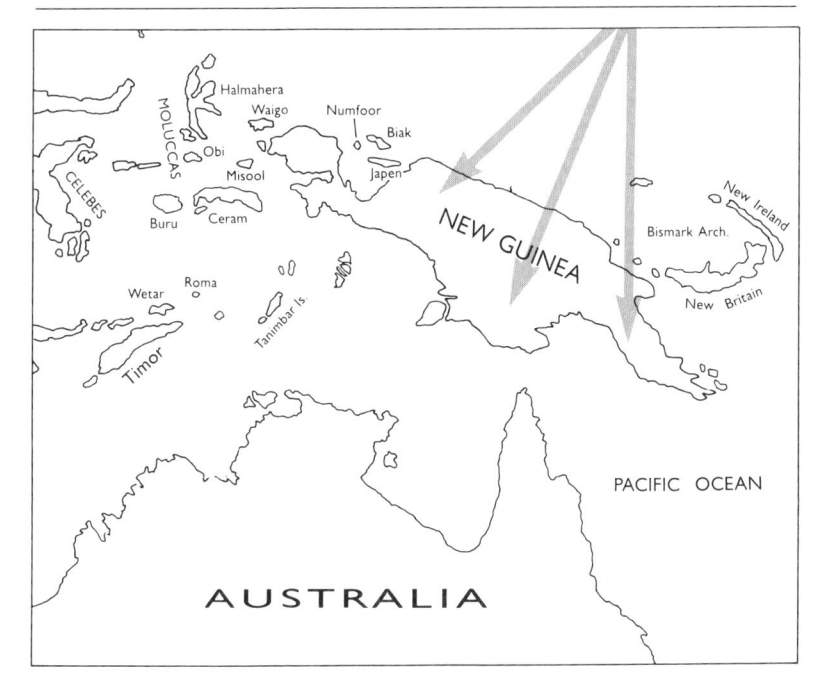

Distribution of the Fairy Lorikeet

wings; stomach blue-black and hind crown violet-black; red breast streaked yellow; thighs and nuchal patch purple-black; tail red becoming green, tipped with yellow; underside entirely yellow; rump blackish-green; beak, legs and iris orange. Dimorphic, even on feathering-up in nest: hen has yellow spots either side of the rump.

Distinguishing features Similar to Sepik Lorikeet (*C.j. sepikiana*) but smaller. Differs from Rothschild's Fairy Lorikeet (*C.p. rothschildi*) in which the upper breast is green. Females harder to distinguish; rump markings of *C.p. rothschildi* are greenish yellow.

Status a-b Fairly common through a large range; small numbers kept in aviculture.

Maturity 12–13 months.
Length 17–19cm (6¾–7½in).
Weight 25–35g (⅞–1¼oz).

Call Short quiet note.
Management Not hardy; needs protection against temperature extremes.
Nest-box A, D, F, G, H, I.
Eggs 2. *Incubation* 25 days.
Ring size 4.2–4.5mm (⁵⁄₃₂in) 'L'.
Fledging 8 weeks.

Practical experience This lorikeet was not available in the UK before the early 1970s, although it had been bred apparently as far back as 1914. Other than in warm climates these lorikeets are best housed inside. If kept in this way, i.e. entirely inside, they will need some additional vitamin D3 and calcium. They require a thin nectar in common with other *Charmosyna* spp.

Heiner Dahne (1992) writes from Germany and I quote extracts:

My birds breed in a cage measuring 30 × 50 × 40 cms. The nesting box (budgerigar size) is mounted on the outside of the cage. This was intended as temporary housing, however since the pair was able to breed there twice successfully I have left this housing unchanged to date.

Later he says:

A second breeding followed immediately. Again, only one chick was raised. This time it was a female. The young bird apart from being paler in colour, and with dark beak and eyes, had the yellowish green specks.

Subspecies There are two subspecies of *Charmosyna pulchella*:

(1) *C.p. pulchella* as described above.
(2) *C.p. rothschildi* (Rothschild's Fairy Lorikeet), from north-central New Guinea, which differs from the nominate in having the upper breast green. There are a very few, mostly single specimens in the UK. Fortunately, some breeders have recently been making up pairs with birds from Europe; it is to be hoped that more of this cooperation will take place in the future.

Red-flanked Lorikeet

Charmosyna placentis placentis
(Plate 6)

Common names
SYNONYM   Pleasing Lorikeet
DUTCH   Roodflanklori
GERMAN   Schonlori
FRENCH   Loriquet joli

Distribution South Moluccas, Kai, Aru Islands, southern New Guinea. In primary forest edges, tall secondary forest, partly cleared land, savannah, coconut plantations, sago swamps and occasionally mangroves; also around gardens, mostly in the lowlands and hills up to 1600m (5250ft). A variety of nesting sites has been recorded (which could give breeders food for thought) and these include moss on trees, the base of ferns, 6m (20ft) up in trees and in tunnels. Nests have apparently usually been found in the vicinity of termites' nests, on which insects they possibly depend in some way. Nesting has been observed in both the wet and dry seasons.
Range M/Is. *Population trend* S. M-L S. *In the field* F.

Description Dimorphic. Cock generally green with a dark blue patch on the rump and a purplish-blue ear-covert patch; cheeks, flanks and sides of breast red; hen predominantly green, darker on the upper side; ear coverts dull bluish-black, strongly streaked with yellow. Beak of both red; legs orange-red; iris is orange.
Distinguishing features Male distinguishable from male Red-spotted Lorikeet (*C.r. rubronotata*) by the absence of red on crown, but presence of red cheeks. Females of the two species can be distinguished by the presence of green ear coverts streaked with yellowish-green in *C.r. rubronotata*.
Status a-b Generally common in the wild, recent fieldwork having been done on some of the subspecies; established to some extent in aviculture.
Maturity 10 months.
Length 15–18cm (6–7in).
Weight 35–45g (1¼–1⅝oz).
Call Quiet.
Nest-box B, D, F, G, H, I.
Eggs 2. *Incubation* About 25 days.

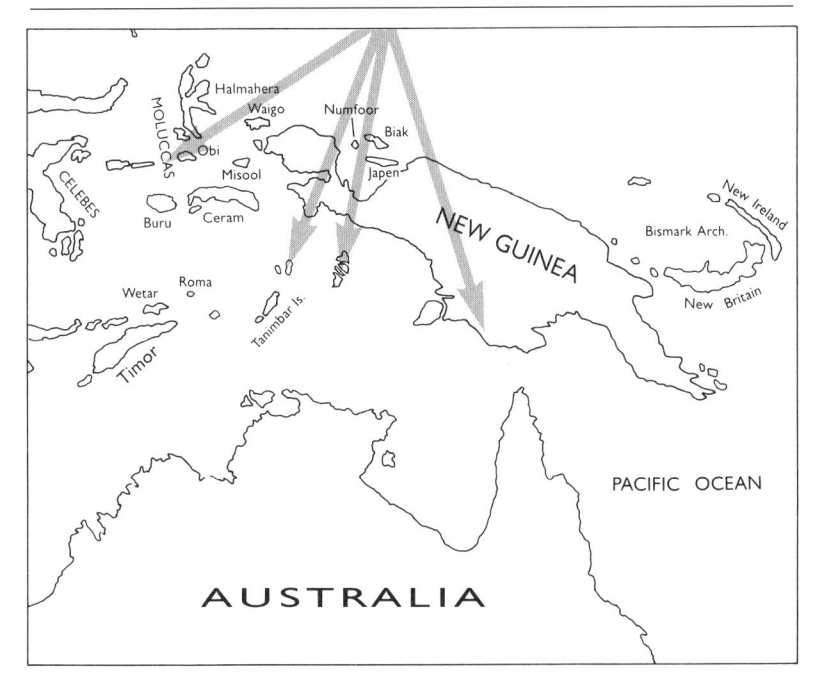

Distribution of the Red-flanked Lorikeet

Ring size 4.5mm (³⁄₁₆in) 'L–M'.
Fledging 6½ weeks.

Practical experience Only a handful of these birds was known in aviculture in the early part of this century and virtually no information was available. A friend of mine in the UK was desperately looking for a hen for his male during the 1970s. At that time some were being bred on the Continent, housed indoors at a temperature of about 21°C (70°F). More recently there have been a few importations and a few dedicated breeders have succeeded in breeding them; in such cases, the birds have been housed in internal flights, with a constant heat of about 21°C (70°F) and extended daylight. I know of some birds kept partly inside and partly outside, in planted aviaries, or living outside for the summer and being brought in before the weather becomes inclement. They would become unhappy below about 10°C (50°F).

Red-flanks do best housed in flights measuring about 1.5m × 0.6m × 0.9m high (5ft × 2ft × 3ft high), of the box type, with a deep litter tray, lined inside with Melamine or other easily cleaned surface. They enjoy being given branches to strip and, indeed, derive benefit from this. Spraying with tepid water is greatly enjoyed and this improves their condition and encourages preening. With birds that live totally indoors, care must be taken to ensure that the atmosphere does not become too dry. Many people believe the birds do best in a really humid atmosphere. Birds that live totally inside, with no access to sunshine, need extra vitamin D3 in order to utilize their calcium intake. This can be administered once or twice a week in the feed, which is what I do routinely for such birds. Alternatively Tru-lite aquarium strip-light can be used to extend the daylight. I believe this helps birds synthesize Vitamin D3.

The nest, of whatever type is preferred, must be readily accessible for cleaning because continual fouling is likely. I believe in accustoming such birds, as soon as they arrive, to daily nest inspection. This reduces the chance of them panicking and means that soiled eggs will not ruin the chances of breeding.

Young can be sexed when no red appears on the flank, as female.

Subspecies There are five subspecies of *Charmosyna placentis*:

(1) *C.p. placentis*, as described above.

(2) *C.p. intensior*, from the North Moluccas including Obi and Gebe in the western Papuan Islands. This is a slightly larger bird at 18cm (7in) long. The rump of the male is violet rather than dark blue, and the forehead more green than yellow. (See Chapter 13 for conservation current work.)

(3) *C.p. ornata*, from the western Papuan Islands except Gebe. The blue of the rump area is larger and the red at the throat extends further.

(4) *C.p. pallidor*, (Solomon Islands Pleasing Lorikeet) has a generally greener appearance and is somewhat smaller. It inhabits Woodlark Island in the Bismarck Archipelago and Bougainville and Fead in the Solomon Islands, where it frequents gardens, coconut plantations and lowland tropical forest up to 3000m (9800ft).

(5) *C.p. subplacens* differs in lacking the blue patch on the rump. It comes from New Guinea, east of Hall Sound in the south and the Sarmi District of Irian Jaya in the north.

Red-chinned Lorikeet

Charmosyna rubrigularis rubrigularis

Common names

ENGLISH	Red-throated Lorikeet
DUTCH	Roodkin Lori
GERMAN	Rotkinnlori
FRENCH	Loriquet aux marques rouges

Distribution In the Bismarck Archipelago: New Britain where it is thought to be still abundant and also New Ireland and New Hanover. It is mainly found in mountain forests from 450m (1500ft) to the summit, at the tops of flowering trees, often in the company of honeyeaters. It is replaced at lower altitudes by Solomon Islands Pleasing Lorikeet (*C.p. pallidor*).
Range Is. *Population trend* S. *M-L* S. *In the field* ?

Description Mainly green with blue-green ear coverts streaked paler green and yellowish below; small streak of red on chin and side of lower mandible; tail green with a yellow tip and some red at base of inner web feathers; underside of flight feathers yellow; beak orange; legs yellowish. Hen is similar to *C.p. placentis*.
Call Quiet.
Length 17cm (6¾in).

Subspecies There are two subspecies of *Charmosyna rubrigularis*:

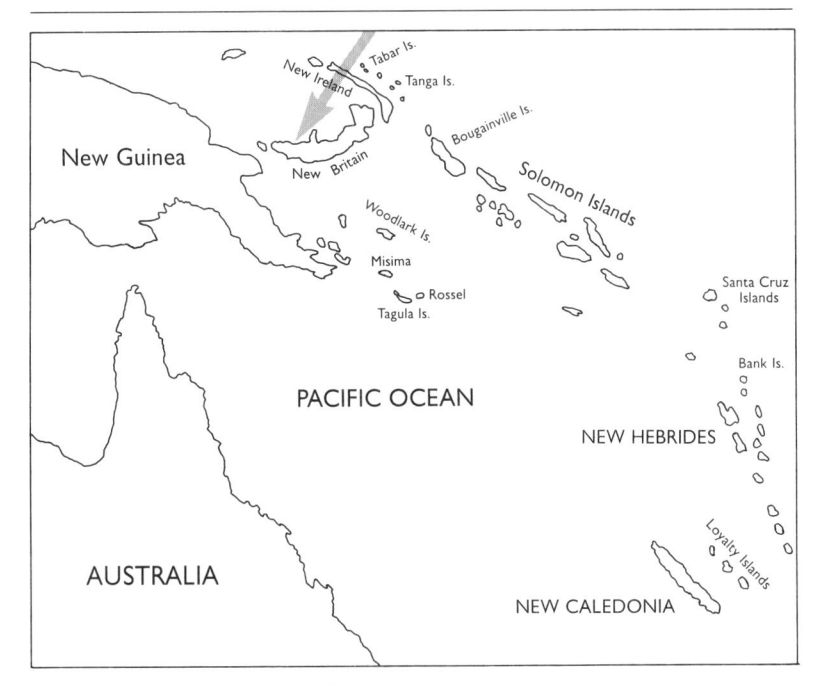

Distribution of Red-chinned Lorikeet

(1) *C.r. rubrigularis*, as described above.
(2) *C.r. krakari*, which is slightly larger than the nominate bird and has a more extensive area of red, bordered by yellow. It inhabits the Karkar Islands to the northeast of New Guinea.

Red-spotted Lorikeet

Charmosyna rubronotata rubronotata
(Plate 5)

Common names
ENGLISH	Red-marked Lorikeet
DUTCH	Roodstuitlori
GERMAN	Rotstirnlori
FRENCH	Loriquet aux marques rouges

Distribution Salawati Island and northwest New Guinea; in lowland forest to 900m (3000ft), inhabiting the high branches of flowering trees and coconut palms, often in the company of Red-flanked Lorikeets (*C.p. placentis*) and Fairy Lorikeets (*C. pulchella*).
Range M/Is. Population trend S. M-L S. In the field ?

Description Dimorphic: cock predominantly green, darker on the back and wings; crown and forehead bright red; small purple ear patch; chest light green suffused with gold; red under wing extends to high on each side of the chest. The hen is a smarter variation of green, much lighter on the chest; cheeks very bright light green with bold yellow streaking; dull red patch on the rump. Both have red beaks, orange iris, and pink

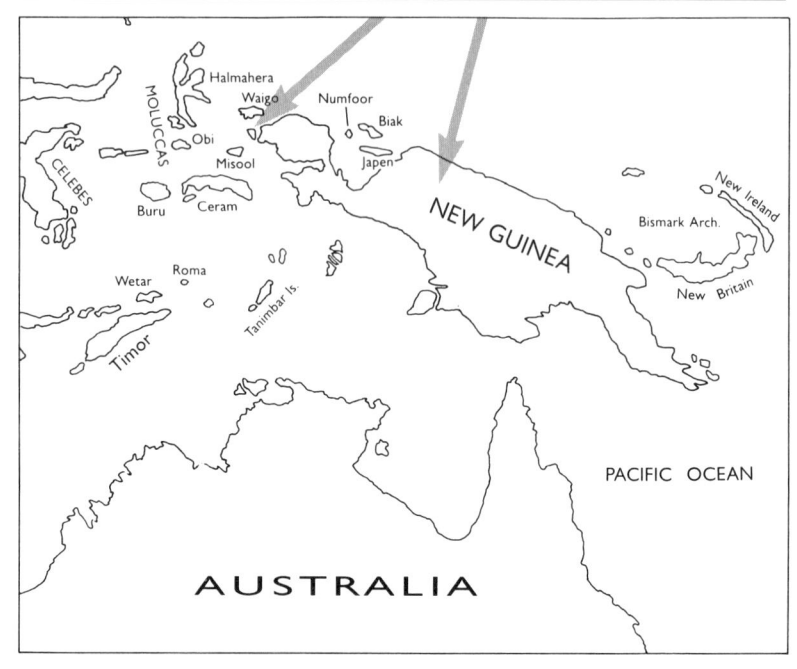

Distribution of the Red-spotted Lorikeet

legs. Young can be sexed in the nest.
Distinguishing features Similar to Red-flanked Lorikeet (*C.p. placentis*) but males have a red crown and no red on the face, while females lack the dull bluish-black ear coverts streaked with yellow, of *C.p. placentis* females.
Status a-b Relatively secure in the wild but less common than *C. pulchella* and *C. placentis* to which it is closely related and with which, to some extent, it competes for food. This species is not at all well established in captivity.
Maturity 10 months.
Length 16cm (6¼in).
Weight 30–35g (1–1¼oz).
Call Quiet.
Management Must have warmth, an inside flight and a constant temperature of 21°C (70°F).
Nest-box B, D, F, G, H, I.
Eggs 2.

Incubation About 23 days.
Ring size 4.2–4.5mm (³⁄₁₆in). 'L'
Fledging Average 40 days (35–59 days have been recorded).

Practical experience Some people still keep these birds all year round in a warm house with a planted flight into which they can go. Others keep them out in summer and move them inside completely when the temperature falls below 10°C (50°F). Generally speaking, however, this species is best kept housed indoors in a flight of about 1.5m × 0.6m × 0.9m high (5ft × 2ft × 3ft high), with a base litter tray; the box type, open only at the front and with an easily washable interior is preferable. There should be plenty of light, probably with extended daylight. The nest-box needs to be proportionately larger than normal for this size of lorikeet; this allows the birds to move to a dry area when the nest becomes saturated, as it inevitably will. It should be positioned by the door or attached to the outside of the flight for ease of inspection, training the birds and maintenance.

Birds kept entirely inside will need extra Vitamin D. The temperature needs to be maintained at a constant 21°C (70°F). Some provision needs to be made to ensure that the atmosphere does not become too dry. Growing plants in the vicinity can be a good idea. The birds should be fed twice daily with nectar (this species needs a thinner mix than usually fed to most lories; see Chapter 7) and a small piece of sponge or bread should be given each day; this should be increased when there are young in the nest. They can also have a dry mix, which they may take only when with young, and some fruit or purée.

Subspecies There are two subspecies of *Charmosyna rubronotata*:

(1) *C.r. rubronotata*, as described above.

(2) *C.r kordoana*, from Biak in Geelvink Bay, in which the red crown is larger and paler.

Following are two members of the genus about which still nothing is known in aviculture although this may soon change with regard to the former.

Meek's Lorikeet

Charmosyna meeki

Distribution Predominantly a mountain bird from 300–1800m (980–59 000ft) on the Solomon Islands, Bougainville, Guadalcanal and Malaita, where its preferred food is flowering *Syzgium*, *Metrosideros* and *Mearnsia*.
Range Is. *Population trend* S. M-L S. *In the field* ?

Description Small (16cm [6½in]) green, darker above and more yellowish below, with darker streakings on ear coverts and sides of neck; mantle tinged with brown; beak and feet orange; some yellow on the underside of the wings.

Wilhelmina's Lorikeet

Charmosyna wilhelminae

Common names
SYNONYM Pygmy Lorikeet

Distribution New Guinea: from the Arfak Mountains in Irian Jaya, east to the Huon Peninsula and southeastern New Guinea, where it occurs mostly at the lower levels of the Owen Stanley Mountains.
Range M. *Population trend* S? M-L S. *In the field* ?

Description The smallest of all lorikeets. Green with yellow streaking on the breast and crown; nape purplish-brown with blue streaks; lower back red; rump dark purple-blue. Dimorphic: cock has red underwing coverts.
Distinguishing features Similar but smaller, particularly when seen in flight or from the underside, to Goldie's Lorikeet (*Trichoglossus goldiei*) and Striated Lorikeet (*Charmosyna multistriata*) but lacks the two-tone beak and red vent and has a distinctive red underwing.
Status a Unknown in aviculture.
Maturity About 9 months.

Length 12cm (4¾in).
Weight 22–25g (⅜–⅞oz).
Call Quiet, high-pitched but hoarse.

A further three members of the genus remain obscure.

New Caledonian Lorikeet

Charmosyna diadema
SYNONYM   Diadem Lorikeet

Distribution   New Caledonia
Range Is. *Population trend* Ex?
M-L C/Ex.   *In the field* F.

Description   Light green with pale underparts; bright blue crown; cheeks and throat yellow, vent red; beak and feet orange.
Status a   Known only from two specimens and thought probably extinct.
Length 18cm (7in).

Palm Lorikeet

Charmosyna palmarum

Distribution   Vanuatu, Duff Santa Cruz and Banks Islands in the Solomons.
Range Is. *Population trend* S?
M-L S.   *In the field* ?

Description   Dimorphic. Light green, more olive-yellow below; red chin and lores; yellow tip to tail; beak and legs orange; iris yellow. The hen has little or no red on chin.
Distinguishing features   Similar to the Red-chinned Lorikeet (*Charmosyna rubrigularis*) but lacking yellow band on underside of flight feathers.
Length 17cm (6¾in).

Blue-fronted Lorikeet

Charmosyna toxopei

Common name
SYNONYM   Buru Lorikeet

Distribution   Buru, Indonesia.
Range Is. *Population trend* S?
M-L V/S?   *In the field* F.

Description   Generally light green darker above, with yellow tinge to upper breast and blue crown; yellow band on underside of primaries and some red on undertail.
Status a   Known only from seven specimens.
Length 16cm (6¼in).

19 Eos

Species	Subspecies	English name	Availability
bornea	bornea	Red Lory	**
	bernsteini	Bernstein's Red Lory	–
	cyanothus	Buru Red Lory	**
	rothschildi	Rothschild's Red Lory	–
cyanogenia	–	Black-winged Lory	*
histrio	histrio	Red and Blue Lory	–
	challengeri	Challenger Red and Blue Lory	–
	tallautensis	Tallaut Red and Blue Lory	*
reticulata	–	Blue-streaked Lory	**
semilarvata	–	Blue-eared Lory	–
squamata	squamata	Violet-necked Lory	**
	riciniata	–	–
	obiensis	Obi Lory	*
6	7	13	

All *Eos* spp., of which there used to be seven, including *E. wallaceii*, are vibrant red lories marked with blues and black, and ranging in size from 23–31cm (9–12¼in). All have orange to orange-red beaks, an orange iris and grey legs. They are all hardy, easy to manage and usually adaptable and free-breeding. Unusually, the length and shape of tail varies considerably within the genus. All have a particularly musky smell, even eggs emit this, and it is particularly noticeable when they are in an incubator.

Red Lory

Eos bornea bornea (Plate 23)

Common names
SYNONYM	Moluccan, Moluccan Red Lory
DUTCH	Rode Lori
GERMAN	Amboina Rotlori, Roter Lori
FRENCH	Lori rouge

Distribution Moluccan Islands of Amboina and Saparua, Indonesia, where it has been observed in flocks around flowering trees, especially *Eugenia* and *Erythrina*.
Range Is. *Population trend* D. M-L S/? *In the field* C/S.

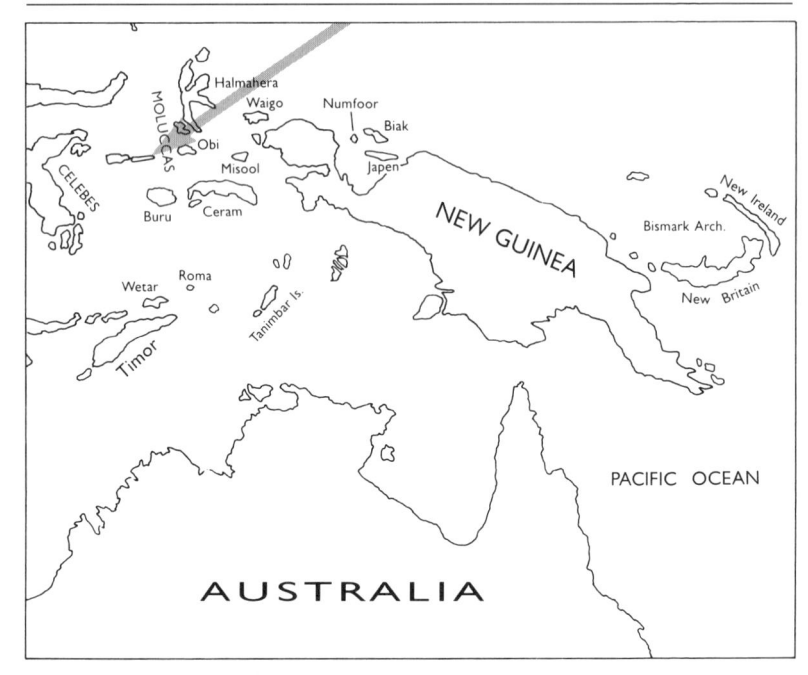

Distribution of the Red Lory

Description Bright red with blue and black on the wings (more accurately primaries are black and speculum red); secondaries red-tipped; black and greater wing coverts blue; vent blue, upper tail dark red and undertail very dark blue. Immatures exhibit varying amounts of blue, particularly blue cheek patches, which usually surprises first-time breeders of this subspecies into thinking they have produced some rarity.
Distinguishing features Larger and a brighter red than the Buru Lory (*E.b. cyanonothus*), which is almost maroon in colour.
Status a-b While declining, it is not certain to what extent but, being an island species, it is at risk. Twenty years ago this was the most freely available lory in aviculture and, although still readily available, it is fairly certain this state of affairs will not continue.
Maturity 3–(4) years.
Length 30cm (12in).
Weight 150–190g (5¼–6¾oz).
Call Harsh and penetrating, or a screech, but generally moderate.
Management Very hardy, easy.
Nest-box A, C, E, H.
Eggs 2. *Incubation* 24–26 days.
Ring size 6.5–7.5mm (¼–⁵⁄₁₆in) 'R–S'.
Fledging 8–9 weeks.

Practical experience The Red Lory is a delightful, cheerful and often confiding bird. My first pair was one of the earliest types of lory I owned; they were immaculate and devoted to each other and were in my possession for nearly 20 years. They reared regularly but usually just one chick at a time. The cock of this pair, who talked quite well, literally dropped dead in my presence when their last chick was a few days old. During that day the hen appeared to be sitting well. Alas, the following morning she was down on the floor, fluffed up and head tucked away. The chick was stone cold and appeared dead. I rushed the hen to a hospital cage, and the chick to an incubator because I had seen it give the minutest twitch. Both revived; the chick took well to hand-rearing in due course and the next day I housed the hen with the only spare cock I had, a Meyer's Lorikeet (*Trichoglossus flavorides meyeri*). They took well to each other. With hindsight I should have left well alone but, in due course, I found a 'proven cock' for her; she never took to this bird and, over a couple of months, seemed to lose interest in food and gave up on life. Subsequently this 'cock' laid eggs!

The chick, a hen, did not begin breeding until 4½ years of age despite being paired since 1½ years of age with an adult cock. She refused to sit the first two rounds of eggs, which were fostered and hand-reared, but then became a model parent. Hand-rearing was obviously vital in this instance; she had been reared with others and, while remaining friendly with people, was not imprinted. I believe it is possible that young birds in the wild may also take time to get used to and perfect parenthood.

Subspecies There are four subspecies of *Eos bornea*:

(1) *E.b. bornea*, as described above.
(2) *E.b. bernsteini* (Bernstein's Red Lory), from Kai, larger than the nominate bird.
(3) *E.b. cyanothus* (Buru Red Lory, Plate 22) is smaller than the nominate bird at 25cm (10in) long and is a darker red, with maroon wings and back. It is a forest- and mangrove-dweller from the island of Buru where, until recently, it was said to be abundant. Now, as the result of recent survey work, it is known to be declining.

The Buru Red Lory is a hardy, easy bird which breeds well and makes an excellent foster parent. Young appear to have little or no blue ear coverts.

A pair of mine once appeared to abandon one of two chicks after about 3 days. I took it in and, regretfully, I did not notice for a further two days that it had a broken thigh. Because the bone appeared twisted by then, I felt I had no choice other than to dispatch it humanely. Subsequent to the remaining chick fledging, the nest was changed from an upright to a sloping variety. I saw them, on occasion, bolting into the nest and this was obviously the cause of the accident.

Before this subspecies became relatively abundant, I housed a male with a Violet-necked female (*E. s. squamata*). They went to nest before I was able to find suitable mates. The resulting chick was taken at a few weeks for hand-rearing with the specific aim of taming it for the pet trade. I had been approached several times by a young medical student who wanted a lory as a pet and I had told him that it would only be in very rare circumstances (such as this) that I would be able to oblige. He did not wish to wait and found one elsewhere but this little crossbreed was not hard to place.

(4) *E.b. rothschildi* (Rothschild's Red Lory), is said to be smaller than those listed above. There are birds on Goram, Cerambulet and the Wetabula Islands which are questionably said to be intermediates.

Black-winged Lory

Eos cyanogenia (Plate 7)

Common names
SYNONYM	Blue-cheeked Lory
DUTCH	Koningslori
GERMAN	Blauohrlori
FRENCH	Lori aux ailes noires

Distribution Indonesian islands of Biak, Numfor, Manim and Moes Num in Geelvink Bay. It feeds in inland forest and roosts in coastal coconut plantations.
Range Is. *Population trend* D. M-L E. *In the field* F/S.

Description Vibrant scarlet with a purple-blue band around the eye and ear coverts; wings, central tail feathers, thighs and a small area on the flank heavily marked with black.
Distinguishing features Heavy black wing markings, black thighs and thick purple blue band each side of head.
Status a-b Seriously threatened. There is urgent need for more intensive *in situ* management. A threat exists from hybridization as well as loss of island habitat. This species has never been well represented in aviculture but, since its arrival in the 1980s in quite large numbers, it has become established to some extent although reproduction is not proving easy due to poor parenting in many cases.
Maturity 3–3½ years.
Length 29–30cms (11½–12in).
Weight 140–180g (5–6¼oz).
Call High-pitched scream, particularly when disturbed and during nesting.
Management Hardy; wild-caught specimens are highly strung.
Nest-box A, C, E, H.
Eggs 2. *Incubation* 26 days.
Ring size 6.5–7.5mm (¼–⁵⁄₁₆in) 'R–S'.
Fledging 11–12 weeks.

Practical experience This species is surely one of the most striking of all lories and one that requires the same sensitive management as Blue-streaked lories (*E. reticulata*); it is, however, even harder to settle and persuade to nest. If/when it does lay, any disturbance can cause eggs or chicks to disappear. The young of those that have been bred in captivity are much less nervous and present a better prospect for the maintenance of this species in captivity. I consider their survival in captivity to be in the balance. With 'wild' wild-caught specimens, the maximum privacy and the minimum disturbance should be afforded. There is, I believe, a case here for hand-rearing or part hand-rearing one clutch from the pairs, at least initially. These are birds for the serious aviculturist.

Red and Blue Lory

Eos histrio histrio (Plate 20)

Common names
SYNONYM	Blue-tailed Lory, Blue-diademed Lory
DUTCH	Diadeem Lori
GERMAN	Diademlori
FRENCH	Lori histrion

Distribution Sangihe, Siau and Ruang in the Sanghi group of islands, north of Sulawesi.
Range Is.
Population trend ?/D/Ex.
M-L C/Ex. *In the field* C/F/S.

Description Predominantly red and blue with characteristic blue breast band and blue band from the blue

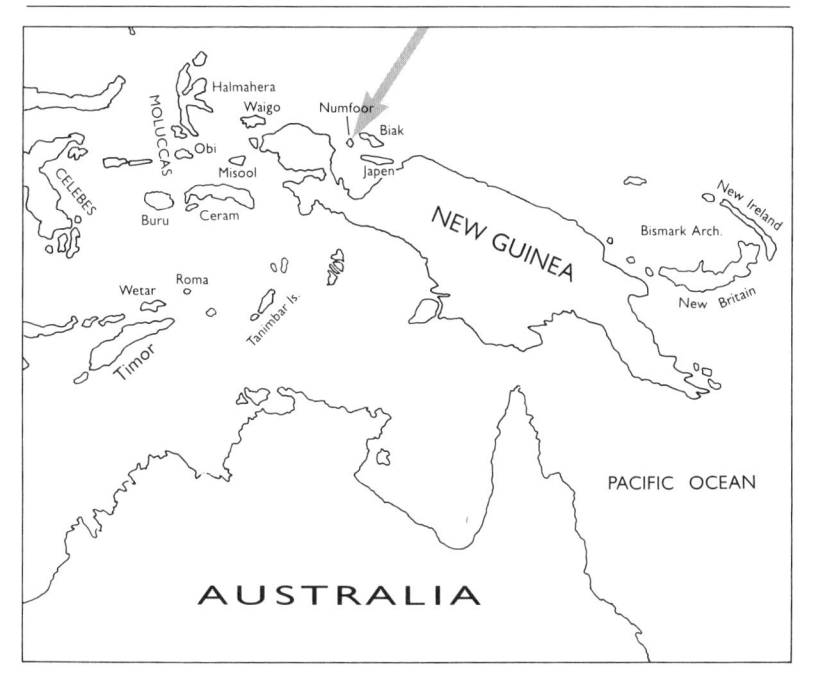

Distribution of the Black-winged Lory

mantle to the eyes, widening across the hind crown; wing coverts red; scapulars, thighs and flight feathers black; tail reddish-purple above and red below; beak and iris red; legs grey. Young birds have a blue crown while the nape, below the eyes and the underside are red with variable blue markings.

Distinguishing features Broad blue bands on breast and hind crown distinguish this from all other *Eos* spp.

Status a-b This lory may already be extinct or at least be in very low numbers (Lambert *et al.*,1992). On Sangihe, by the late nineteenth century, it had retreated to the mountainous interior as a result of the spread of coconut plantations (Forshaw and Cooper, 1989). A recent survey by Bishop in 1986 failed to locate any specimens, and only a tiny area of forest habitat remains. Siau and Ruang were not visited during the 1986 survey but, judging by the size of these islands and the extent of deforestation, they were not expected to hold a viable population. (Whitten, cited in Bishop, 1992). Late in 1995 Frank Lambert hopes to return in conjunction with IUCN and Bird Life International. He has welcomed the idea tht the Lory Group could provide a selection of slides of the various species. *E.h. histrio* is virtually unknown in captivity. At the 9th meeting of the Conference of the Parties to CITES in Florida in November 1994 *Eos histrio* was moved to Appendix 1.

Maturity 3–4 years.

Length 30–31cm (12–12¼in).

Weight 150–190g (5¼–6¾oz).

Call Medium for *Eos* spp., with occasional outbursts.

Management Similar to other larger members of the genus.

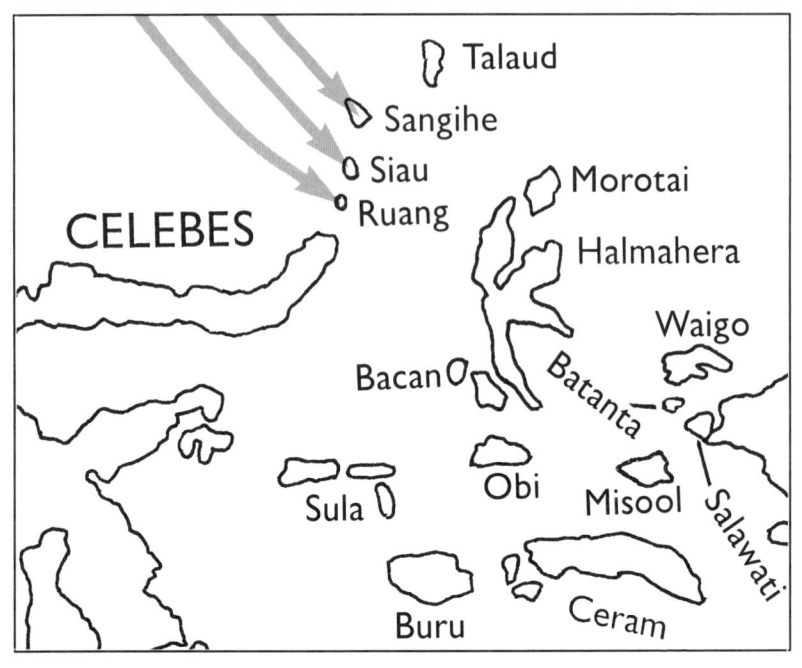

Distribution of the Red and Blue Lory

Nest-box B, C, E, H.
Eggs 2. *Incubation* 25–27 days.
Ring size 6.5–7.5mm (¼–⁵⁄₁₆in).
Fledging 12 weeks.

Practical experience At present there is, I believe, only a single bird in Walsrode, Germany, and another of the same sex in Los Angeles.

Subspecies There are three sub-species of *Eos histrio*:

(1) *E. h. histrio*, as described above.
(2) *E. h. challengeri* (Challenger Red and Blue Lory) from the tiny island of Miangas in the Nenusa Islands northeast of the Talaud Islands, is much smaller but otherwise almost identical to the nominate lory. The blue on the breasts of this subspecies is less extensive and variably mingled with red. The blue line from the eyes does not meet the blue mantle. The population of this subspecies is thought to be very small because the island is tiny but as some have been observed in trade, there must be at least a few left. The M-L criteria is E/C.
(3) *E. h. talautensis* (Talaut Red and Blue Lory), from the Talaud Islands northeast of the Sangihe Islands, including Karakelong, Salebabu and Kabaruang. It has a narrower purple eye and crown stripe and much more red on the wing coverts and flight feathers than the nominate bird. There has been recent fieldwork on the taxon. The population of this bird is declining and estimates indicate fewer than 2000 birds, with the probability of extinction within 20 years. The M-L criterion is C/E. (See also Chapter 13.)

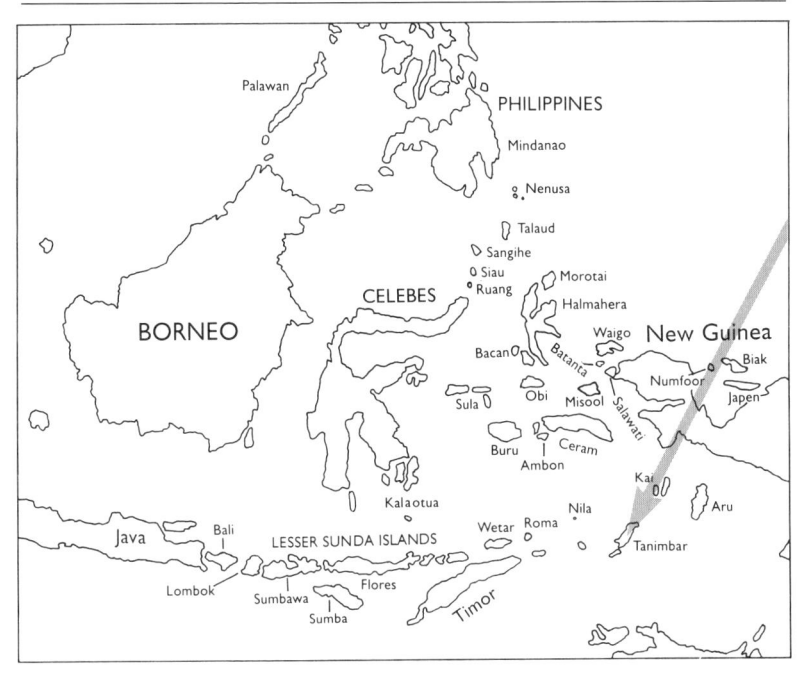

Distribution of the Blue-streaked Lory

York University is mounting a research expedition. We are supplying them with slides and data. They, in turn, will give us a full report on their return. *E. h. talautensis* have quite recently arrived with a few aviculturists. Possibly with this foundation stock, some relocation may one day be possible. There are none in the UK although zoos may mount a programme in the future. Those in the USA have not yet reproduced, but in the Philippines where these have been some for a while, they breed freely, as they are now beginning to do in Africa and Europe.

Blue-streaked Lory

Eos reticulata (Plate 10)

Common names
ENGLISH   Blue-necked Lory
DUTCH   Blauwgestreepte Lori
GERMAN   Blaustrichellori
FRENCH   Lori strié bleu

Distribution Indonesian islands of Tanimbar and introduced to the Kai and Damar Islands; frequenting mainly coastal areas.
Range Is.   *Population trend* D.
M-L V/E.   *In the field* S.

Description Generally bright red, often somewhat darker on the front; wide blue band encompassing the eye and crossing the ear coverts to the mantle, where there is distinctive blue streaking; back and rump red with variable blue streaking; red wings irregularly marked and tipped with black; red thighs possibly with black marks; tail, which is somewhat long and pointed, brownish-black above and red below. Young, apart from less well-defined blue mantle streaking, are similar in size and colour but for the darker beak.

Distinguishing features Vivid blue mantle and hind-neck streaking.

Status a-b Until recently thought to be declining dangerously and many zoos have adopted a policy of putting aside aviaries in order to set up breeding pairs as a matter of urgency. However, good numbers have now been found by Birdlife International surveys. In aviculture they are fairly freely available.

Maturity 3-4 years.

Length 31cm (12¼in).

Weight 140-180g (5-6¼oz).

Call Somewhat raucous screech from time to time and when disturbed.

Management Hardy, often flighty or nervous but can be good breeders when they settle – usually a year at least after reaching maturity.

Nest-box A, C, E, H.

Eggs 2. *Incubation* 24-26 days.

Ring size 6.5-7.5mm (¼-⁵⁄₁₆in) 'R-S'.

Fledging 12 weeks (or longer).

Practical experience The Blue-streaked Lories depicted in Plate 10 are probably the most productive pair of birds I have ever had. The hen was part of an exchange with Chester Zoo over 10 years ago. She had previously been part of an exchange with Naples Zoo. She had lost her mate at Chester and I had been warned that she had few feathers. As these had gone from her head as well I was hopeful that, with a new mate, this might not recur. This proved to be the case; within months she looked immaculate and was given a choice of males. Within a couple of months they laid the first of what was to prove their six annual eggs, more if the couple of occasions on which I have taken the young are included. The hen lays invariably within a month of the previous chicks departing the aviary.

My chosen method for giving this pair a 'rest' is to leave the last clutch with them for a couple of months. After the first such rest, the hen laid within a week or so of the youngsters being taken and, amazingly, again at 21 and 23 days. Naturally these eggs were removed and given to another hen; one was fertile but the chick made very poor growth rate, feathered up poorly and in a brick colour, and died shortly before fledging. I think it amazing that this should occur at all and it showed that a hen needs a period of time to replete her resources. Meanwhile the first two eggs hatched and were reared normally.

Another pair of mine are badly plucked down the front and their chicks grow and feather-up poorly comparatively. I have switched the young to see if different rearing would alter this.

Most Blue-streaked Lories with which I have been acquainted are comparatively wild birds, more so than any other species. Even ones I have reared wish to sever their link with me at fledging and act as though they were wild-caught (which is a good thing). It is interesting that, however long I have had them, they always have a desire to keep out of sight and inevitably screech when caught unawares. Nervousness, or wildness, evidenced itself in the Naples/Chester

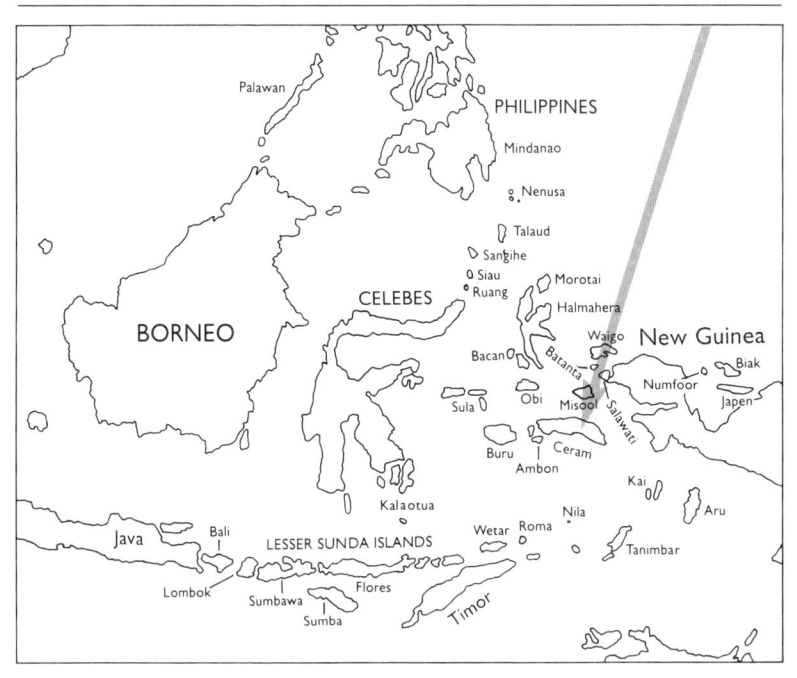

Distribution of the Blue-eared Lory

pair, which killed their chicks when visitors proved too noisy for their liking; another pair, when new to me, threw out two rounds of eggs before being 'trained'.

I find it impossible to build a rapport with this species but their indifference, almost arrogance, I find fascinating because it appears so marked and specific. (I could make a pet of one by different management, but obviously I have no intention of doing this.)

Blue-eared Lory

Eos semilarvata

Common names
SYNONYM Half-masked Lory, Ceram Lory
DUTCH Halfmaskerlori
GERMAN Halbmasken-Lori
FRENCH Lori aux joues bleues

Distribution Ceram's central montane forests from 1500m (4900ft), where it replaces the Red Lory (*E.b. bornea*).
Range Is. *Population trend* S.
M-L V. *In the field* F.

Description Generally bright red with white bases to the body feathers; upper cheeks, ear coverts and a band down the sides of the neck violet-blue.
Distinguishing features Violet-blue band down the sides of the neck.
Status little known in aviculture.
Length 24cm (9½in).

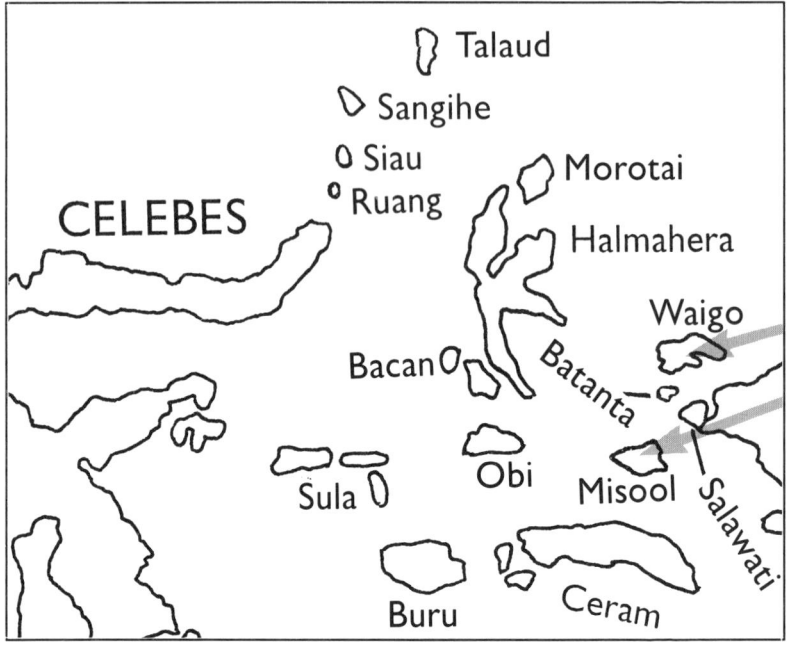

Distribution of the Violet-necked Lory

Violet-necked Lory

Eos squamata squamata (Plate 24)

Common names
SYNONYM   Violet-naped Lory
DUTCH   Violetneklori
GERMAN   Kapuzen Lori
FRENCH   Lori à nuque violette de Bechstein

Distribution Western Papuan islands of Gebe, Waigeu, Batante and Mysool, and the Indonesian Schildpad Islands.
Range Is. *Population trend* S? M-L S? *In the field* S.

Description Mainly red with variable violet-blue collar; abdomen and undertail purple; tail purple-red above and red-grey below; scapulars dull purple, tipped with black; greater wing coverts and flight feathers red, tipped with black; primaries black.
Distinguishing features Violet collar reaching the hind crown prevents confusion with the Obi Lory (*E.s. obiensis*) which lacks this.
Status a-b Currently thought probably safe after all, as the result of recent fieldwork which has been done with two of the subspecies. More work is called for with the nominate bird which is well established in captivity.
Maturity 3 years.
Length 27cm (10½in).
Weight 120–140g (4¼–5oz).
Call Infrequent, high-pitched.
Management Hardy, easy, placid, and a willing breeder.
Nest-box B, C, F, H.
Eggs 2. *Incubation* 26 days.
Ring size 6mm (¼in) 'P–R'.
Fledging 9–10 weeks.

Practical experience I kept this subspecies for several years, finding it easy and tolerant in every way. I was surprised to find that such a relatively small lory takes approximately 3 years to mature. Once, while waiting for a cock with the distinct collar to become available (there seems to be two types – one with the distinct collar and another with a mottled purple and red effect down the front), I placed the hen with a cock Buru Red Lory (*E.b. cyanonothus*) until maturity. I failed to notice time passing and a chick was duly produced. Being a crossbreed it was taken at a few weeks for hand-rearing and turned into a delightful pet bird, looking much like a Buru but with a mottled chest.

Subspecies There are three subspecies of *Eos squamata*:

(1) *E.s. squamata*, as described above.
(2) *E.s. obiensis* (Obi Lory), see p. xx.
(3) *E.s. riciniata*, from Weda and the North Moluccas, which has a well pronounced grey-purple collar extending to the hind crown. It is thought that a large proportion of the 'Violet-necked Lorikeets' that are in captivity are in fact members of this subspecies. Birdlife International has carried out a recent census on the latter two subspecies and found *E.s. obiensis* to be 'Declining' and 'Vulnerable', with a need for more taxonomic and geographic investigation (see Chapter 13).

Until recently, there was a fourth subspecies, *E. s. atrocaerulea*, which has now been combined with *E.s. riciniata*.

Obi Lory

Eos squamata obiensis (Plate 25)

Common names
DUTCH   Obilori
GERMAN Obi Lori
FRENCH Lori à nuque violette d'Obi

Distribution Obi in the North Moluccas.
Range Is. *Population trend* D/S. *M-L* V. *In the field* C.

Description Similar in size and shape to the nominate subspecies but lacks any collar and is brighter crimson on the head, neck, back, breast and thighs; abdomen to vent purple; scapulars black and remainder of wings black marked with red; underwings red; tail dark red; eyes brown; beak orange; legs dark grey.
Distinguishing features Lack of any collar distinguishes this from the Violet-Necked Lory (*E.s. squamata*).
Status a-b Since recent fieldwork was undertaken, the plight of this lory is not thought to be quite so dire. It is becoming quite well established in aviculture.
Maturity Approaching 3 years.
Length 24cm (9½in).
Weight 120–130g (4¼–4⅗oz).
Call Similar to but quieter than the nominate bird.
Management As for the nominate bird, with the exception of incubation time.
Nest-box A, C, F, H.
Eggs 2. *Incubation* 24–25 days.
Ring size 6mm (¼in) 'P–R'.
Fledging 9–10 weeks.

Practical experience This lory arrived on the avicultural scene in the late 1980s, amid fierce debate as to what it was. Many people referred

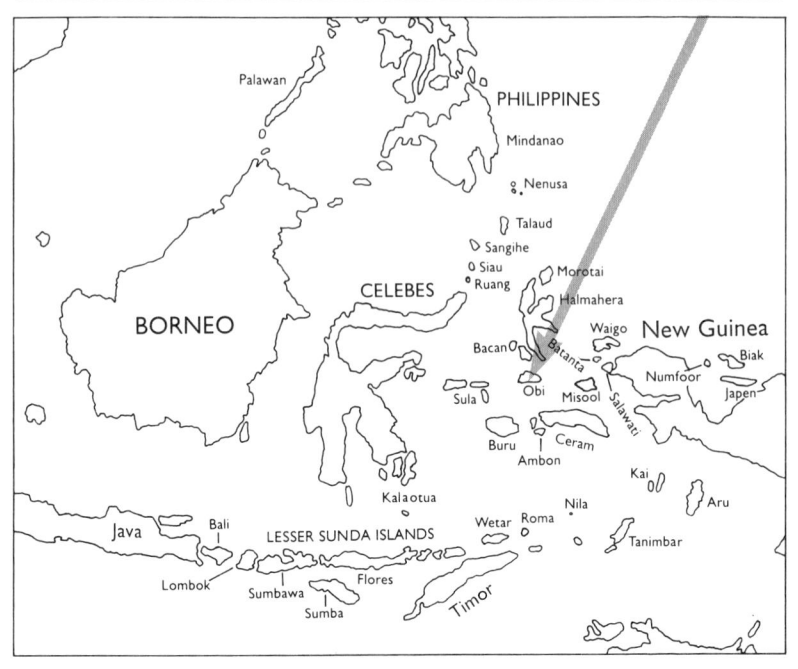

Distribution of the Obi Lory

to it as 'Wallace's Lory' for a time. Management is the same as for the nominate bird. It is much sought after, has adapted well and reproduces quite freely, but demand always exceeds supply from the relatively few pairs. My own pairs have remained wild, but are good parents.

20 Glossopsitta

Species	Subspecies	English name	Availability
concina	–	Musk Lorikeet	*†
porphyrocephala	–	Purple-crowned Lorikeet	†
pulsilla	–	Little Lorikeet	†
3	0	3	

There are three species within the genus *Glossopsitta*; all are found in Australia and are subject to Australian laws restricting their export. Outside that country they are virtually unknown and are never likely to be seen to any extent. The wild populations are healthy and, over the last decade or so, their situation in Australian aviculture has also improved. They can be seen in pairs, small parties and sometimes large flocks in their search mainly for nectar, pollen and insects on leaves, although they sometimes take fruit and cereal as well. They have a few features in common:

(1) Small size.
(2) Particularly fine beaks.
(3) Pointed tail feathers.

Musk Lorikeet

Glossopsitta concina (Plate 45)

Common names
DUTCH   Musklori
GERMAN   Moschuslori
FRENCH   Loriquet musque

Distribution Australia: Queensland south from Rockhampton, eastern New South Wales to Victoria, and in the southwest to the Eyre Peninsula; also, Kangaroo Island, Tasmania. It frequents open dry terrain and dense, wet forest near the coast. Around Adelaide it is a common pest in orchards and among maize crops.
Range M/Is. *Population trend* S M–L S *In the field* F

Description Possibly dimorphic. Green with a blue hue, darker above; scarlet forehead and cheeks divided by the eye; turquoise blue crown and bronze mantle; some yellow on the sides of breast and thighs and some red undertail; beak coral. Hen usually exhibits less blue on the crown.
Distinguishing features Scarlet on the face divided by the eye.
Status a-b Safe in Australia in both the wild and aviculture; elsewhere quite scarce.
Maturity 13–14 months.
Length 23cm (9in).
Weight 50–60g (1¾–2⅛oz).

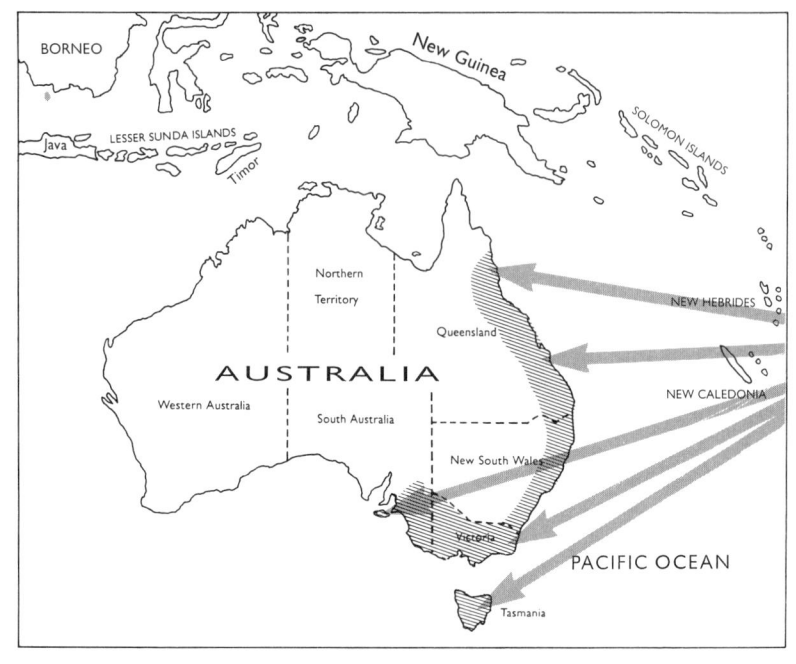

[Distribution of the Musk Lorikeet]

Call Constant, quiet, low-pitched chatter.
Management Easy in Australia where it is a free breeder and good parent.
Nest-box 24cm × 14cm × 18cm high (9½in × 5½in × 7in high), with a spout entrance in Australia.
Eggs 2(3) eggs.
Incubation 24 days.
Ring size 5–5.5mm (¼in) 'N'.
Fledging 6–7 weeks.

Practical experience Some specimens arrived in Europe a few years ago with some scaly-breasted Lorikeets (*Trichoglossus chlorolepidotis*) and were welcomed to the avicultural scene, where they proved to be quite easy, hardy and free-breeding. The total numbers in Europe are so small, however, that they cannot be considered established here.

Purple-crowned Lorikeet

Glossopsitta porphyrocephala
(Plate 51)

Common names
SYNONYM   Zip Parrot
DUTCH   Purperkoplori
GERMAN   Porphyrlori
FRENCH   Loriquet de Florent

Distribution Southern Australia, extending north to Shark Bay in Western Australia and, in the southeast, extending north to Eden in New South Wales. Its range is broken by the barren area of Nullarbor Plain. This is a bird of the treetops and, unusually, a community nester which frequents the tall karri and jarrah forests and dry mallee country, but is seldom seen near the coast. It has

GLOSSOPSITTA

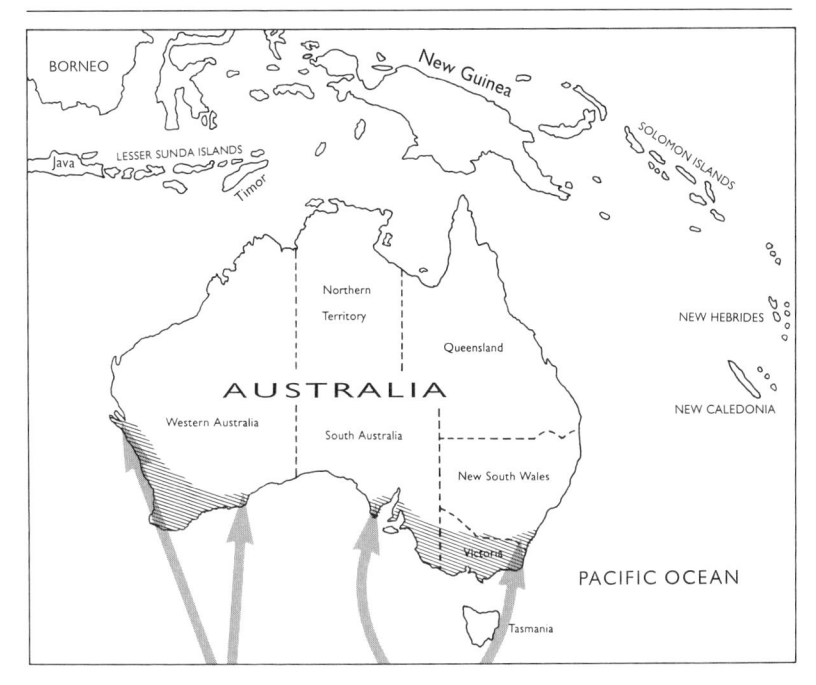

Distribution of the Purple-crowned Lorikeet

been recorded doing damage to ripening pears.
Range M *Population trend* S
M–L S *In the field* F

Description Basically pale lime-green, with turquoise blue at the bend of wing and a paler blue sheen to the chest; forehead and ear coverts bright orange and the crown deep purple; mantle light brown; under-wings red, only revealed during flight, yellow patches to the side of the chest; small black beak.
Distinguishing features Deep purple crown and black beak.
Status a-b Less often seen than some years ago; safe in Australian aviculture.
Maturity 6 months.
Length 16cm (6¼in).
Weight 45g (1⅝oz).

Call Light screech.
Management This is relatively easy; tendency to become overweight.
Nest-box Lovebird-type 30cm × 13cm × 17.5cm high (12in × 5in × 7in high).
Eggs 3–4.
Incubation 17–22 days.
Ring size 4.5mm (³⁄₁₆in) 'L–M'.
Fledging 6½–8½ weeks.

Practical experience In the last decade, since the advent of modern lory diets and improved avicultural techniques, these little gems have become the most prolific of the small lories in Australian aviculture. Before this trappers had tried, and failed, to maintain them on a diet of seed. Breeding takes place at any time of year and there has been considerable success with flock breeding. They can safely be kept in a mixed collection

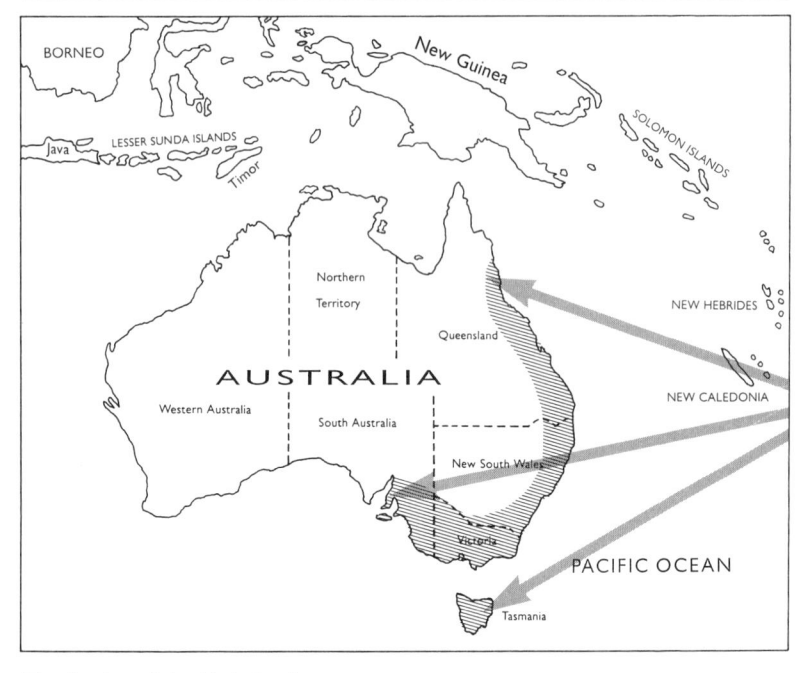

Distribution of the Little Lorikeet

of non-psittacines. It has been noted that the cock does not feed the hen until after the first egg has been laid, and the hen alone feeds the young for the first week.

Little Lorikeet

Glossopsitta pulsilla (Plate 49)

Common names
SYNONYM   Red-faced Lorikeet, Jerryang
DUTCH   Dwerglori
GERMAN   Zwerglori
FRENCH   Loriquet nain

Distribution Throughout east and southeast Australia, from Cairns in north Queensland through the York Peninsula in South Australia, to northeast Tasmania. These nomadic lories are extremely fast fliers.
Range M/Is. *Population trend* S M–L S *In the field* F

Description Possibly dimorphic. Bright red forehead, lores and throat; generally bright grass-green, with bronze mantle and a lighter shade of bronze on the abdomen; cheeks and crown slightly darker green with yellow streaking; wings a darker green again; some red to the base of the tail; beak black and feet pink. The hen has a smaller mask and less bronze on the mantle.
Distinguishing features Tiny, appearing all-green but for red face.
Status a–b Now secure in both.
Maturity 11 months.
Length 15cm (6in).
Weight 44g (1½oz).

Call It is excitable and noisy for its size in flight.
Management Quite easy if special attention is paid to diet.
Nest-box Should be an oblong, lovebird-type preferably, with spout entrance in Australia.
Eggs 3–5 laid at 2–3 day intervals.
Incubation 20–22 days.
Ring size 4.5mm (³⁄₁₆in).
Fledging 6 weeks.

Practical experience Stan Sindell observed that these lories in the wild prefer to nest between 6–12m (20–40ft) off the ground, with an entrance via a very small knot hole. He has simulated this in his aviaries by providing a hollow log, or an oblong African-Lovebird-type nest, and attaching a spout to it. The oblong nest should be slightly tilted to prevent the eggs from scattering. With the development of diets more suited to the specialized requirements of this species, they are now more commonly kept and successful breedings are regularly recorded, although it is still the least commonly kept of the native lorikeets.

21 Lorius

Species	Subspecies	Common name	Availability
albidnuchus	–	White-naped Lory	–
amabilis (?)	–	New Britain Lory	–
chlorocercus	–	Yellow-bibbed Lory	*
domicellus	–	Purple-capped Lory	*
garrulus	garrulus	Chattering Lory	*
	flavopalliatus	Yellow-backed Lory	*
	morotaianus	Morotai Yellow-backed Lory	–
hypoinochrous	hypoinochrous	Purple-bellied Lory	–
	devittatus	Devittatus Lory	–
	rosselianus	Rossel Island Lory	–
lory	lory	Black-Capped	*
	cyanauchen	Biak Lory	–
	erythrothorax	Erythro Black-capped Lory	**
	jobiensis	Jobi Lory	*
	salvadorii	Salvadori's Lory	*
	somu	Somu Lory	–
tibialis (?)	–	Blue-thighed Lory	–
8	9	17	

These lories are easily recognized as belonging to the genus *Lorius*. They are somewhat thickset birds with short, slightly rounded tails. All have green wings (which easily distinguishes them from *Eos* lories, which have red, black and blue wings). The main body colour is red. Their flight – which is at no great height – consists of rapid, shallow wing beats. *Lorius* spp. love human company, can be excellent, clear talkers, and are avid bathers and searchers for toys; lightweight food-pots, ponds and nest-lids will be removed and tossed about unless well secured.

Yellow-bibbed Lory

Lorius chlorocercus (Plate 17)

Common names
DUTCH Groenstaartlori
GERMAN Grunschwanzlori
FRENCH Lori à queue verte

Distribution Eastern Solomon Islands, which form a republic consisting of six main islands, the largest of which is Guadalcanal, on which is the capital Honaira. This, as well as Malaila, San Cristobal and a few of the smaller islands, is home to the Yellow-bibbed Lory. This lory inhabits the lower

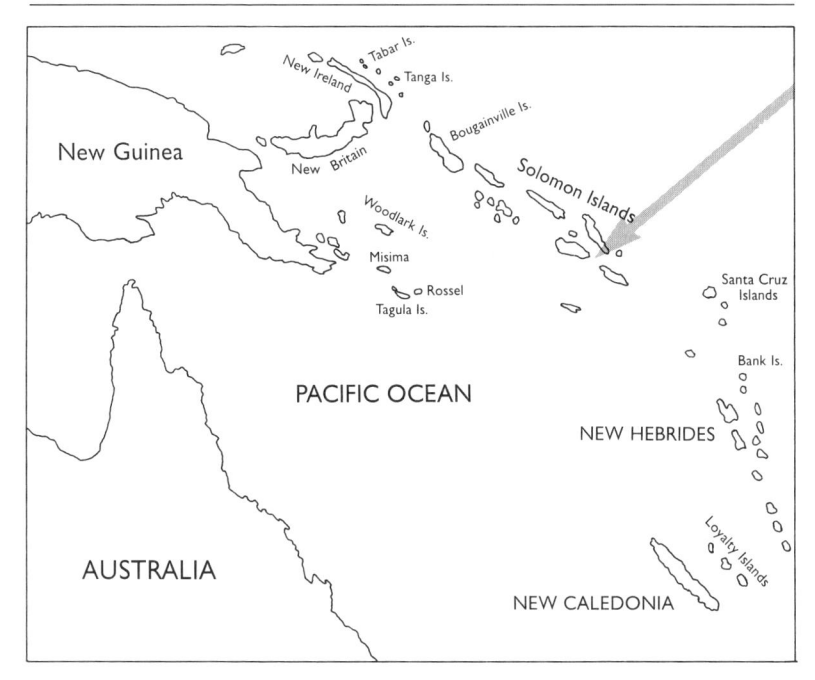

Distribution of the Yellow-bibbed Lory

canopies of primal rainforest and lower mountains, seldom frequenting lowland. Its diet is believed to consist of seeds, larvae and caterpillars.
Range Is. *Population trend* S/D.
M-L V. *In the field* F.

Description Less large and heavy than the *Lorius lory* subspecies. Similar to, but smaller than, *L. domicellus* but basically red, with green wings and black cap, with no purple; also a distinctive and much wider yellow bib, with a black spot on each side; beak and iris orange.
Distinguishing features Wide yellow bib with a black spot at each side differentiates this species from the Purple-capped Lory from (*L. domicellus*).
Status a-b Protected in the Solomons. Quite rare in captivity, except in New Zealand. Recently a few pairs have started to reproduce in Europe and the USA. Possibly, small numbers may be exported from the Solomons.
Maturity 3½ years.
Length 27–28cm (10½–11in).
Weight 160–200g (5⅝–9oz).
Call Medium.
Management Probably omnivorous; takes time to establish and breed initially.
Nest-box A, C, E, H.
Eggs 2. *Incubation* 25–26 days.
Ring size 7mm (⁵⁄₁₆in) 'P–R'.
Fledging 8–9 weeks.

Practical experience This lory is very intelligent and seems hardy once established. It is an avid bather and a very active aviary bird. In New Zealand, where there are the largest numbers in aviculture, it was several years before it commenced breeding, which it now does well there. A few breeding pairs are gradually becoming established in the USA and Europe. I have heard of breeders rearing them on a basic diet of bread and milk; others treat them as totally nectivorous and yet others, and this includes myself, as omnivorous feeders. Tony Silva arranged for me to buy some from Wolfgang Keissling of Loro Parque during the spring of 1991. The others arrived as black-beaked babies from New Zealand the following winter. In New Zealand the males have been found to be somewhat aggressive at breeding time, and are placed in cages adjacent to the females' flight. Each winter I observe aggression among the pairs I have set up, but by separating the males to a cage for a while, and always feeding individual nectar and fruit-pots for each bird, this aggression has so far been kept to a minimum. With two pairs which have tried to breed I have noticed that the onset of breeding can be told well in advance by some feather-plucking. These feathers are meticulously used to line the nest; we are going to experiment with collecting feathers and lining the nest ourselves in an attempt to avoid the plucking.

In the only pair to lay fertile eggs the cock was offered a choice of females. He made his preference known in no uncertain terms, with serious danger to the unfavoured female (who was removed forthwith). Then ensued mating, plucking, laying and finally rearing what I have learned is the first Yellow Bib to be raised in the UK. It was DNA-sexed as a male and is now some seven months old and in an adjacent flight to two females from which he can make a choice in due course. Another pair has just started nesting. They laid clear eggs last year, and the original parent birds are on eggs again – so here's hoping!

Purple-capped Lory

Lorius domicellus (Plate 11)

Common names
ENGLISH   Purple-naped Lory
DUTCH   Purperkaplori
GERMAN   Erzlori
FRENCH   Lori des dames

Distribution Ceram and, according to old records, Ambon and Buru. This lory prefers primary forest at 500–1000m (1600–3250ft) but, today, it is more likely to be found in secondary vegetation, where it forages amongst banana and papaya trees. *Range* Is. *Population trend* D. *M-L* E. *In the field* S.

Description Mainly deep red with a variable yellow necklace, some yellow chest flecking and a cap of black tapering to violet; wings green; eyes and beak orange-red.
Distinguishing features Similar to, but usually larger than the Yellow-bibbed Lory (*L. chlorocercus*) with a narrower yellow bib and violet at the hind part of the cap.
Status a-b Threatened with extinction, and probably *still* being trapped mainly for the local pet trade. Conservation protection is called for and research in captivity into its requirements and management. In Europe, while the number is quite small, it is big enough for a basis population. Ambon is heavily populated and has suffered a great deal of deforestation;

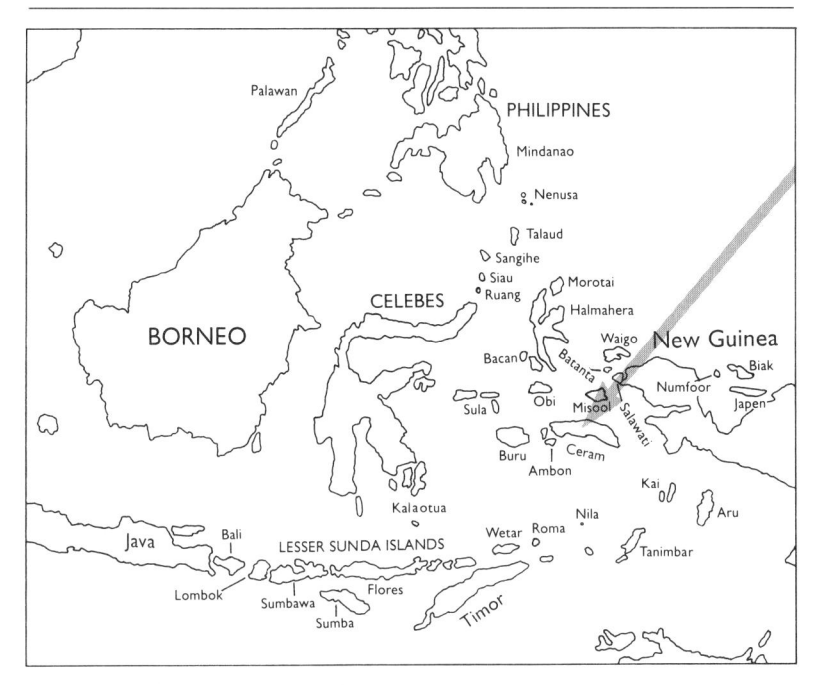

Distribution of the Purple-capped Lory

these lories can no longer be found there. (It is thought that Buru no longer supports any breeding birds, if it ever did; the one documented sighting was of a bird with a leg thong, probably an escaped pet bird.) Even in the Manusela National Park, its long-term protection is not guaranteed because of the infeasibility of patrolling the boundaries against trappers. The results of recent research expeditions suggest that its numbers here are now also low.
Maturity 3½ years.
Length 28–29cm (11–11½in).
Weight 200–250g (7–9oz).
Call Loud; a distinctive repeated clicking, and hammering with the beak.
Management Hardy when established; management as for *Lorius chlorocercus*.

Nest-box A, C, E, H.
Eggs 2. *Incubation* 24–26 days.
Ring size 7–8mm (⅜in) 'S–T'.
Fledging 12–13 weeks.

Practical experience Purple-capped Lories used to be thought of as common, possibly because they were a common pet locally. Not much information has been gathered; often, the more common a bird appears to be, the less effort is spent on research or conserving it, either in the wild or captivity. We see time and again how quickly that scenario can change. A breeding programme was set up in 1989 aimed at survival of this species, at least in captivity, and it would be appreciated if anyone owning these lories would contribute information. I hear from the USA that there is a risk of inbreeding there due to the small gene pool. The same, surely, will follow in Europe. Armin Brockner, who holds the Studbook in Germany, would be pleased to be contacted via the publishers or author.

I was fortunate to acquire a young pair in May 1993. They are truly magnificent and take pleasure in associating with people. Early on the cock twice gave cause for some concern: he became quiet, appeared to be depressed and just sat, all of which were not at all characteristic. His mate seemed incredibly concerned and attentive. On both occasions, however, he responded to the application of a heat lamp overnight. Some five months later, both appeared to have settled into one of my conventional 'large lory' aviaries and seemed to be hardy. Once quarantine was over, I shut them away at night for a week or so but they quickly learned to put themselves away. Now they always greet me with the distinctive sounds mentioned above. They eat well and seem particularly fond of fruit and vegetables, as well as bread and other solids; they empty their fruit and drypots quickly each day. I feel they would be unhappy with just nectar alone.

During the summer of 1994 an egg was laid, but disappeared. In February 1995 two more eggs were laid, one of which was fertile, and was hatched and reared by the parents until it was four weeks old. During a cold spell (the chick had been all right at the 8.00 a.m. nectar feed) it appeared abandoned, unfed and pecked on the back by mid-morning fruit-time. After a week of strenuous effort, including maintenance of the skin, this chick appears to have stabilized in the brooder, with company which was introduced after four days when the skin appeared to have healed without infection.

I was fortunate to receive another magnificent young pair from Tony de Dios of B.I.I. in the Philippines during January 1994. They were quite hard to acclimatize, coming from such an extreme climate compared with ours. Eventually, just after the worst of the following winter had settled in March 1995, at under two years old they laid two eggs, but made only an intermittent attempt to sit. I was sure with such young and large birds that neither would be fertile. However, both were brought in on day three to the incubator, and were fertile. They went 'wrong' at about two weeks, probably due to the erratic sitting at the start. There is always something to learn and next time (hopefully) we will switch the eggs the day they are laid and attempt training with china ones. These pairs are important to the captive gene pool, being totally unrelated. I will only, hopefully in due course, mate them on Armin Brockner's advice.

Chattering Lory

Lorius garrulus garrulus (Plate 15)

Common names
DUTCH   Molukkenlori
GERMAN   Gelbmantellori
FRENCH   Lori des Moluques

Distribution Halmahera, Weda in the North Moluccas.
Range Is. *Population trend* D.
M-L E. *In the field* F.

Description Mostly vibrant red; deep in colour, almost maroon, on the mantle; wings, upper side of tail and thighs green; iris and beak orange-red, darker in youngsters.
Distinguishing features It is almost

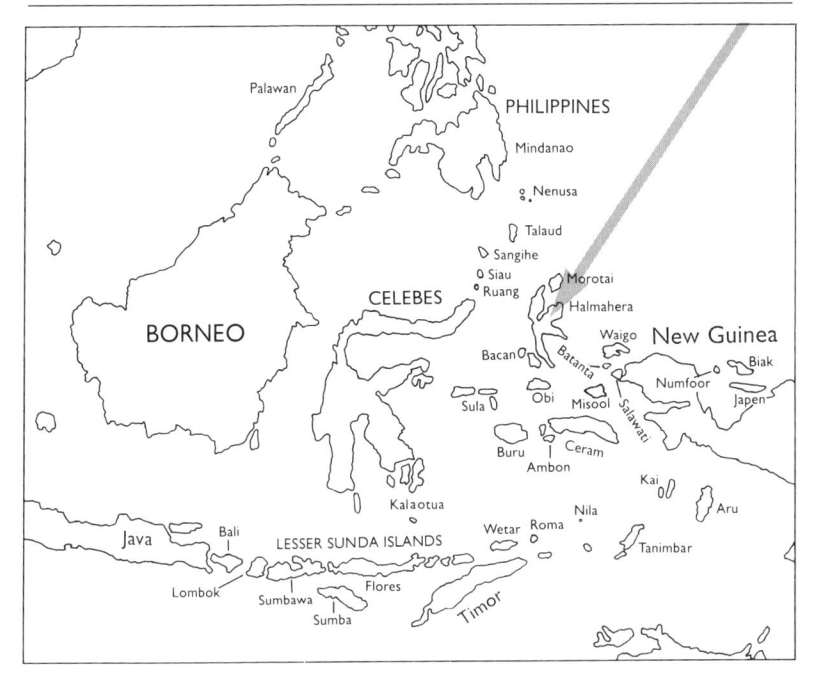

Distribution of the Chattering Lory

identical to the Yellow-backed Lory (*L.g. flavopalliatus*) but lacking the yellow mantle.
Status a-b Threatened (see also Chapter 13). It is imperative to breed pure stock now (avoiding crossbreeding with *L.g. flavopalliatus*) from those birds still in captivity.
Maturity 3½ years.
Length 30cm (12in).
Weight 200–250g (7–9oz).
Call Loud.
Management Easy and hardy; free-breeding when available and a good parent.
Nest-box A, C, E, H.
Eggs 2. *Incubation* 28 days.
Ring size 7–8mm (⅜in) 'S–T'.
Fledging About 11 weeks.

Practical experience These magnificent lories are among the most popular everywhere, not only for their colour and ease of management but for their vibrant personalities and their delight in human company. I have kept and enjoyed this species for well over 20 years. Please note that they are affectionate towards people but can be treacherous towards other birds.

I recently had a very large hen which I had thought to be a Chattering Lory (*L.g. garrulus*) and for which I had searched in vain for a cock. (The owners of the few that I found were, understandably, not prepared to split them from their Yellow-backed mates – an attitude with which I sympathize, as I know to my cost that splitting a bonded pair can cause death from time to time through pining.) My hen tried to kill successive Yellow-backed males, before taking a fancy to a little Obi Yellow-backed Lory (*L.g. flavopalliatus*). I had bought this bird to save it from a life in a cage. It had become too aggressive for the owners even to feed, and they had not been able to clean it out for a long while. After having it sexed – it was a male (and having its double-looped nails cut short while under the anaesthetic) – I tried my usual adjacent-cages introduction, offering him a hen on each side, this big Chattering Lory and a little Obi Lory. His preference was immediately apparent; it was love at first sight and I was able to dispense with the cages the next day, although I naturally kept a very close eye on them. I need not have worried; they are devoted, but they are an odd-looking couple; she is half as big again as him.

Because their love was apparent for all to see, and because of their tricky personalities and the lack of Chattering males, I made an exception, on humanitarian grounds and kept them together. Six weeks after putting them in an aviary in May, they laid two infertile eggs, which in due course I candled and removed. Six weeks later they laid another two, one of which was fertile; this duly hatched and was raised immaculately by the parents.

Interestingly the cock's personality has totally changed since becoming an aviary bird. He is no longer aggressive towards people (nor is the hen, to her mate or their young); in fact they both avoid people totally, being quite self-sufficient. I believe this miraculous change is the result of joy at having a compatible mate and an aviary.

Subspecies There are three subspecies of *Lorius garrulus*:

(1) *L.g. garrulus*, as described above.
(2) *L.g. flavopalliatus* (Yellow-backed Lory), from two distinct islands (see p. 185).
(3) *L.g. morotaianus* (Morotai Yellow-backed Lory), from the island of Morotai; said to be slightly smaller than (2) and with less yellow.

Yellow-backed Lory

Lorius garrulus flavopalliatus
(Plate 16)

Common names
DUTCH   Geelmantellori
GERMAN   Prachtgelbmantellori
FRENCH   Lori des Moluques à dos jaune

Distribution There appear to be two races of this lory, one from Bacan (Batjan) (A) and one from Obi (B). *Range* Is. *Population trend* D. *M-L* E? *In the field* C.

Description As for the nominate Chattering Lory (*L.g. garrulus*) with the addition of a yellow mantle patch. Birds from Bacan and birds from Obi should not be paired together, nor with the nominate race. (There are too few purebred birds left in aviculture, the result, no doubt, of years of crossbreeding, possibly because of lack of information on the subspecies generally and to the dominance of the Yellow-backed Lory (*L.g. flavopalliatus*). The Obi race is a smaller bird with a relatively much larger patch of yellow. If both specimens are seen together they cannot be confused. Jos Hubers (pers. comm.) believes it should be classed as a distinct subspecies (i.e. *L.g. obiensis*). Crossing *L.g. garrulus* and *L. g. flavopalliatus* can result in offspring that, in general,

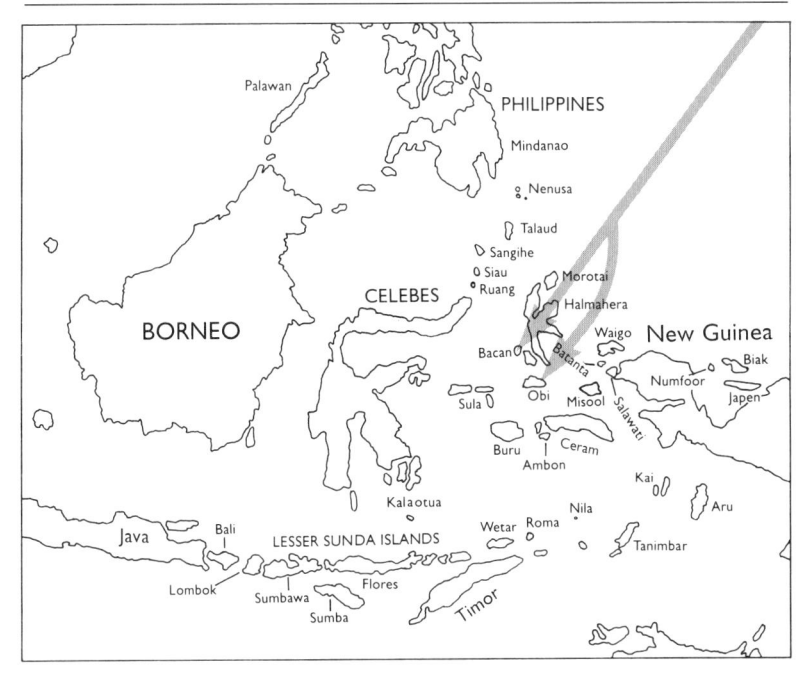

Distribution of the Yellow-backed Lory

resemble the Morotai Lory (*L.g. morotaianu)s*. Hubers also believes that a large individual with a small patch of yellow is not purebred.
Distinguishing features A is larger than B, most often with a smaller yellow mantle patch. Both are easily distinguished from the nominate bird which has no yellow.
Status a-b Threatened in the wild (see also Chapter 13). Relatively secure in captivity; in the UK, zoos are running a breeding programme.
Maturity 3½ years.
Length A 30cm (12in), B 27cm (10½in).
Weight A 200–250g (7–9oz) B 190–220g (6¾–7¾oz).
Call Loud.
Management Very easy and hardy; free-breeding and usually good parents.

Nest-box B, C, E, H.
Eggs 2. Incubation 26–28 days.
Ring size A 7–8mm (⅜in) 'S–T'; B 7mm (⁵⁄₁₆in) 'R–S'.
Fledging 11–12 weeks.

Practical experience The Yellow-backed Lory, being more abundant than the Chattering Lory (*L.g. garrulus*), and more colourful, is even more popular. Its management in every respect is exactly the same as for the nominate bird.

Before the advent of surgical sexing, it once took me literally weeks to pair up four hens that I had kept together as pairs with newly acquired cocks that had been similarly kept. In fact one hen was killed. Eventually I made up two pairs which have bred well ever since, but I think I paid the penalty for keeping birds of the same sex together for too long. These pairs have been with me for 10 years and are peaceful by nature, if not by voice, and regularly give me four to six chicks annually. I inspect the nest daily, topping it up while the adults feed, and I am often watched by them.

I also have a small Obi Yellow-backed pair, bought at an auction that, during the 2 years which I have kept them, have sat at opposite ends of the aviary quite amicably. They have been most confiding and gentle with people, regularly perching on the shoulders of those bearing food and other essentials. In May 1993 things changed quite suddenly. They had become adult and both became aggressive towards us; the cock in particular was *lethal*, dive-bombing, biting, and holding on and shaking whatever he managed to sink his beak into. She layed egg(s). We decided to leave them well alone, not out of fear for ourselves so much as fear of the damage that could be wreaked in the form of broken eggs or squashed chicks. This was the first time *ever* I had to make an exception to my rule about daily inspections. In fact the chick (for there was just one, when, at 3½ weeks, I decided I must investigate and had to catch up both parent birds) was fine, but the nest was dangerously sodden and I decided to take the bird in for hand-rearing.

Purple-bellied Lory

Lorius hypoinochrous hypoinochrous

Common names
SYNONYM   Eastern Black-capped Lory, Louisiade Lory
DUTCH   Violetstaart Lori
GERMAN   Schwarzstersslori
FRENCH   Lori à bande violette

Distribution The eastern Papuan islands of Misima and Tagula in the Louisiade Archipelago, where it flies low through trees (particularly coconut plantations), foothills and primary forest, usually at sea level and rarely to 1600m (5250ft).
Range Is. *Population trend* S? *M-L* S. *In the field?*

Description Stocky; crimson; crown and nape purplish black; abdomen, thighs and undertail dark purple and wings green; dark red half-collar (which is purple in the Western Black-caps); tail red, tapering to blue-green on top and olive below; cere white.
Distinguishing features White cere of the three subspecies and their distinctive call distinguishes them from the Black-capped Lories.
Status a-b Considered safe, generally common, locally abundant in the wild. Rare in captivity but it is believed to have been incorrectly identified on several occasions.
Maturity 3–3½ years.
Length 26cm (10¼in).
Weight 200–240g (7–8½oz).
Call Very distinctive; long drawn out nasal whistles and coarse whinnying.

Practical experience This species has been recorded in the UK, but Peter Odekerken (1992) believes that the specimen recorded at Chester Zoo in 1973 was probably in fact an error and, although there were photographs of specimens at Kelling Park Aviaries, there were no subsequent details of these available. Eric Lindgren has kept both *L.h. hypoinochrous* and *L.l. lory* and notes that, in the former, the peri-orbital skin graduates from cream to black, unlike the pure black of *L.l. lory*, and that the upper mandible is considerably heavier. No

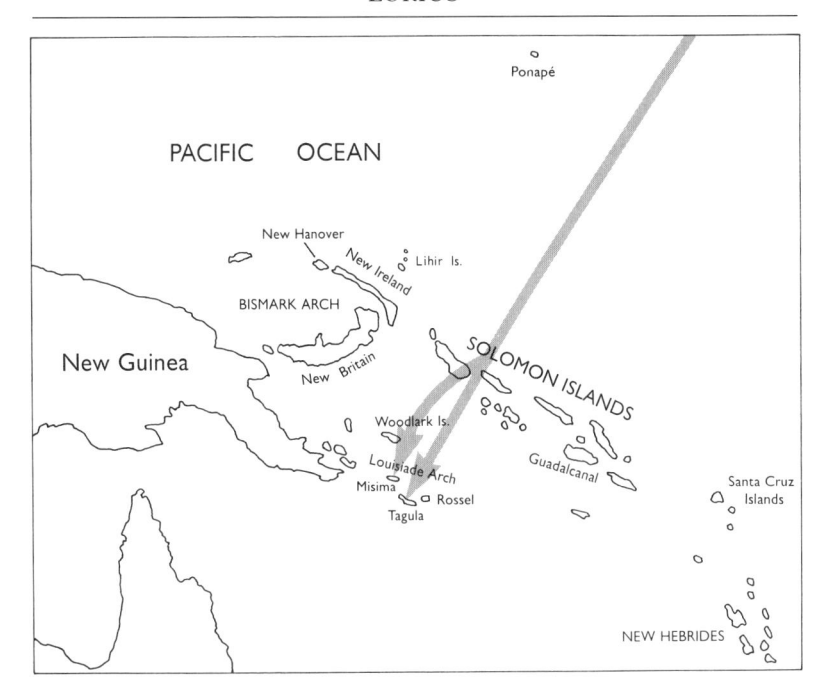

Distribution of the Purple-bellied Lory

doubt this is an adaptation for a specific item of diet.

Peter Odekerken has seen one in a collection at Rulolo, Morobe Province, New Guinea, and the photograph which he was able to take appears in his article (1992). The bird's primaries had been removed and it wore a leg ring of coconut husk to prevent its escape. This single specimen had been purchased from local people in the nearby coastal region and released in an aviary where it had paired up with one of a number of *L.l. erythrothorax*.

Subspecies There are three subspecies of *Lorius hypoinochrous*:

(1) *L.h. hypoinochrous*, as described above.

(2) *L.h. devittatus* (Devittatus Lory), from Trobriand and Woodlark Islands, Bismark and D'Entrecasteaux Archipelagos and southeast New Guinea, is larger than the nominate bird and differs in having a purple band on the upper back and, supposedly, lacking the black margins on the greater underwing coverts.

(3) *L.h. rosselianus* (Rossel Island Lory), from Rossel Island in the Lousiade Archipelago, also has the purple band on the upper back and both the breast and abdomen are deep crimson. It has a black line on the underwings.

Black-capped Lory

Lorius lory lory (Plates 13 and 52)

Common names

SYNONYM	Western Black-capped Lory
DUTCH	Zwartkoplori

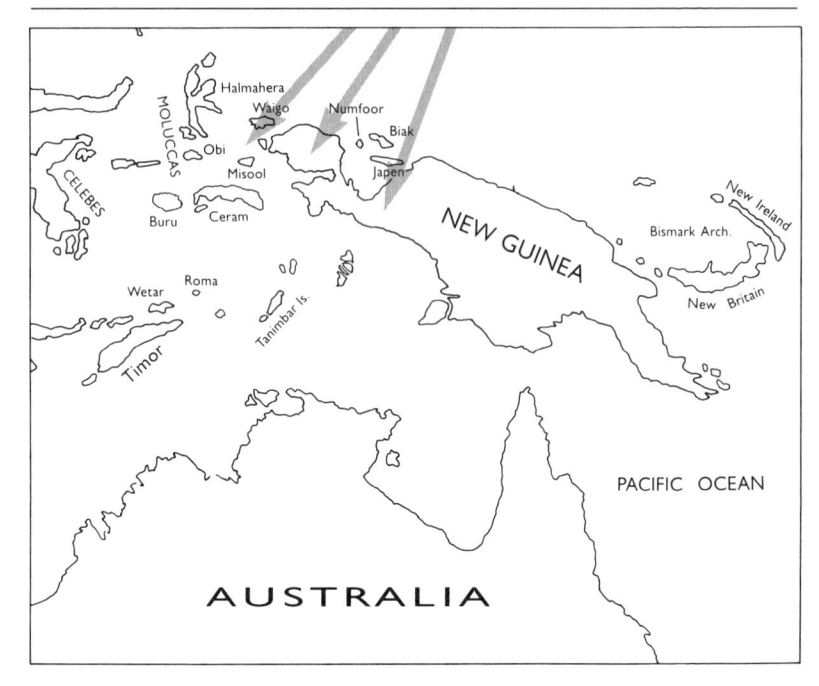

Distribution of the Black-capped Lory

GERMAN Frauenlori
FRENCH Lori à calotte noire

Distribution Vogelkop in Irian Jaya and in the western Papuan islands of Batanta, Salawati and Misool, where it inhabits lowland forest up to 1550m (5000ft); it feeds on pollen, nectar, insects, fruiting trees and possibly some seed. It is said to be particularly fond of the blossom of the climbing *Freycinetia*. It is noticeably absent from monsoon forest and coconut plantations.
Range M. *Population trend* S. M-L S. *In the field* ?

Description A truly vibrant broad-tailed lory: upper breast and head red, except for the large black cap; underparts and mantle, which forms a large collar and adjoining chest bib, dark purple to royal blue; a narrow red band below the blue on the mantle; lower abdomen, thighs and undertail turquoise blue; rump red and upper tail royal blue-turquoise. Wings green above and red underneath.
Distinguishing features Full collar joining and extending over the chest to the abdomen distinguish this from the Erythro Black-capped Lory (*L.l. erythrothorax*). It is red on the underwing, unlike the Jobi Lory (*L.l. jobiensis*) which is blue-black here.
Status a-b Considered safe throughout its large range, although there is believed to be some threat from hybridization; becoming scarcer in captivity.
Maturity 3–3½ years.
Length 31cm (12¼in).
Weight 200–240g (7–8½oz).
Call Variety of loud whistles; a noisy

species, particularly in late afternoon.
Management Hardy and easy when available.
Nest-box A, C, E, H.
Eggs 2. *Incubation* 26–27 days.
Ring size 7–8mm (⅜in) 'S–T'.
Fledging 8–9 weeks.

Practical experience Every attempt should be made to pair the subspecies correctly. This has not been done in the past owing to the shortage and inaccuracy of information. It is hoped that Plate 52 will lay any confusion to rest.

The Black-capped Lory is not only beautiful but has one of the most lively personalities, and can become one of the best talkers. I find that even youngsters in a communal flight with other species will start to talk and imitate other sounds within a few months. They are, however, not the most athletic of fliers and, for that reason, too long a flight is not to be recommended; they are less in control of their 'brakes' than most. I would say 2.74m (9ft) is long enough. They tend to be very keen on their food and can easily become overweight. They seem more intolerant of high levels of lactose than any other lory. When recognized the problem can be quite easily overcome (see p. xx).

Black-caps sometimes breed earlier than stated, particularly if one is placed with an older partner. I have found in two instances that Black-caps took a little time to settle to the job of reproducing – either breaking eggs or attacking chicks – but in due course all was well. I think, if research were done in the wild, that there would be evidence of the same thing with early clutches.

In common with some other big lories, really stout china or other heavy food-pots are required; otherwise they will be overturned with subsequent loss of food. Anything with hooks, and most revolving feeders, may be rendered useless. To keep these intelligent birds' minds active I give them plenty of branches and toys. This is particularly vital for youngsters and maybe why, to date, there have been no instances of Black-caps intimidating other species in my adolescent flights, although I have heard that this often happens. At least twice a day long swings, cut from branches, with dog-leads or old belts knotted at each end, are hung from the roof. Most lories play contentedly with these for hours, but Black-caps will undo the knots, then call to you to come and put the toy up again. Contrary to what I have heard, I do not find breeding Black-caps are unduly aggressive.

Subspecies There are seven subspecies of *Lorius lorius*:
(1) *L.l. lory*, as described above.
(2) *L.l. cyanauchen* (Biak Lory), from Biak in Geelvink Bay is similar to *L. l. erythrothorax* but with no red on the hind neck, i.e. the purple-blue joins the black cap directly. This subspecies is blue and black under the wing and a blue band extends across the upper abdomen to under the wings as it does in *L.l. jobiensis*. It is unknown in aviculture and seriously endangered. An island species, its population is declining and it is now categorized as vulnerable. Urgent field surveys need to be done.
(3) *L.l. erythrothorax* (Red-breasted Lory), see p. xx.
(4) *L.l. jobiensis* (Jobi Lory), see p. xx.
(5) *L.l. salvadorii* (Salvadori's Lory) is 32cm (12½in) long, weighs 200–230g (7–8oz), and comes from

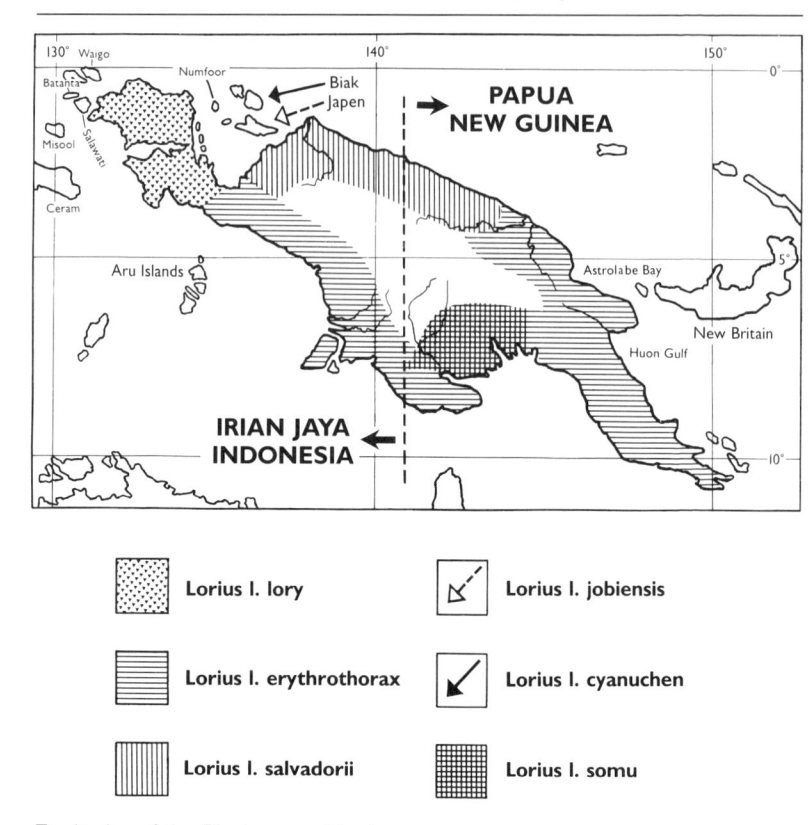

▦ Lorius l. lory	⬚ Lorius l. jobiensis
≡ Lorius l. erythrothorax	⬚ Lorius l. cyanuchen
||| Lorius l. salvadorii	▦ Lorius l. somu

Territories of the Black-capped Lories

northeast New Guinea, from Astrolabe Bay west to the Aitape area. It is similar to *L.l. erythrothorax* in size and colour but is blue and black on the underwing, has a wide dark blue band on the hind neck and across the lower chest, and is basically red as opposed to the rose-pink of *L.l. jobiensis*. The abdomen is blackish-blue. (I have followed Trevor Buckell's advice here as in all matters pertaining to Blackcaps) and included *L.l. viridicrissalis* as synonomous with *L.l. salvadorii*.

(6) *L.l. somu* (Somu Lory), from south New Guinea, around the Fly River, Lake Kutubu, the Purari River and the Karimui Basin. This bird is unknown in aviculture but, while resembling *L.l. erythrothorax*, is easily distinguished in having red from the cap down the back with no blue hind collar.

Erythro Black-capped Lory

Lorius lory erythrothorax
(Plates 14 and 52)

Common names

SYNONYM	Red-breasted Lory
DUTCH	Rodeborstlori
GERMAN	Salvadori Frauenlori
FRENCH	Lori à calotte noire de Salvadori

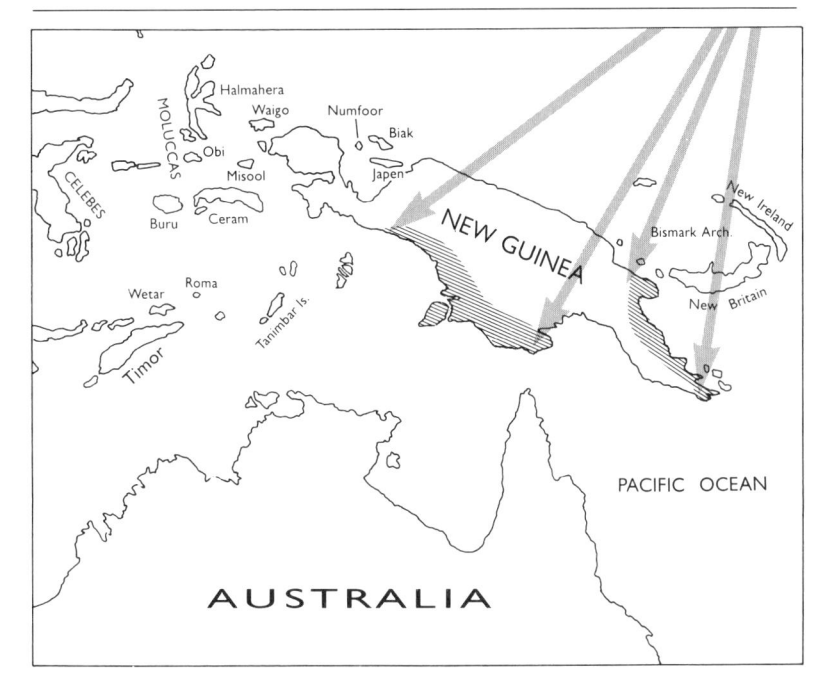

Distribution of the Erythro Black-capped Lory

Distribution Southern parts of Geelvink Bay and from the Onin Peninsula, Irian Jaya, east to southeastern Papua and the Huon Peninsula.
Range S. *Population trend* S.
M-L S. *In the field* ?

Description Chest entirely red; half-collar of vibrant blue on the hind neck; lower abdomen also blue; red on the underwing.
Distinguishing features Red chest with no collar and red on the underwing.
Status a-b Considered safe. In aviculture now the most common of this species, but still not always correctly identified and paired.
Maturity 3+ years.
Length 30cm (12in).
Weight 200–220g (7–7¾oz).
Call Not as loud as the nominate bird.

Management Hardy and easy.
Nest-box A, C, E, H.
Eggs 2. *Incubation* 26 days.
Ring size 7–8mm (⅙in) 'S–T'.
Fledging 8–9 weeks.

Practical experience Management is identical to that of the nominate birds, but its personality and voice is a little less boisterous, as is its character. This is now the most common subspecies in aviculture today, an intelligent and uncomplicated bird.

Jobi Lory

Lorius lory jobiensis (Plates 12 and 52)

Common names
SYNONYM   Jobi Black-capped Lory
DUTCH   Jobilori

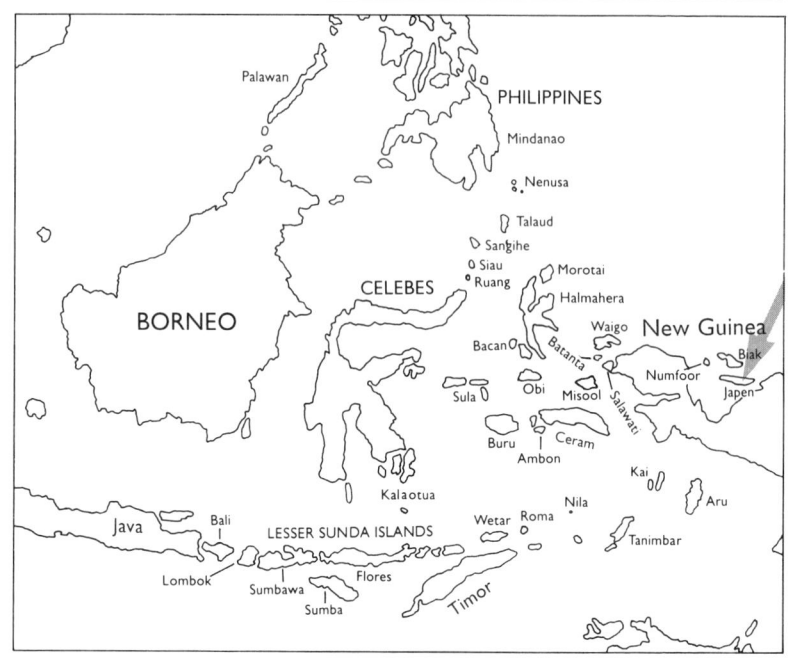

Distribution of the Jobi Lory

GERMAN Jobi Frauenlori
FRENCH Lori de Jobi

Distribution The islands of Japen (formerly Jobi) and Meos Num in Geelvink Bay; in dense rainforest, swamp and forest edge to 1600m (5250ft).
Range Is. *Population trend* S.
M-L S. *In the field* ?

Description Large and substantial; breast rose- or brick-pink light blue; hind half-collar and narrow band between chest and abdomen, reaching to the underside of wings; abdomen purple; pale pink stripe behind the black cap; blue and black on the underwing.
Distinguishing features Blue and black on underwing, not red. Rose-coloured breast, not red, and pale pink-white at the nape.

Status a-b Possible still safe; rare in captivity.
Maturity 3–3½ years.
Length 32cm (12½in).
Weight 220–250g (7–9oz).
Call Loud.
Management Hardy and easy, although can be aggressive.
Nest-box A, C, E, H.
Eggs 2. *Incubation* 25–26 days.
Ring size 7–8mm (⅜in) 'S–T'.
Fledging 9 weeks.

Practical experience Every attempt should be made correctly to identify and pair these birds. Being island birds it cannot be long before they become rare in the wild as well as in aviculture.

Two doubtful species follow.

White-naped Lory

Lorius albidinuchus

Distribution New Ireland in the Bismarck Archipelago, Papua New Guinea, where it inhabits forests from 500–2000m (1650–6500ft).
Range Is. *Population trend* S/D. M-L V. *In the field*?

Description Predominantly red with green on the upper wings, red on the underwings and a yellow band across the flight feathers; broken yellow collar; black cap; white nape.
Distinguishing features White nape.
Length 26cm (10¼in).
Status a Currently, little is known of this bird in the wild and, so far, it is not known in aviculture, although there is a glimmer of hope in this direction.

New Britain Lory

Lorius amabilis

Common name
SYNONYM Stresemann's Lory
Known only from one specimen from Nakanai, New Britain, this is probably not a valid species. Birdlife International do not consider it so and Forshaw (1973) thought it a likely mutation.

Blue-thighed Lory

Lorius tibialis
This is probably not a true species, being known only from one specimen and not recognized by Birdlife International. It is thought to have been a mutant form of *L. domicellus*, but lacking the black crown.

Summary of Black-capped Lories

Differences in the Black-capped Lories have not been correctly recognized until recently, and have resulted in many crossbreeds. It is however important that, as aviculturists and conservationists, we breed only pure lories. The confusion came about through incorrect information and lack of knowledge, including much of that given in even the most recent books. I am indebted to Trevor Buckell – a foremost expert on *Lorius* spp. – for his Black-cap map and for the idea which gave rise to Plate 52. He initially helped me to recognize the differences in my own collection and has been a patient source of help with all 'Black-cap' matters.

The Black-caps can be divided as follows:

(1) Eastern Black-capped Lories (*Lorius hypoinochrous*)
(2) Western Black-capped Lories (*Lorius lory*)

Within the second category we are likely to see only three subspecies and it is confusion among these which it is particularly important to avoid. This category can be further broken down into:

(2i) Red underwing *L.l.* (a) *lory* and (b) *L.l. erythrothorax*
(2ii) Blue and black underwing *L.l. jobiensis* (see p. 191)

The two species in (2i) can be distinguished as follows:

(a) Full collar and bib of blue extending from the upper chest to the vent *L.l. lory* (see p. xx)
(b) Half- or hind-neck blue collar and red chest *L.l. erythrothorax* (see p. 190)

22 Neopsittacus

Species	Subspecies	English name	Availability
musschenbroekii	musschenbroekii	Musschenbroek's Lorikeet	*
	major	–	–
pullicauda	pullicauda	Emerald Lorikeet	*
	alpinus	Alpine Lorikeet	–
	socialis	–	–
2	3	5	

Neopsittacus spp. comprise small, heavy-billed, red-fronted, green mountain lorikeets that live on a particularly varied diet. This needs to be taken into account in an avicultural situation, as does their lack of tolerance to change. They are swift in flight, when red flashes of underwing show, but spend much time busily twittering and running around branches like mice.

Musschenbroek's Lorikeet

Neopsittacus musschenbroekii musschenbroekii (Plate 46)

Common names
DUTCH   Musschenbroeklori
GERMAN   Gualori
FRENCH   Loriquet de Musschenbroek

Distribution Vogelkop, Irian Jaya from 1250–2800m (4100–9200ft) upwards. It inhabits fruiting and flowering trees being particularly fond of casaurinas, but also taking annual weeds, insects, larvae and seeds of the mid-mountain forest trees. It is found in the company of Emerald Lorikeets (*N.p. pullicauda*) at about 3000m (9850ft) on the Owen Stanley Mountains, and with Mount Goliath (Stella) Lorikeets (*Charmosyna papou goliathina*) at about the same altitude in Irian Jaya.
Range M. *Population trend* S. *M-L* S. *In the field* ?

Description Olive-green upper parts and lighter olive below; yellow streaking on head and cheeks, divided by a black eye stripe; throat, breast and abdomen variably red; tail tipped with yellow, and thighs and undertail olive; proportionately large beak horn-coloured; iris brown; legs grey; broad band of red on the underwing. Immatures are similar in size and colour but with less red and with brown beaks.
Distinguishing features Larger and more olive-green than the Emerald

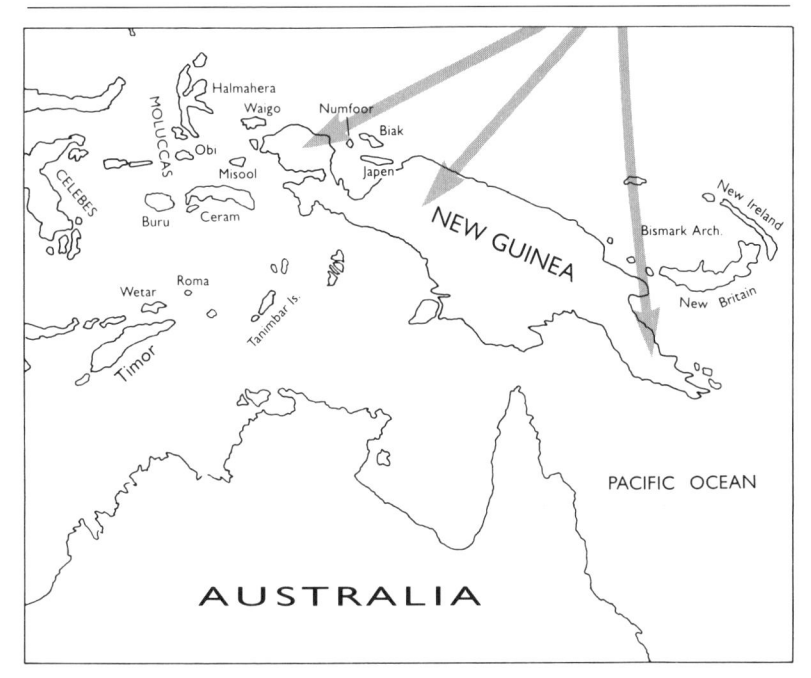

Distribution of Musschenbroek's Lorikeet

Lorikeet (*N.p. pullicauda*), less red on front and with a larger beak, horn not orange.
Status a-b Safe in its habitat which spreads over a wide range; too few breeding pairs left in aviculture to ensure its long-term survival there.
Maturity 2 years.
Length 21–23cm (8¼–9in).
Weight 48–52g (1¾–1⅞oz).
Call Quiet squeak and twitter.
Management Hardy; requires specialized feeding.
Nest-box B, D, F, G, H.
Eggs 2. *Incubation* 22–24 days.
Ring size 5mm (¼in) 'Mu–N'.
Fledging 7–7½ weeks.

Practical experience These lorikeets are among my personal favourites. I have kept this species since 1986 and love them. They appear and behave in a totally different way from any other lory and present a challenge in aviculture. They were virtually unknown in aviculture until 1986 and we know now that they cannot reproduce on a diet consisting entirely of nectar or entirely of seed. Some pairs take a little nectar and all love seeds but they should not be maintained on this diet alone. Most fruits are also enjoyed, and a variety of other items (see Chapter 7).

They are the most destructive of lories if everything does not suit them. When I kept mine in an indoor flight, the woodwork was demolished and nests became riddled with holes in no time at all. After they were moved to outdoor aviaries, the chewing virtually ceased. Nevertheless, when they found a small rotten hole in a house wall, it was enlarged hazardously quickly so that they could nest between the wall and lining. Next, a choice of nest-box was given, the most popular of which was an L-shape with a divider, the intention being that they should climb to the bottom and thence over to the nesting and inspection area. During the first 24 hours this divider, which was 2.5cm (1in) thick, was chewed down; it has not been altered since. Young have been reared to independence in this nest, all four birds returning to roost at dusk. I now provide some pairs with outside suspended aviaries 1.8m × 0.9m × 0.9m high (6ft × 3ft × 3ft high) with attached totally unheated houses while others have conventional full-height 1.8m × 0.9m × 1.8m high (6ft × 3ft × 6ft high) aviaries with access to a house kept above freezing. I find this vital for first-year birds which seem to need time to toughen up. When I tried to keep them without heat during the first year, they appeared fluffed and unhappy whenever it became damp or cold. A number of captive-bred birds die at this time. Those reaching their second year seem impervious to cold.

During my early years with this species (at that time I fed nectar and seed) I lost young ranging from 12 hours to 6 weeks of age. In the first chicks – which at hatching have very unique long white down except for a brown patch on the head – I noticed the crops appeared to be filled with what I thought was shredded wood from the nest. When they died I had them necropsied and it was found to be regurgitated non-identified larvae. The adults were then wormed at intervals with a broad-spectrum wormer (as opposed to just the tape-wormer routinely given to newly imported lories). The crops of subsequent chicks were observed to have normal fluid contents, but the chicks continued to make poor growth and die young. At this stage I switched one chick with an Edward's Lorikeet (*T.h. capistratus*) chick. The Edward's chick was reared for 10 days by the Musschenbroek's Lorikeets when it was found to have an impacted crop. This I cleared in the routine way (see Chapter 14) and thence hand-reared it. Meanwhile the Edward's Lorikeet reared the Musschenbroek chick for about the same time, after which it just faded away. I tried to hand-rear the next chicks. They appeared very anaemic; one faded away at a few days and the other, which never grew in step with the other young lories, died at 6 weeks of age.

At about this time I began to use the diet mentioned in Chapter 7 and, from then on, things went well. Chicks have been parent-reared ever since, with one exception, that of a cockbird dying while the chicks were hatching, which caused the hen to abandon the nest. I reared one of these from the egg and gave the other to the same Edward's Lorikeet because I was not sure whether either of us would manage the task. At 10 days both chicks looked well and there was no difference in size, but I felt there was a better chance of long-term survival on the more varied diet that proved to be suiting the adults; so both were hand-reared from then on. The hand-rearing formula was amended by the addition of equal parts of ground, hulled seeds. The chicks appeared identical at fledging and, as another pair had reared their own at virtually the same time, I had the pleasure of having all four young in an aviary together for a while. I placed a different-coloured plastic leg-ring on each chick

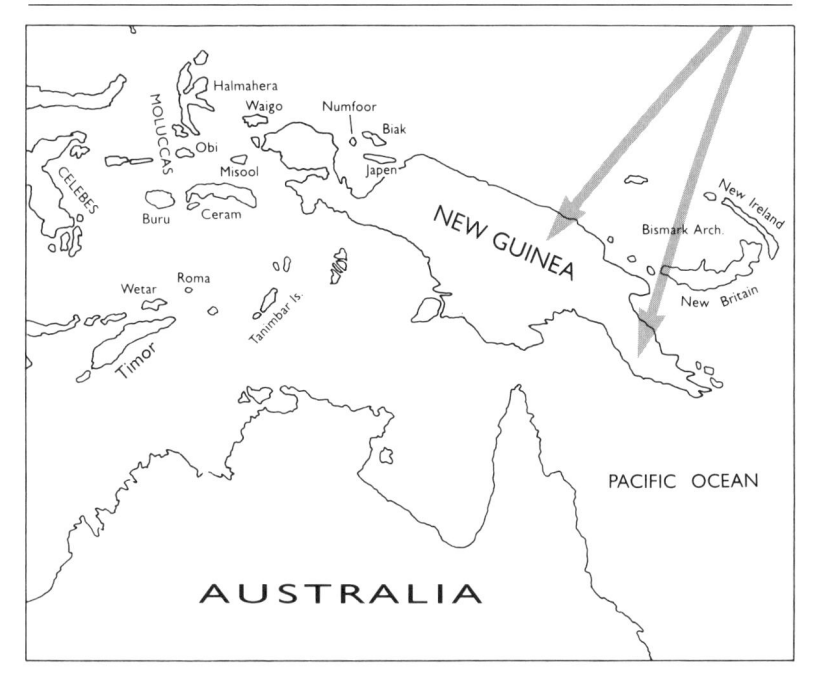

Distribution of the Emerald Lorikeet

for ease of comparison. Despite the chicks' strong beaks none of the rings was removed and without them I could not have told one chick from another although I did clip tails differently as a safeguard.

Subspecies There are two (previously three) subspecies of *Neopsittacus musschenbroeki*:

(1) *N.m. musschenbroekii*, as described above.
(2) *N.m. major*, from southeast New Guinea from the Sepik Region to the Huon Region of south Papua, which has paler plumage and green cheek streaking.

N.m. medius, from the Snow Mountains of Irian Jaya, is no longer believed to be a distinct subspecies and is classified with *N.m. major*.

Emerald Lorikeet

Neopsittacus pullicauda pullicauda

Common names
SYNONYM Alpine Lorikeet
DUTCH   Emeraldlori
GERMAN   Smaragdgualori
FRENCH   Loriquet de Victoria

Distribution The mountains of southeast New Guinea, west to the Sepik Region between 2400–3800m (7900–12 500ft), in flocks of 28–30 birds, where it frequents mossy forest and partly cleared areas. In the lower parts of its range it is often found in the company of Musschenbroek's Lorikeets.
Range M. Population trend S.
M-L S. In the field ?

Description Bright green unstreaked head, back and wings; and an unbroken red throat, chest and abdomen; orange beak; underside of tail olive-green, red at the base.
Distinguishing features Smaller and brighter green than the Musschenbroek's Lorikeet (*N.m. musschenbroekii*) with a more solid red front, smaller, orange beak and no yellow tip to the upper surface of the tail.
Status a-b Common with a wide range of mainland habitat. Known in aviculture now, but in very small numbers which are not sustainable.
Maturity 20–23 months.
Length 18cm (7in).
Weight 30–40g (1–1⅜oz).
Call Quiet squeak and twitter.
Management Quite hardy; requires special feeding (as for Musschenbroek's).
Nest-box B, D, F, G, H.
Eggs 2. *Incubation* 25 days.
Ring size 4.2–4.5mm (³⁄₁₆in) 'L'.
Fledging 7 weeks.

Practical experience Unfortunately these lovely little birds came into aviculture only just before importation from the wild virtually ceased. Their numbers were so small that, although a handful have been bred, they cannot be maintained and so the risk of inbreeding is very real, giving aviculturists almost no chance to meet the full challenge of understanding this subspecies. The management is virtually the same as for *N.m. musschenbroeki*, but they are thought not to be quite as hardy; or perhaps the few lucky owners have just not been prepared to risk them. Peter Clear, who won an Avicultural Society 1st UIC Breeding Award with this species in 1992, finds their management similar in all respects similar to that of the *N.m. musschenbroekii*.

Subspecies There are three subspecies of *Neopsittacus pullicauda*:

(1) *N.p. pullicauda*, as described above.

(2) *N.p. alpinus* (Alpine Lorikeet), from the Snow Mountains east to the Fly River, which is a darker green and has an orange-red chest.

(3) *N.p. socialis*, from the Herzog Mountains and the mountains of the Huon Peninsula, which is also dark green but with ear coverts streaked with red.

23 Oreopsittacus

Species	Subspecies	English name	Availability
arfaki	arfaki	Whiskered Lorikeet	–
	grandis	–	–
	major	–	–
1	2	3	

The sole species of this genus is small and slim with a very fine, pointed beak, and is unique in having 14 tail feathers as opposed to the normal 12. Its distribution covers the mountains of New Guinea from the Vogelkop, Irian Jaya, east to the Huon Peninsula and southern Papua.

Whiskered Lorikeet

Oreopsittacus arfaki arfaki

Common names
ENGLISH   Arfak Alpine Lorikeet
DUTCH   Arfaklori
GERMAN   Arfakbergzierlori
FRENCH   Loriquet des Monts Arfak

Distribution Vogelkop, Irian Jaya. This very swift-flying, acrobatic lorikeet is found only in forest between 2000–3750m (6600–12 300ft), where it apparently roosts in epiphytic moss and sometimes visits salt-pools on the ground. It can be found in the company of honeyeaters and flowerpeckers and feeds almost silently.

Range M. *Population trend* S. M-L S. *In the field* ?

Description Dimorphic. Green, yellowish below; forehead and crown red; lores and cheeks purple, above which a double row of white streaks; abdomen and lower flanks orange-red; undertail coverts yellow; underwing coverts and sides of breast red; a yellow band across the underside of the secondaries; tail green with tip and underside rose-red; beak black. Hen has the forehead and crown green.
Status a Little is known.
Status b Virtually unknown in captivity.
Length 15cm (6in).
Weight 20–25g ($^{11}/_{16}$–$^{15}/_{16}$oz).
Call Quiet, plaintive; like the sound of coins clinking together.
Ring size 4.0–4.5mm ($^3/_{16}$in) 'L'

Subspecies There are three subspecies of *Oreopsittacus arfaki*:

(1) *O.a. arfaki*, as described above.
(2) *O.a. major* only from the Snow Mountains of the Vogelkop, Irian Jaya. This is said to be slightly larger,

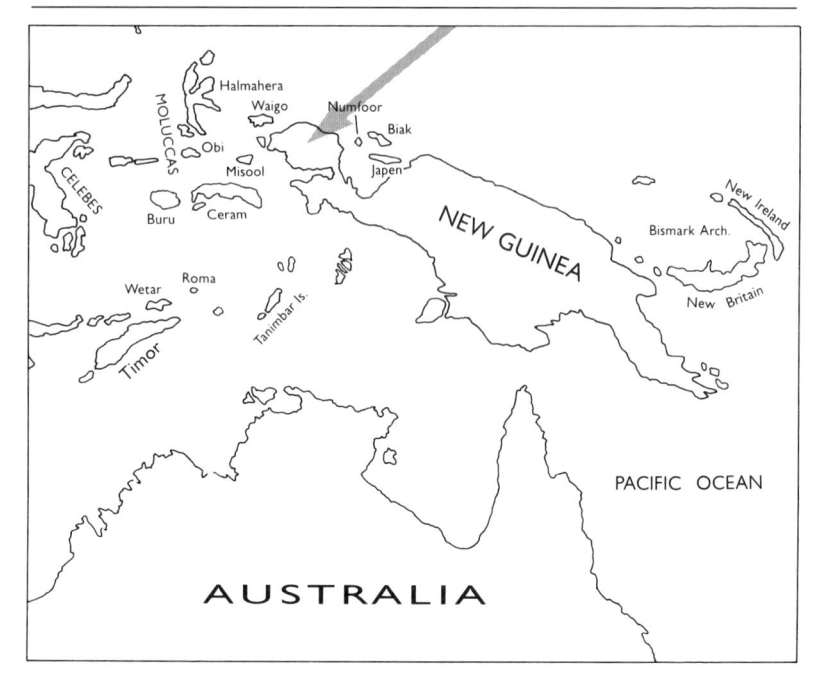

Distribution of the Whiskered Lorikeet

with the facial red extending beyond the eye and the tail tipped scarlet.
(3) *O. a. grandis*, which is distributed throughout the mountains of south-east New Guinea, west to the Huon Peninsula and the Sepik Region. This subspecies differs in having the abdomen and lower flanks green.

24 Phigys

Species	Subspecies	English name	Availability
solitarius	—	Collared Lory	—
1	0	1	

Collared Lory

Phigys solitarius

Common names
SYNONYM Ruffled Lory
DUTCH   Gekraagde Lori
GERMAN   Einsiedlerlori
FRENCH   Lori solitaire

Distribution The single member of this genus inhabits Fiji, with the exception of the southern Lau group of Islands and Samoa, in any type of habitat but particularly in the vicinity of *Erythrina* blossoms and gardens; it is fearless of man.

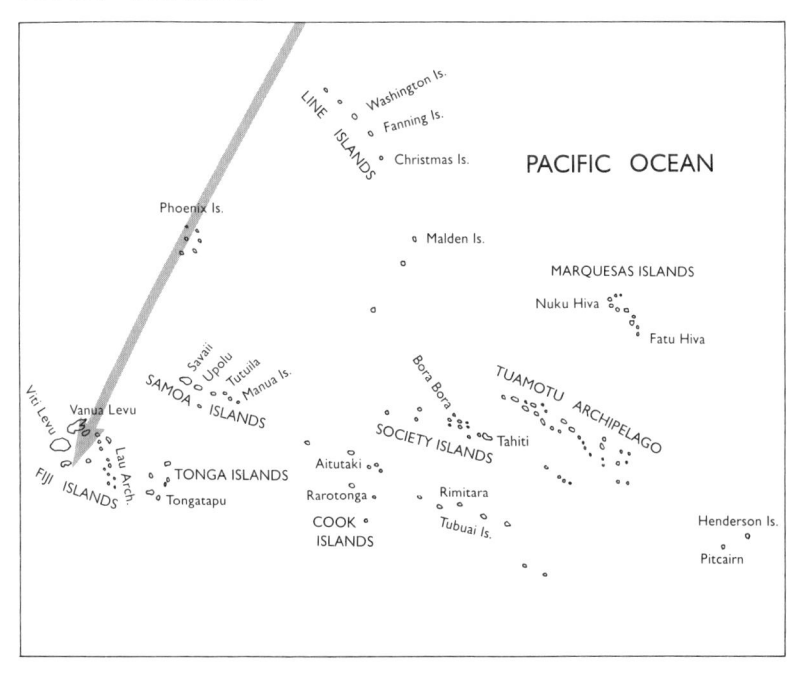

Distribution of the Collared Lory

Range Is. *Population trend* S. M-L S. *In the field* ?

Description A breathtakingly beautiful small lory, stocky and agile like a small Erythro Black-capped Lory (*L.l. erythrothorax*) in shape but more like *Vini* spp. in personality. Purple crown tapering to black towards the nape where the elongated feathers trail over the vivid green hind collar; lower back, wings, rump and tail are the same green; upper back, face, chest and upper abdomen scarlet; lower abdomen and thighs purple; beak and legs orange.

Distinguishing features Elongated nape feathers on the vivid green hind collar.
Status a-b Considered safe, although Viti Levu, the largest of the Fijis, has suffered greatly from increased population and deforestation. The scarlet feathers were highly prized by the Samoans and Tongans for edging mats and considerable trade existed in live birds, which were periodically plucked. This is prohibited today but still persists intermittently. Hardly ever known in captivity so far.
Length 20cm (8in).
Call Penetrating screech.

25 Pseudeos

Species	Subspecies	English name	Availability
fuscata	—	Dusky Lory	**
1	0	1	

This is now a monotypic genus. There were previously though to be two subspecies, including *P.f. incognita*, a somewhat larger bird, also from New Guinea.

Dusky Lory

Pseudeos fuscata (Plates 8 and 9)

Common names
DUTCH   Witruglori
GERMAN Weissburzel Lori
FRENCH Lori à dos blanc

Distribution New Guinea, Salawati, Japen. This lory is nomadic and widespread. It frequents rainforests, inhabited regions, deforested areas, coconut and teak plantations and savannah, and is seen at all months high above the Brown River, mainly in lowland and hills up to 2400m (7900ft). It is often seen in large noisy flocks, in the company of Rainbow Lorikeets (*T.h. haematodus*) but flying higher.
Range M/Is. *Population trend* S. M–L S. *In the field* ?

Description Two recognized colour phases; orange and yellow, although some appear almost red and others a mixture of all these colours; one thing is certain; none could be described as 'dusky'. Upper parts brown; front appears brown, barred with either orange or yellow; undertail blue and the beak, which looks massive, orange with some bare skin around the lower mandible; iris red; wings brown; rump varying cream colour; crown orange or yellow.
Distinguishing features Brown with wide orange or yellow chest stripes.
Status a–b Safe in both.
Maturity 2½ years.
Length 25–27cm (10–10½in).
Weight 145–190g (5⅛–6¾oz).
Call Loud, high-pitched and piercing.
Management Easy in all respects.
Nest-box A, C, E, H.
Eggs 2. *Incubation* 24 days.
Ring size 6.5–7.5mm (5⁄16in) 'R–S'.
Fledging 10–11 weeks.

Practical experience I consider Duskys to be one of the easiest lories to look after and breed, as they are hardy and not fussy in any way. I had two pairs for many years. The orange pair were prolific breeders and very good parents, while my yellow pair, although immaculate, never

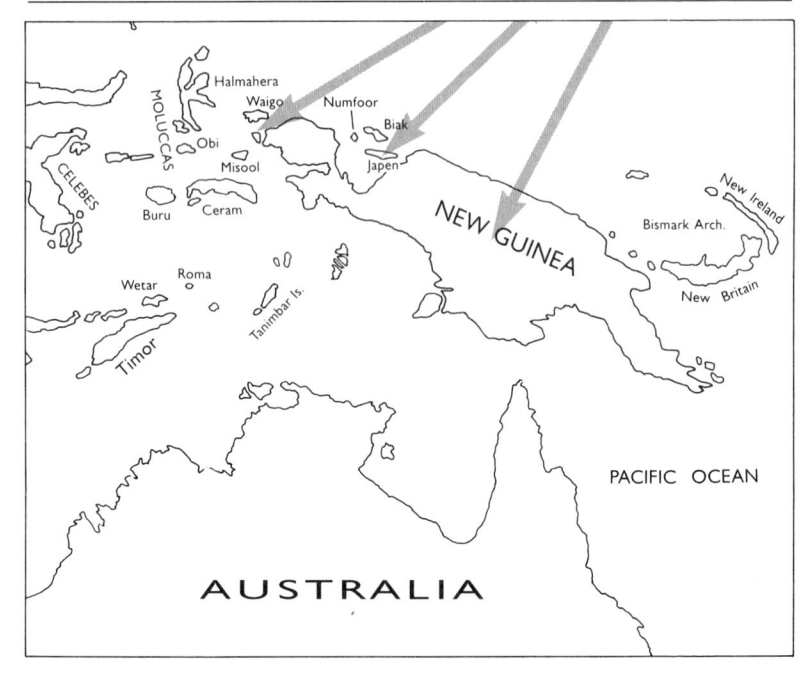

Distribution of the Dusky Lory

produced a fertile egg but instead reared everything, from Goldies Lorikeet (*T. goldei*) upwards in size, over the years. If they had been rare birds, I would have endeavoured to find a fertile cock but, as they are common, their value to me lay more in their capabilities as foster parents. Most foods will be readily accepted, although they are less willing to take dry feed than most and, in my experience, do not like seed of any sort. Duskys are avid bathers and are also extremely aggressive towards other birds. Should they, in error, get into an aviary with others, a death will most probably occur. To put it more graphically, from the shredded remains of the poor unfortunate, you might think a rat had intruded. Previously, it was thought that the rump colour denoted sex, but this is now known to be false.

26 Trichoglossus

Species	Subspecies	Common name	Availability
chlorolepidotus	–	Scaly-breasted Lorikeet	*†
euteles	–	Perfect Lorikeet	**
flavouiridis	*flavoviridis*	Yellow and Green Lorikeet	*
	meyeri	Meyer's *Lorikeet*	**
goldiei	–	Goldie's Lorikeet	**
haematodus	*haematodus*	Green-naped Lorikeet	**
	brooki	Brook's Lorikeet	–
	caeruleiceps	Blue-headed Lorikeet	*
	capistratus	Edward's Lorikeet	**
	deplanchii	Deplanche's Lorikeet	–
	djampeanus	Djampea Lorikeet	–
	flavicans	Olive-green Lorikeet	–
	flavotectus	Yellow-breasted Edward's Lorikeet	*
	forsteni	Forsten's Lorikeet	
	fortis	Sumba Lorikeet	
	massena	Coconut Lorikeet	*
	micropteryx	Southern Green-naped Lorikeet	–
	mitchellii	Mitchell's Lorikeet	*
	moluccanus	Swainson's Lorikeet	**†
	nigrogularis	Black-throated Lorikeet	*
	rosenbergii	Rosenberg's Lorikeet	*
	rubritorquis	Red-collared Lorikeet	*†
	stresemanni	Stresemann's Lorikeet	*
	weberi	Weber's Lorikeet	*
iris	*iris*	Iris Lorikeet	*
	wetterensis	Wetar Iris Lorikeet	–
johnstoniae	–	Mount Apo Lorikeet	*
ornatus	–	Ornate Lorikeet	*
rubiginosus	–	Cherry-red Lorikeet	–
versicolor	–	Varied Lorikeet	†

10   20   30

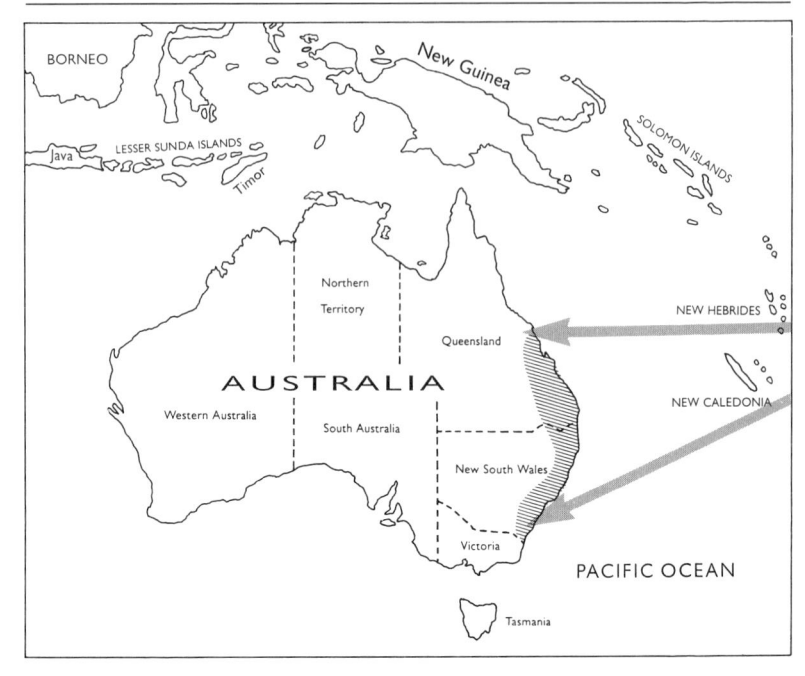

Distribution of the Scaly-breasted Lorikeet

The 10 species of this genus are small- to medium-sized lorikeets with relatively long, tapering tails. Most species available to aviculture adapt well and are hardy and easy.

Scaly-breasted Lorikeet

Trichoglossus chlorolepidotus (Plate 43)

Common names
SYNONYM	Greenie, Green and Yellow Lorikeet
DUTCH	Schubbenlori
GERMAN	Schuppenlori
FRENCH	Loriquet écaillé

Distribution Most of Eastern Australia, from Cooktown in the north, where the birds are found to be smaller, to just south of Sydney. These lories are found in most types of country, including parks and gardens.
Range M. *Population trend* S. *M-L* S. *In the Field* F.

Description Bright green, with yellow scalloped effect over the chest, abdomen, upper mantle and thighs resulting from yellow feathers edged with green; underwing red; beak red-orange.
Distinguishing features Only scallop-fronted lory with a green head.
Status a-b Plentiful and safe in both.
Maturity About 12 months.
Length 24cm (9½in).
Weight 70–90g (2½–3⅛oz).
Call Quiet.
Management Easy and hardy.
Nest-box B, D, F, G, H, 22.5cm^2 × 30cm high. (9in^2 × 12in high) in Australia.

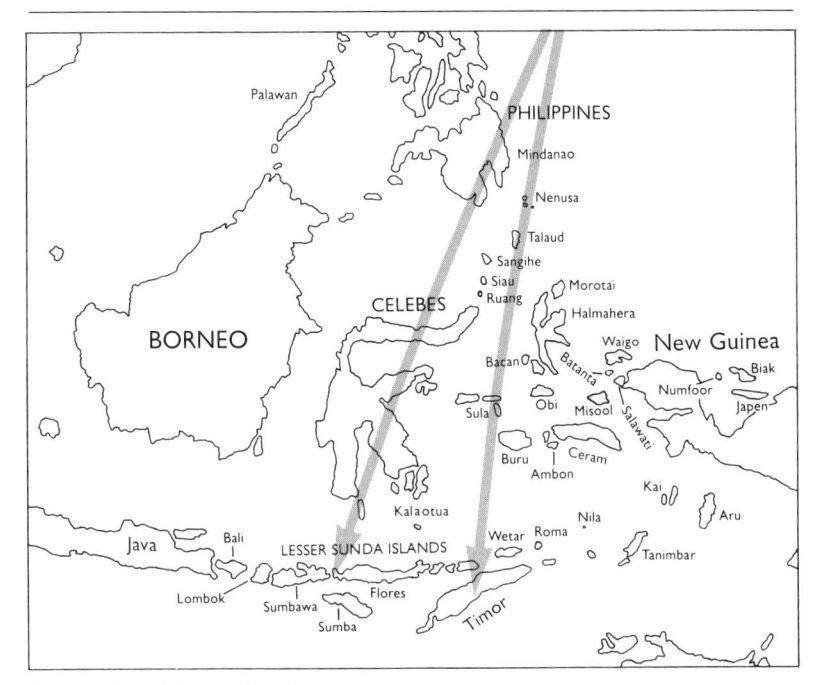

Distribution of the Perfect Lory

Eggs 2 or 3. *Incubation* 22 days.
Ring size 5.5–6mm (¼in) 'P'.
Fledging 8–8½ weeks.

Practical experience This lorikeet is rare outside Australia, where it is regularly kept and bred. A few years ago some arrived in Europe. It appears to fare better in an indoor aviary but swift inexplicable losses occur and the small numbers have not really become established.

Perfect Lory

Trichoglossus euteles (Plate 42)

Common names
SYNONYM   Yellow-headed Lorikeet, Plain Lorikeet
DUTCH   Geelkoplori
GERMAN   Gelbkopflori
FRENCH   Loriquet à tête jaune

Distribution Lesser Sunda Islands and Timor, Indonesia.
Range Is. *Population trend* S/D?
M-L   S?   *In the field* ?

Description Upper body green; underside olive-yellow; undertail and flight feathers yellow; head olive-yellow, nuchal collar lime-green, beak orange; iris red; legs grey.
Distinguishing features Olive-yellow and green with no feather scalloping, distinguish this from the Yellow and Green Lorikeet (*T.f. flavoviridis*). It differs from Weber's Lorikeet (*T.h. weberi*) which is dark and light green.
Status a-b Probably declining. Still available in aviculture but care is needed lest they are lost.
Maturity 1 year.

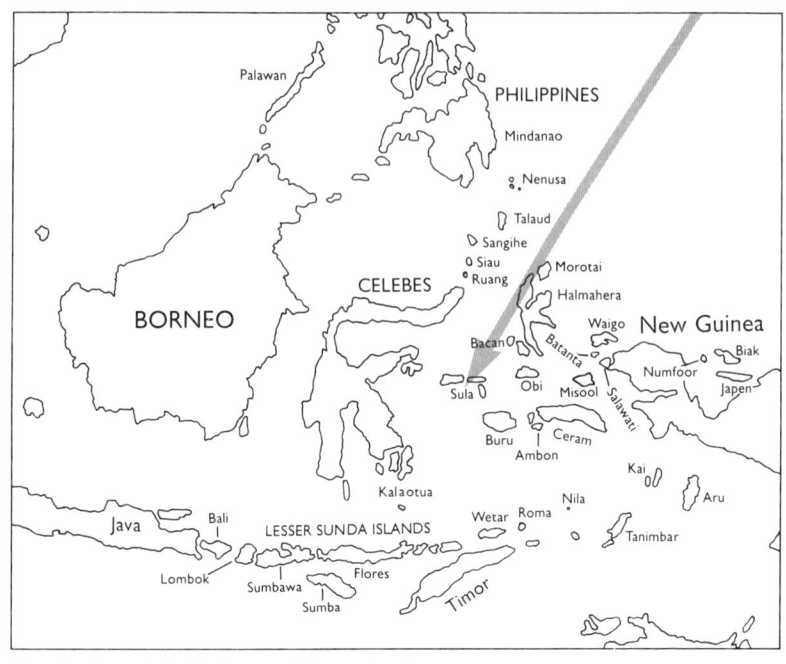

Distribution of the Yellow and Green Lorikeet

Length 25cm (10in).
Weight 85–90gm (3–3⅛oz).
Call Quiet, with occasional shrill screech which is still not loud.
Management Fairly hardy; easy and prolific breeders.
Nest-box A, D, F, G, H.
Eggs Usually 3.
Incubation 23 days.
Ring size 5.5mm (7/16in) 'P'.
Fledging 9 weeks.

Practical experience These lorikeets have never been very popular in aviculture. This could be because they lack bright colours but, when I kept a pair for some years, I found it impossible to build up a rapport with them as they behaved in a most indifferent way. Possibly it was just that pair. They have a greater following in Europe than in the UK.

Yellow and Green Lorikeet

Trichoglossus flavoviridis flavoviridis
(Plate 41)

Common names
ENGLISH	Sula Lorikeet
DUTCH	Geelgroene Lori
GERMAN	Gelbgruner Lori
FRENCH	Loriquet vert de Sula

Distribution Sula, Indonesia, at altudes of 500–2000m (1650–6600ft), in the almost entirely uncleared rainforest of this still relatively undisturbed island.
Range Is. *Population trend* D?
M-L S? *In the field* F.

Description Upperside green from nape to tail; head, face and entire front heavily scaled yellow feathers

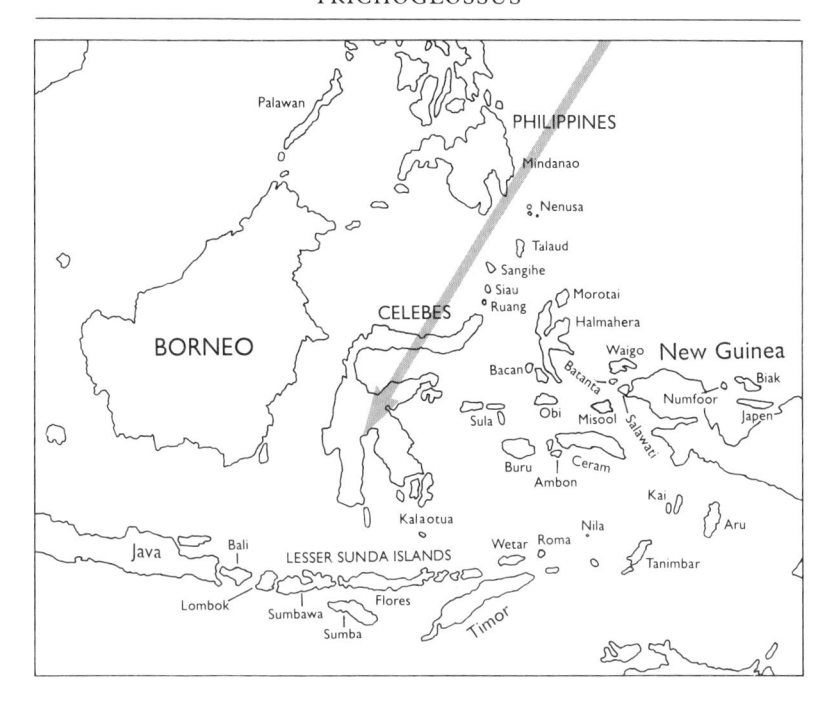

edged with green (this colouring comes right up over the head, giving a hood effect); face varyingly darker; unique, yellow peri-orbital skin; beak and iris orange; feet grey.
Distinguishing features Scaled front, hood and bare *yellow* eye ring.
Status a-b Possibly safe in the wild; uncommon so far in aviculture.
Maturity 12–14 months.
Length 21cm (8¼in).
Weight 50–60g (1¾–2⅛oz).
Call Comparatively strong and loud.
Management Relatively hardy and easy.
Nest-box B, D, F, G, H, 22cm² × 35cm high (9in² × 14in high) in Holland.
Eggs 2–3. *Incubation* 23–24 days.
Ring size 5–5.5mm (¼in) 'N'.
Fledging 8½–9 weeks.

Practical experience Jos Hubers has recently acquired a few pairs from Germany and finds them fairly similar to Meyer's Lorikeet (*T.f. meyeri*) to manage; he keeps some indoors and some outdoors with inside shelters. So far just one pair has bred. He notes some aggression from the males when they are housed in small flights.

Meyer's Lorikeet

Trichoglossus flavoviridis meyeri
(Plate 44)

Common names
SYNONYM   Lory of Bonthain
DUTCH   Meyerlori
GERMAN   Meyer's Gelbgruner Lori
FRENCH   Loriquet de Meyer

Distribution Sulawesi, Indonesia.

It is found in low to mid-lying dense forest in flocks that stay well hidden in the foliage. At the lower reaches of its range it can be seen in the company of the Ornate Lorikeet (*T. ornatus*).
Range Is. *Population trend* S.
M-L S. *In the field* ?

Description Dimorphic. Upper parts, nape, and wings to tail dark green; no nuchal band. The crown and face are olive, tinged golden in the male, more brown in the female. The front yellow with green scalloping from beak to vent; bright yellow ear patches; beak and iris orange; feet grey.
Distinguishing features Bright yellow ear patches distinguish this from the Yellow and Green Lorikeet (*T.f. flavoviridis*) which is larger, displays much more yellow.
Status a-b Considered safe, both in its habitat and in aviculture.
Maturity 10–11 months.
Length 18cm (7in).
Weight 50–55g (1¼–2oz).
Call Constant low-pitched chatter.
Management Fairly hardy; usually shy and preferring a weaker nectar.
Nest-box B, D, F, G, H.
Eggs 2. *Incubation* 22–23 days.
Ring size 5mm (³⁄₁₆in) 'N'.
Fledging 7 weeks.

Practical experience Originally I kept pairs from spring to autumn in outdoor aviaries (with access to internal houses) but later settled, as with the Goldie's Lorikeet (*T. goldeii*), for internal flights; as with the Goldies breeding then commenced. I maintained them on a general diet but with extra sponge in honey-water during rearing. At one time I found them to be prone to candidiasis, which at that time did not respond in the long term to Daktarin gel, and in due course both hens died. I believe, had I used nystatin, as I now do, which travels down and deals with the problem throughout the system rather than just treating the cheese-like growth locally, I could probably have saved them; I have succeeded in saving subsequent birds which have shown similar symptoms.

One always hears how shy this subspecies is, but I should just note here, that I once took on a young Meyer's whose entire top mandible had been ripped off. He was not a pretty sight but was able to take nectar quite satisfactorily as well as to shovel up softened sponge and other items. He was one of the most confiding, endearing and communicative pets we have had and lived with us for many years.

Goldie's Lorikeet

Trichoglossus goldiei (Plate 38)

Common names
DUTCH Viooltjeslori
GERMAN Veilchenlori
FRENCH Loriquet de Goldie

Distribution From the Weylands Mountains near Geelvink Bay, Irian Jaya, to southeast Papua New Guinea. This is a bird mainly of the mid-mountain forests around 1400–2200m (4600–7200ft), frequenting the highest branches. Goldies enjoy eucalyptus and casuarina flowers and have been noted nesting in dry foliage in tall pandans. It is an annual visitor to lowland forest and has been observed at sea level and at 2800m (9200ft), flying in pairs and in large flocks.
Range M. *Population trend* S.
M-L S. *In the field* ?

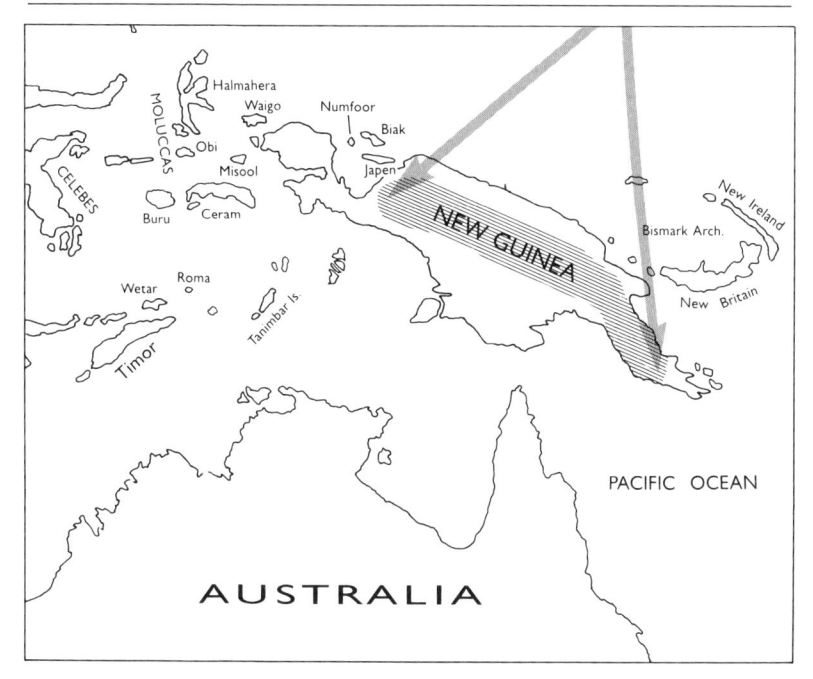

Distribution of Goldie's Lorikeet

Description Forehead and crown scarlet (some think more so in the male); black eye streak and perimeter to the crown; nape dark purple-blue behind, with pale lilac around the chin and throat; light green mantle, chest and abdomen with darker green streaks; wings darker green; beak black; legs and iris brown.
Distinguishing features Lilac-edged scarlet 'hood' distinguishes this from Striated Lorikeet (*Charmosyna multistriata*) which has a two-tone beak.
Status a-b Because of the diversity and size of its range, considered safe in its habitat. Still safe in aviculture.
Maturity 11–12 months.
Length 19cm (7½in).
Weight 50–55g (1¾–2oz).
Call Quiet, wheezing hisses with occasional high-pitched screech, but not loud.

Management Easy in all respects but not the hardiest; free-breeding.
Nest-box B, D, F, G, H.
Eggs 2. *Incubation* 23–24 days.
Ring size 5mm (⅟₁₆in) 'Ma–N'.
Fledging 7–8 weeks.

Practical experience At one time this lorikeet was a rarity in captivity, then it became one of the commonest in the UK, and now, as so often happens because it is thought to be easy and abundant, we are beginning to see a slight decline in numbers.

Goldies are still classified by some as *Psitteuteles*; others believe it is due for further reclassification, based on new evidence coming to light as the result of DNA experiments. They are real little characters as well as being very beautiful, quiet of voice and easy to manage and breed. George

Anderdon, who has bred this species to eight generations in the UK in the 20 years they have been available in aviculture (a unique achievement, I think), has always correctly sexed mine visually, but I must admit to not being able to see any dimorphism – although obviously George does.

Goldies enjoy a small internal/external aviary. In the past I have kept a colony in a planted aviary successfully but they breed best for me in an indoor flight. Surprisingly for such small birds, normal feeding suits them well. They usually make excellent parents, and even foster parents, but I once had a cock which virtually severed the leg of a hen. In time, with hospitalization, she recovered and was paired successfully with a younger cock. The aggressive cock I could never trust, even with a proven hen. I regard him as an exception, one that could happen in any species.

Another exception, after several years of successful experience with several pairs of a species, occurred one summer when I lost a hen from egg-binding. She had bred successfully at all seasons and, while I knew she was laying, I did not wish to disturb her unduly. I found her dead with a large egg stuck in the aviduct. On opening this I found two yolks. I had never seen this before nor since, until this winter, when one of my Red-collared Lorikeets (*T.h. rubritorquis*) hens suffered from the same problem, but with happier results.

Green-naped Lorikeet

Trichoglossus haematodus haematodus
(Plates 33 and 53)

Common names
SYNONYM Rainbow Lorikeet

DUTCH Groenneklori
GERMAN Breitbinden Allfarblori
FRENCH Loriquet à nuque verte

Distribution Western New Guinea, Buru, Ambon, Ceram, Ceramlaut, Goram, Watubela, western Papuan Islands, and the Geelvink Bay Islands, except Biak. It inhabits a huge range, from village gardens and savannah to primary forest, but is rarely seen above 1980m (6500ft). It develops a favourite roost high in the trees; it is believed to roost only in eucalyptus, despite the presence of other tall trees, to which flocks will regularly return over long periods. It is a very opportunistic feeder, having been seen opening cocoons to feed on moth pupae.
Range M. *Population trend* S.
M-L S. *In the field* ?

Description Forehead, lores and chin mauve-blue; rest of head blackish with a yellow collar; green mantle with some red flecks, and green wings and upper tail; breast red-barred (each feather edged with black); thighs and undertail green and yellow; abdomen green; underwing coverts red with a broad yellow band across the underside of flight feathers which is typical of this species; beak and iris orange; legs grey-green.
Distinguishing features Red-barred breast reduces the number of subspecies with which the nominate bird could be confused (see p. xx).
Status a-b Abundant. This is the most common and free-breeding lory.
Maturity 14–18 months.
Length 27cm (10½in).
Weight 120–140g (4¼–5oz).
Call Medium and some hissing.
Management Hardy and easy in all aspects; a good beginner's lory.
Nest-box A, C, E, H.

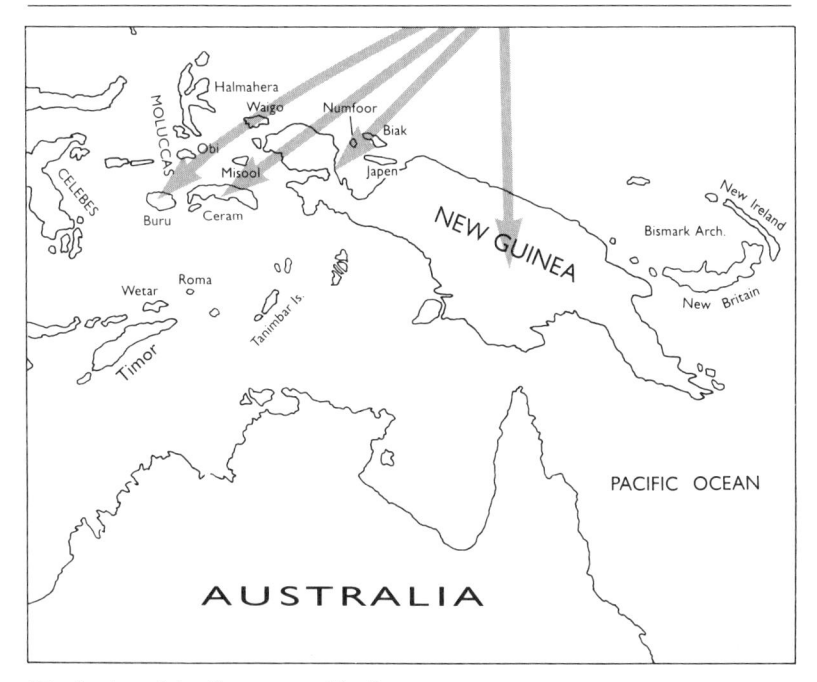

Distribution of the Green-naped Lorikeet

Eggs 2. *Incubation* 25 days.
Ring size 6mm (¼in) 'P–R'.
Fledging 9–10 weeks.

Practical experience Like most people the Green-naped was one of the first lories I kept. I found it to be tolerant of my mistakes and an excellent parent and foster parent. (I began to keep lories exclusively after weasels began, uncontrollably, to climb through the 1.25cm × 2.5cm (½in × 1in) mesh of my aviaries and destroy Australian parakeet chicks. The two pairs of Green-napeds I had at the time were able to defend themselves against this pest.) Because the parakeets had been given hollow logs of different depths, the lories were given these too (as well as conventional ones). To give height to the Green-napeds' hollow log, it was placed upside-down on another surplus log. Thus the sawn V-shaped nest-hole was on the ground. It surprised me to find that these lories chose to nest in this and to lay directly on the soil. I did not interfere by adding substrate. The aviaries at this time were underwired but I did fear chewing attacks by rats. Chicks were duly reared, after which this nesting site was removed. They next selected the conventional nest in preference to the hollow log which was now positioned on the ground but with a base on it.

Subspecies The 18 (some doubtful) subspecies of *Trichoglossus haematodus* are feathered in a variety of bright colours, which accounts for their common collective name of 'Rainbow Lorikeets'. They can be among the most difficult of lorikeets to distinguish. Variations occur between individual birds and between mature and young specimens (the latter are duller and have dark beaks for the first few months). There are also the size- and colour-related geographical variations found within a subspecies from mainland Australia and New Guinea and the island species have more distinct variations. This genus contains some species which are under current taxonomic debate.

The subspecies are broadly similar in size and habit and require the same management. For the purpose of this section I follow Forshaw (1973). The following is a breakdown of the subspecies into the five different breast-colour groups. Those most commonly available in aviculture are described separately and certain of them are featured in Plate 53.

The following is a breakdown of the subspecies into the five different breast colours.

(A) *Red-bar-fronted subspecies*:
(1) *T.h. haematodus*, see p. xx and Plate 53.
(2) *T.h. brooki* (Brook's Lorikeet), a doubtful subspecies most similar to *T.h. nigrogularis* from the Aru Island of Spirit.
(3) *T.h. caeruleiceps* (Blue-headed Lorikeet, Plate 53), from south New Guinea between the lower Fly River and Princess Marianne Straits, is just beginning to be represented in captivity. It is somewhat like *T.h. moluccanus*. It has a blue head, orange breast and green, possibly with some black, abdomen. Jos Hubers (pers. comm.), who has several pairs, found on having them sexed, that all the hens had a bluer head than the males and a green abdomen, whereas those of the cocks all showed some black. It is early days yet with this species, but Jos Hubers' birds had chicks in 1994.
(4) *T.h. deplanchii* (Deplanche's Lorikeet), from New Caledonia and Loyalty Islands, differs from *T.h. massena* in having more blue on the head, less brown on the nape and occiput, and less yellow on thighs and undertail.
(5) *T.h. flavicans* (Olive-green Lorikeet), from New Hanover and Admiralty Islands is variably marked with upper parts, under tail-coverts and tail bronze-yellow to olive. The occiput is reddish-brown, forehead and lores violet-blue and the remainder of the head streaked greyish-green. There is a little barring on the red breast.
(6) *T.h. massena* (Coconut Lorikeet), see p. xx and Plate 53.
(7) *T.h. micropteryx* (Southern Green-naped Lorikeet), another mainland New Guinea lory, is found east of the Huon Peninsula, the Wahgi Range and Hall Sound, but also on Misima Island and in the Louisiade Archipelago. This lory, which has generally paler plumage than the nominate, may not be distinct from *T.h. massena*.
(8) *T.h. nigrogularis* (Black-throated Lorikeet, Plate 53), from Aru and the eastern Kai Islands. Fairly recently a specimen arrived at a UK Lory Group meeting to make a pair. The owner thought it an outstanding 'Green-Naped'. It was a splendid individual, larger than the nominate bird, with a bluer head and black throat. Fortunately Trevor Buckell was on hand, and a set of the three Dutch lory posters which cover all species of lory, so positive identification was possible.
(9) *T.h. rosenbergii* (Rosenberg's

Lorikeet, Plate 53) from Biak in Geelvink Bay. Its population is considered to be declining and it is thus classified as 'Vulnerable'.

This lorikeet is very distinctive with its extremely wide yellow nuchal collar, bordered by a narrow band of red, and the exceptionally broad barring on the breast. Until 1993 there was a solitary specimen in the UK. It was sent to a mate in Holland. They bred, and an unrelated pair was sent to the UK donor in 1994.

(B) *Red-fronted subspecies*
(10) *T.h. djampeanus* (Djampea Lorikeet), doubtfully distinct from *T.h. forsteni*, is thought by Birdlife International to be declining and is thus classified 'Vulnerable'. It is said to have a darker head, more strongly streaked with violet-blue and with dark purple on the hind neck below the collar.

It comes from Djampea Island in the Flores Sea.
(11) *T.h. forsteni* (Forsten's Lorikeet), see p. 219 and Plate 53.
(12) *T.h. mitchellii* (Mitchell's Lorikeet), see p. 220 and Plate 53.
(13) *T.h. stresemanni* (Stresemann's Lorikeet, Plate 53) from Kalaotua in the Flores Sea, is also thought to be declining and is classified as 'Vulnerable'.

It is similar to, but larger than *T.h. forsteni*, but has a more orange breast. For years there was a single specimen in the UK for which a mate was never found.
(C) *Flame-fronted subspecies*
(14) *T.h. moluccanus* (Swainson's Lorikeet), see p. 221 and Plate 53.
(15) *T.h. rubritorquis* (Red-collared Lorikeet), see p. 223 and Plate 53.
(D) *Yellow-fronted subspecies*
(16) *T.h. capistratus* (Edward's Lorikeet), see Plate 53.
(17) *T.h. flavotectus* (Yellow-breasted Lorikeet), see p. 217 and Plate 53.
(18) *T.h. fortis* (Sumba Lorikeet), from Sumba, has the forehead and cheeks streaked violet-blue, the lores, throat, line above the eye and the occiput green, and an orange-yellow-washed breast. The abdomen is dark green sometimes tinged with black and the underwing coverts are yellow.
(E) *Green-fronted subspecies*
(19) *T.h. weberi* (Weber's Lorikeet), see p. 225.

Edward's Lorikeet

Trichoglossus haematodus capistratus
(Plate 32 and 53)

Common names
SYNONYM Rainbow Lorikeet
DUTCH Bloedvleklori
GERMAN Blauwangen Allfarblori

Distribution Timor.
Range Is. *Population trend* D. M-L S? *In the field* ?

Description Forehead, cheeks and chin blue; remainder of 'hood' green; nuchal collar yellow; nape, upper wings and back green; breast varyingly orange to orange-yellow; underwings orange; abdomen dark green; flanks, thighs and vent green and yellow; beak orange; iris red; feet grey.
Distinguishing features Green hood distinguishes this from all except the yellow-fronted subspecies (see p. 217) and, within that group, from the Yellow-breasted Lorikeet (*T.h. flavotectus*) by the orange breast and orange underwing.
Status a-b Believed to be declining on Timor island; safe still in aviculture.
Maturity About 16 months.

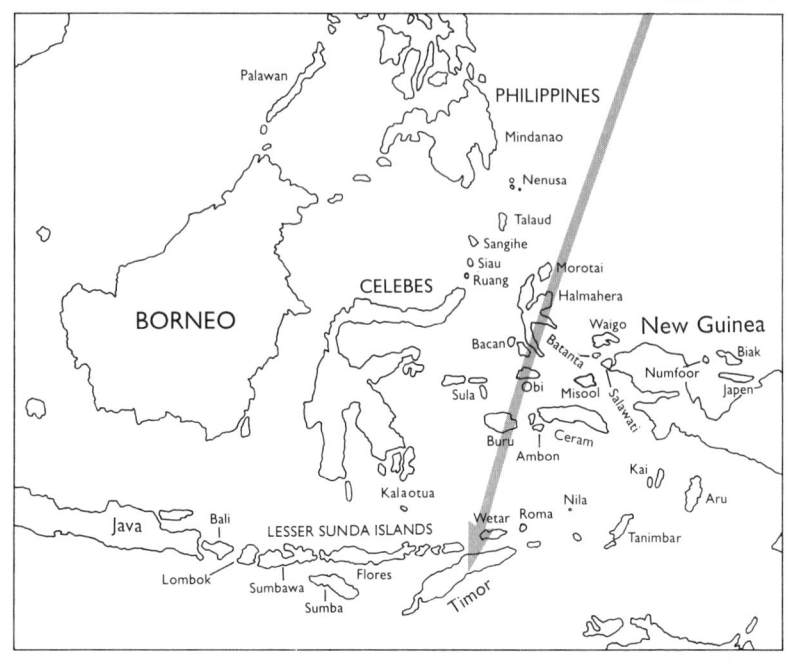

Distribution of Edward's Lorikeet

Length 27cm (10½in).
Weight 120–140g (4¼–5oz).
Call Low-volume whistles and bursts of screeches; not intrusive.
Management Hardy and easy, but plucking may occur; usually free-breeding.
Nest-box A, B, C, E, H.
Eggs 2. *Incubation* 24–25 days.
Ring size 6mm (¼in) 'P–R'.
Fledging 9–10 weeks.

Practical experience I cannot imagine not having Edward's Lories. They are gentle and affectionate creatures, less boisterous than some of the subspecies. I find them excellent parents with the proviso that, because of plucking, chicks usually have to be taken for hand-rearing by 4 weeks of age; after this the wings may be damaged so seriously that the birds can never fly. This is a subspecies to avoid if provision cannot be made for hand-rearing, should feather-plucking occur.

There are exceptions to this behaviour. I had a 22-year-old hen (which sadly I lost in 1993) that had been with her importer for 12 years before I acquired her. She was always naked on the breast, abdomen and mantle and, latterly, all her eggs were infertile, but she only had to be shown an egg or chick and she would brood it. You could even replace a 4-week-old chick with a newly hatched one with no complaint. Lories as diverse as Erythro Black-caps (*Lorius lory erythrothorax*) and Goldies (*Trichoglossus goldiei*) have been fostered to fledging and emerged immaculate. Birds like 'Mother Edward' play a vital role in aviculture.

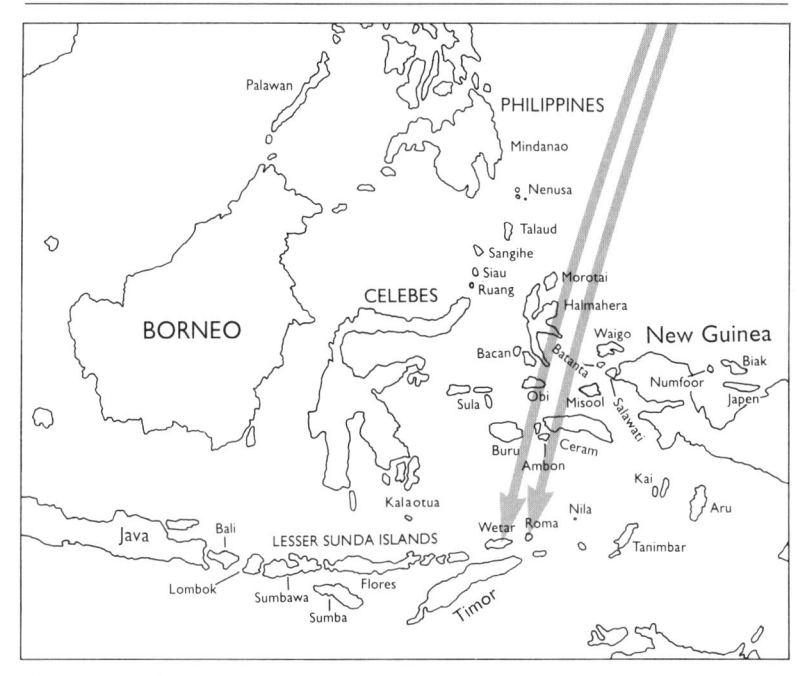

Distribution of the Yellow-breasted Lorikeet

Part of the challenge with these lories is the plucking. So far everything I have tried has been to no avail. Why does this subspecies so often pluck and yet others generally do not?

Yellow-breasted Lorikeet

Trichoglossus haematodus flavotectus (Plate 53)

Common names
SYNONYM   Wetar Lory, Rainbow Lory, Yellow-breasted Edwards' Lorikeet
DUTCH   Geelborstlori
GERMAN   Belbburst Allfarblori
FRENCH   Loriquet de Wetar

Distribution The islands of Wetar and Roma (near Timor).
Range Is. *Population trend* D?
M-L S? *In the field* ?

Description Identical to *T.h. capistratus* except that there is no orange on the underside of the wing and the chest is yellow, not orange.
Distinguishing features Yellow breast and underwing.
Status a-b An island species of which little is currently known; scarce in aviculture, particularly as few are true pairs.
Maturity 14–18 months.
Length 27cm (10½in).
Weight 120–140g (4¼–5oz).
Call Mostly quiet whistles with occasional bursts of low screeching.
Management Hardy and easy, but plucking may occur.
Nest-box A, B, C, E, H.
Eggs 2. *Incubation* 24–26 days.
Ring size 6mm (¼in) 'P–R'.
Fledging About 9½ weeks.

Practical experience Several years ago, on going to a dealers to collect some Forsten's Lorikeets (*T.h. forsteni*) for which I had paid a deposit, I found that they had orange and yellow breasts! They were, however, splendid specimens and, after several telephone calls by the dealer to check on my information, I was allowed to take three birds, the value apparently of the two Forsten's that I had booked. This was before surgical sexing had really taken off, and I spent a considerable time choosing one with the most orange breast and two with yellow breasts for male and females respectively. It was possibly a fluke that they turned out to be as I had chosen. At that time I was not even aware of the subspecies *T.h. flavotectus*. It was only a couple of years ago, and after much wonderment that none of these birds plucked themselves at all, that I decided to make an effort to split the pairs and place yellow to yellow.

During the subsequent 9 months neither the new-paired oranges or yellows went to nest whereas, before the change, each pair had nested about three times a year. Eventually, after detecting no alteration in the indifference shown by what were previously devoted birds, I gave in and returned them to their original partners. At about 4 and 6 weeks, each pair layed. Unfortunately a yellow hen was lost during the rearing of the chicks. Bonding in this instance, I believe, was too strong and the separation accounted for considerable stress. The new pairings might have worked if I had been able to place the pairs totally out of earshot of their original partners.

From my experience with this subspecies in aviculture, I would think there is a very great threat to them in the wild from hybridization, as Birdlife International have noted. By breeding *T.h. capistratus* to *T.h. flavotectus* aviculturists have produced what appears, by colour, to be approximately 10 of the former to one of the latter; showing a dominance of the former. (They are not pure, regretfully.) The latter have all been female, which may or may not be coincidence.

Coconut Lorikeet

Trichoglossus haematodus massena
(Plates 34 and 53)

Common names
ENGLISH   Massena Lory, Rainbow Lorikeet
DUTCH   Massenalori
GERMAN   Massena Allfarblori
FRENCH   Loriquet de Massena

Distribution Bismark Archipelago, Solomon Islands, and New Hebrides, in coconut plantations where it feeds primarily on coconut but also on the flowers of myrtacae.
Range Is. *Population trend* ?
M-L ? *In the field* ?

Description Hood brown, heavily streaked blue at the front and distinctively rufous behind; red breast feathers pale with a narrow edging; narrow nuchal collar of slightly dirty yellow.
Distinguishing features Brown 'hood' and rufous behind, paler and smaller than in the nominate.
Status a–b Not identified, but being an island species, albeit with a range of more than one island, numbers are presumed to be declining. Not common in aviculture.
Maturity About 16 months.
Length 25cm (10in).

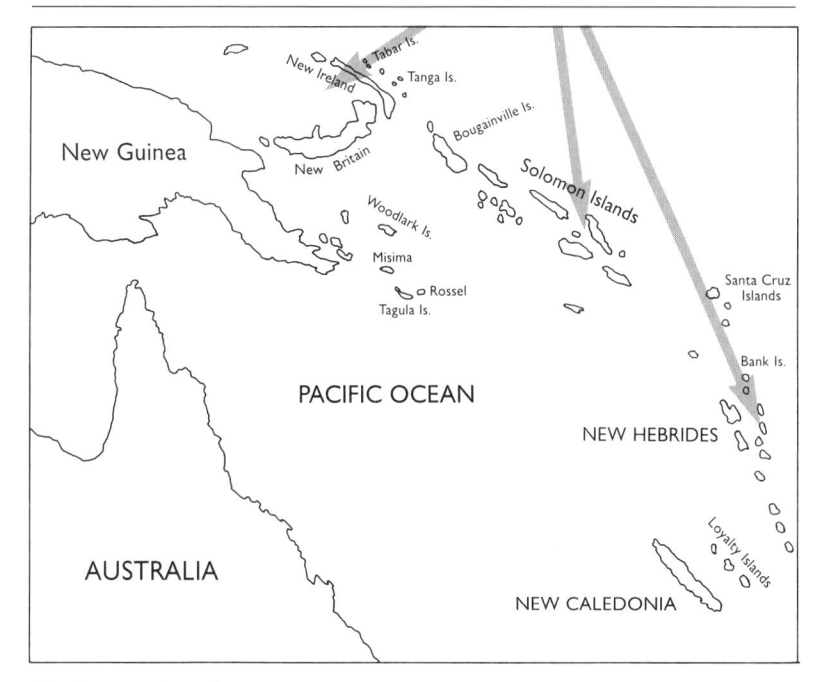

Distribution of the Coconut Lorikeet

Weight 110–120g (3⅞–4¼oz).
Management Hardy and easy.
Nest-box B, C, E, F, H.
Eggs 2. *Incubation* 25 days.
Ring size 6mm (¼in) 'P'.
Fledging 8½–9 weeks.

Practical experience There are some pairs breeding in captivity but, because of confusion about the subspecies, not all are correctly mated.

Forsten's Lorikeet

Trichoglossus haematodus forsteni
(Plates 35 and 53)

Common names
SYNONYM   Red-breasted Lorikeet
DUTCH   Forstenlori
GERMAN   Forsten Allfarblori
FRENCH   Loriquet de Forsten

Distribution Sumbawa Island where it inhabits open rainforest up to around 1000m (3250ft).
Range Is. *Population trend* D?
M-L V. *In the field* S.

Description Green above; red breast completely unbarred; crown, forehead and cheeks streaked dark purplish and abdomen purple; nuchal collar more yellow than usual; red underwing.
Distinguishing features Unbarred darker red breast distinguishes this from Mitchell's Lorikeet (*T.h. mitchelli*).
Status a–b Pending the result of survey, but thought to be declining; there is always the added risk of hybridization. Declining in aviculture.
Maturity 14–18 months.
Length 23cm (9in).
Weight 110–120g (3⅞–4¼oz).
Call Quiet for a 'Rainbow' lorikeet.

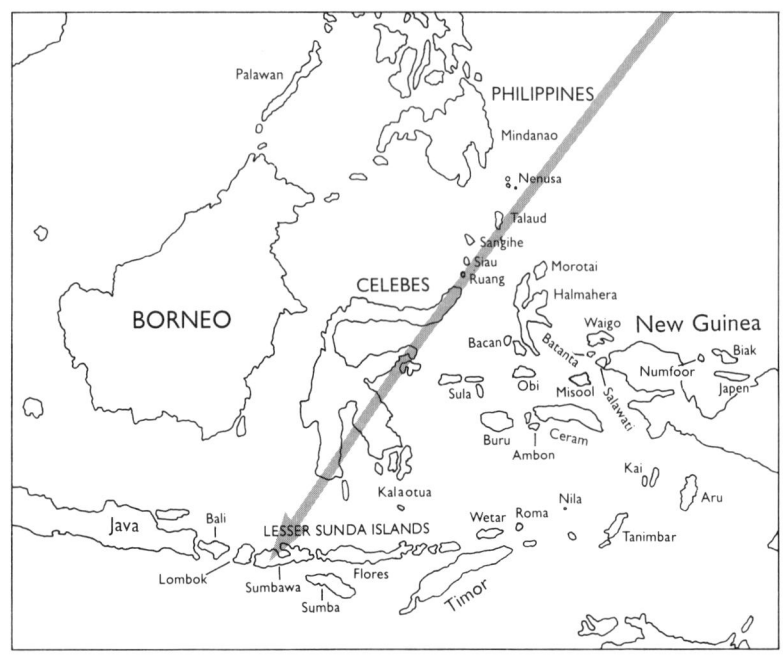

Distribution of Forsten's Lorikeet

Management Hardy; special care usually necessary because of plucking.
Nest-box B, C, E, F, G, H.
Eggs 2. *Incubation* 24–26 days.
Ring size 6mm (¼in) 'P'.
Fledging 8–8½ weeks.

Practical experience I find this species to be gentle, quiet and affectionate. Badly plucked specimens need protecting from the cold and young, because they may also be plucked, need to be removed for partial hand-rearing to ensure their future flying ability. If time is at a premium, bear this in mind.

Mitchell's Lorikeet

Trichoglossus haematodus mitchellii
(Plates 36 and 53)

Common names
SYNONYM Red-breasted Lorikeet
DUTCH   Mitchell Lori
GERMAN   Mitchell Allfarblori
FRENCH   Loriquet de Mitchell

Distribution Bali and Lombok, although this lorikeet is believed to be extinct on the former island.
Range Is. *Population trend* D.
M-L V/E. *In the field* S.

Description Head, nape, cheeks and throat dark brown with some olive-brown on the forehead and reddish-brown occiput; breast red and only very faintly barred with blue; abdomen dark purple; red underwing.
Distinguishing features Brown head, paler red and barred breast differentiate this from Forsten's Lorikeet (*T.h. forsteni*).

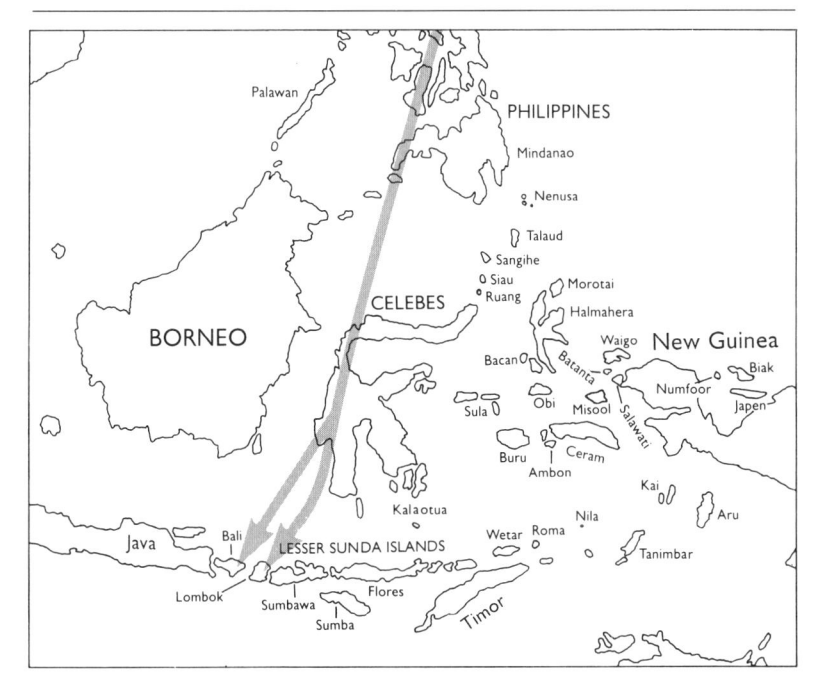

Distribution of Mitchell's Lorikeet

Status a–b This is a lorikeet right on the edge, threatened by the local population explosion and hybridization as well as extensive logging. Lack of numbers in aviculture means its future there looks equally bleak.
Maturity 14–16 months.
Length 21–22cm (8¼–8½in).
Weight 100–110g (3½–3⅞oz).
Call Gentle for a 'Rainbow' Lorikeet.
Management Quite hardy and easy, except for plucking.
Nest-box B, C, E, F, G, H.
Eggs 2. *Incubation* 24 days.
Ring size 5.5–6mm (³⁄₁₆–¼in).
Fledging About 8 weeks.

Practical experience This delightful, gentle lorikeet which Rosemary Low (1977) refers to as 'fairly frequently imported' at that time, has suddenly slid to the very verge of extinction, both in the wild and aviculture (see also Chapter 13).

Swainson's Lorikeet

Trichoglossus haematodus moluccanus
(Plates 30 and 53)

Common names
SYNONYM   Blue mountain Lorikeet, Rainbow Lorikeet
DUTCH   Lori van de Blauwe Bergen
GERMAN   Gerbirgs Allfarblori
FRENCH   Loriquet de Swainson

Distribution Eastern and southeastern Australia, south to Tasmania, Kangaroo Island and Eyre Peninsula and islands in the Torres Strait.
Range M/Is. *Population trend* I.
M–L S *In the field* F

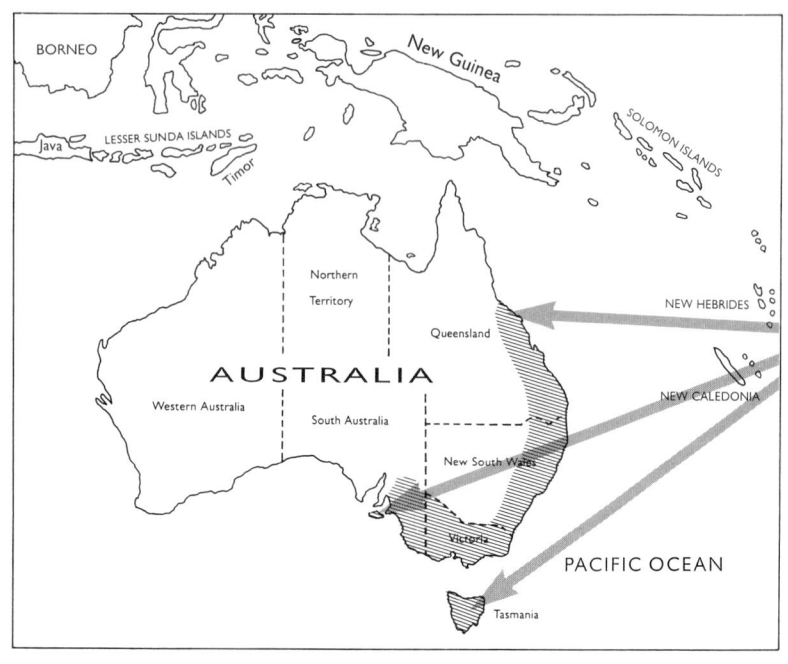

Distribution of Swainson's Lorikeet

Description Head rich vibrant bright blue; breast flame red to orange, varying to yellow-orange; abdomen deep purple; nuchal collar lime green; underwing coverts orange washed with yellow; upperparts and flanks green; undertail greenish-yellow; iris and beak red-orange; legs grey; underwing grey.
Distinguishing features Lime nuchal collar immediately distinguishes this lorikeet from the Red-collared Lorikeet (*T.h. rubritorquis*).
Status a-b Abundant, increasing its numbers and extent of range. Still readily available. This is the only lorikeet to be known to be increasing in numbers.
Maturity 1–2 years.
Length 30cm (12in).
Weight 130–150g (4⅝–5¹⁄₁₀oz).

Call High-pitched screech, hiss or contented twitter.
Management Hardy, easy.
Nest-box A, C, E, H.
Eggs 2. *Incubation* 27 days.
Ring size 6mm (¼in) 'P–R'.
Fledging 8–9 weeks.

Practical experience None has been imported since Australia imposed its ban on exporting native species in 1961. The fact that it is still fairly freely available without showing any signs of inbreeding says a lot about the bird's hardiness and willingness to breed, and the fairly wide gene pool that still exists in captivity outside Australia today. Swainson's Lorikeet is a truly gorgeous bird with an almost unique iridescence to the feathers and among the prettiest of rainbow colouring. They have mischievous, lively personalities, and sometimes talk well.

The display of this, and the Australian *T.h. rubritorquis*, is the most pronounced I have encountered. Both partners blaze their eyes and arch their necks, ruffling their feathers and stretching out their wings while intermittently hissing and bobbing. Poses are struck this way and that, and much deliberate pounding of the perch, nest-box roof or floor takes place, followed by copious preening, often ending in mating.

Several times when looking for an individual bird, I have been assured that I was being offered a Swainson's, only to find on arrival that it was a bird of the nominate subspecies. I doubt whether there have been many crosses between the two, because it is impossible to confuse them when they are side by side. With the increasing interest in, and journalistic coverage of lories in general, this situation should no longer occur; the same applies to diet. Once, on being offered a pair of these birds, the vendor told me that they had lived happily, but solely, on sunflower and water for a couple of years. He rejected the idea of nectar as being unnecessary. I felt that they must be living on borrowed time (liver-wise) and declined the offer.

In my experience both Australian subspecies, when hand-reared, become particularly familiar and pushy as they reach maturity, and they can be downright dangerous to people at breeding time. For this reason I handle any that have to be even partially hand-reared far less than most, in fact as little as possible. (I also do this with certain *Chalcopsitta* spp., but for different reasons.) I have not encountered this trait with other *T. haematodus*.

Red-collared Lorikeet

Trichoglossus haematodus rubritorquis
(Plates 31 and 53)

Common names
SYNONYM   Red-necked Lory, Orange-naped Lory
DUTCH   Rodeneklori
GERMAN   Rotnacken Allfarblori
FRENCH   Loriquet à collier rouge

Distribution Northern Australia from the Kimberley Division in the west to the Gulf of Carpentaria in Queensland.
Range M.   *Population trend* S.
M–L S   *In the field* F

Description Head rich, vibrant, bright blue with a line on the throat and fore neck dividing the blue from the flame-coloured breast; nuchal collar of same flame-orange to red; mantle blue-green with some orange barring and back and wings green; thighs and undertail coverts yellow-green; abdomen dark green to navy; beak and iris orange; feet grey; underwing grey.
Distinguishing features Red collar is unique.
Status a-b Safe. Rare in captivity outside Australia.
Maturity 18–20 months.
Length 29cm (11½in).
Weight 120–150g (4¼–5¼oz).
Call Similar to, but quieter than, Swainson's Lorikeet (*T.h. moluccanus*).
Management Not totally hardy I find; requires dedicated management.
Nest-box A, B, C, E, H, I.
Eggs 2.   *Incubation* 25 days.
Ring size 6mm (¼in) 'P–R'.
Fledging 8–10 weeks.

Practical experience This is a

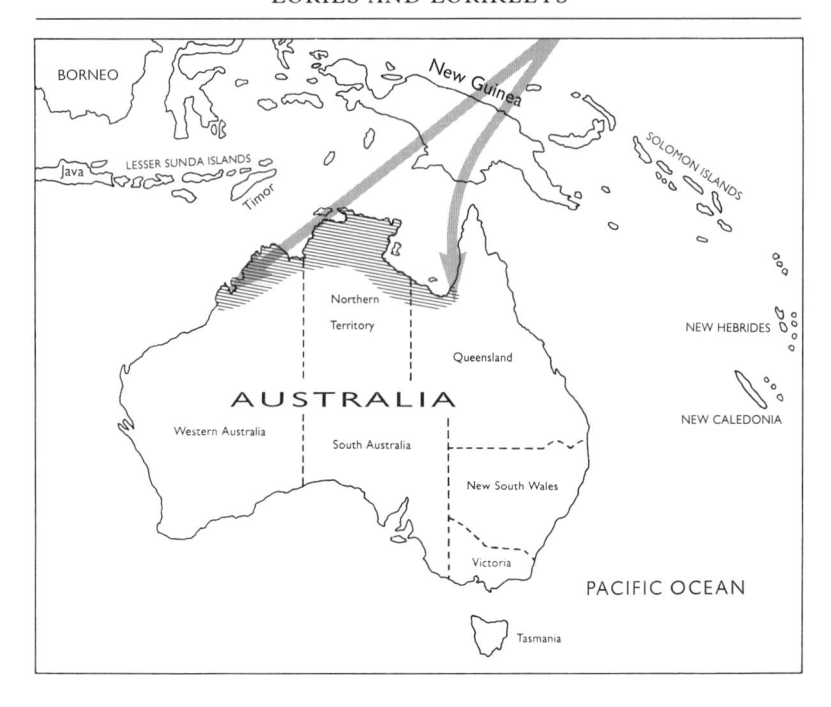

quite strikingly beautiful lory that has not been exported from its native Australia since the ban was imposed on exporting native species. However, I hear that there is the possibility of some pairs coming from North Australia. It is now quite rare in captivity, which reflects how different it is in many respects from *T.h. moluccanus*. It does not become as hardy and is not such a free-breeder. It does however, have the same lively inquisitive personality, rushing to greet visitors, rolling playfully together in the pond, on the swing or even on the ground.

Mine, however, are overexuberant, verging on the aggressive; they work visibly as a team and launch at us in such a way that, as soon as the door opens, they fall straight through and all over you. Once they land you are soon made aware that their idea of fun is a little sinister. Personally I enjoy the challenge of keeping one step ahead and not being outwitted. A glove or catching net is merely snatched and shaken; a water spray held them at bay for a while as they enjoyed it so much but now they have learned how to keep their minds on two things at once and wait their chance to pounce. Revolving feeders were inserted but servicing the nests involved feeding a piece of fruit through the flight net, rushing in and plugging the nest-hole; this was seen as a challenge speed-wise, which they inevitably won. Where possible it now seems best to wait until there is a second person around to distract them.

This pair never used their nest-box until the eggs were laid, and then they never sat on the eggs until day 21,

(Thankfully I had switched them to the incubator.) I returned the one fertile egg prior to hatching, but they worried me as they were always much more interested in fooling around with people than paying full attention to their responsibility in the nest-box; nevertheless I felt I had to give them the chance. The chick was found dead at 7 days. They sat their second round somewhat better, commencing properly at about 10 days. Again I did not return the eggs until just before hatching. This time both eggs were fertile but only one chick hatched. This was looked after well for 3½ weeks, when the parents were again observed playing like puppies out of the nest. This happened too often, so the chick was taken in for hand-rearing.

Another hen, which arrived with a drooped wing (and was consequently a non-flier), was beaten up by my two cocks over a period and had to be removed. In due course the young cock from the other pair was put with her and they appeared to bond. So had the first two for a while but this hen has now laid eggs (albeit infertile) and I feel more optimistic for this union. I hope that the eggs were infertile because the cock is only 1 year old. A third hen, which has had a horn-coloured beak since she arrived, has laid several rounds of infertile eggs with both cocks; the two facts may or may not be related. There is certainly inbreeding with these lories because the gene pool in captivity is so small.

I mentioned losing a *T. goldiei* some summers ago from egg-binding with a double yolked egg. This winter one of my Red-collared hens looked very stressed and fluffed and subsequently laid her second egg which weighed 10g (⅜oz). The first weighed 7g (¼oz). By adding the attachment shown in Fig. 6 (p.30), heat was applied and the resulting egg was also found to be double-yolked. Being nervous after the previous experience I asked Peter Sutton, a retired veterinary surgeon and loriculturist what he felt the prognosis for this bird was. Peter, who is most generous with his help and advice, felt that keeping extra heat for a longish time was my best option. The hen was shut in her own aviary with no access to the flight and, initially, a lot of heat was applied. This seemed preferable to putting her into a hospital situation, as she is very attached to the cock. After 6 weeks she appeared quite well again and in due course laid normally (albeit still infertile).

Weber's Lorikeet

Trichoglossus haematodus weberi
(Plate 21)

Common names
DUTCH   Weberlori
GERMAN   Weber's Allfarblori
FRENCH   Loriquet de Weber

Distribution The island of Flores, Indonesia, in rainforests from lowlands up to 1200m (3900ft).
Range Is. *Population trend* D?
M-L S? *In the field* S.

Description General plumage green, darker above, as is the abdomen; forehead and lores suffused with blue and with lighter green streaking; chest variably light green to yellow, as is the nuchal collar; beak and iris red.
Distinguishing features Similar but much greener than Perfect Lory (*T. euteles*).

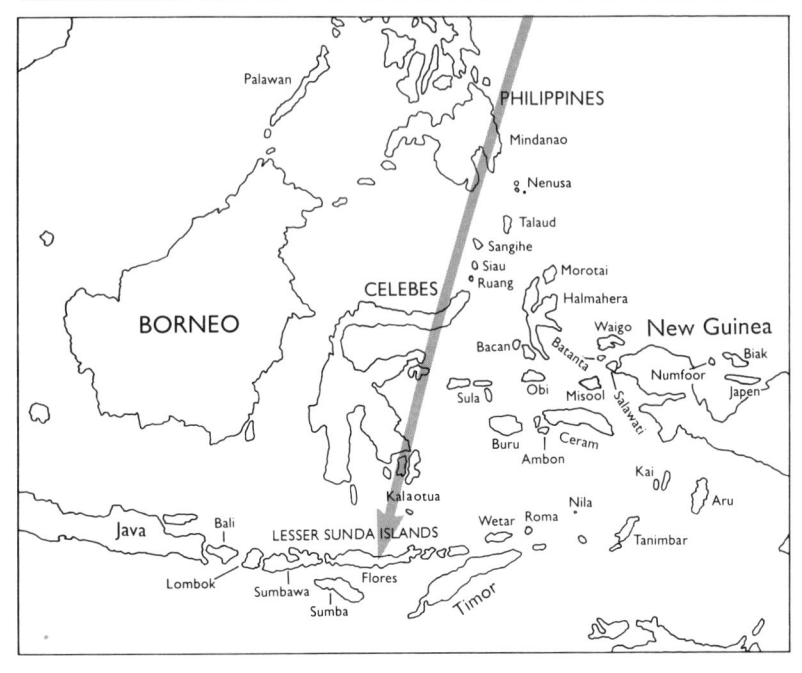

Distribution of Weber's Lorikeet

Status a-b Possibly still safe; never common, thus not secure.
Maturity About 1 year.
Length 23cm (9in).
Weight 100–110g (3½–3⅞oz).
Call Quiet.
Management Fairly hardy; requires management as for Perfect Lorikeet (*T. euteles*).
Nest-box B, D, F, G, H.
Eggs 2–3. *Incubation* 25–26 days.
Ring size 5.5–6mm (¼in) 'P'.
Fledging 8–9 weeks.

Practical experience In recent years, by working with other countries, aviculturists have been able to set up a very few pairs. This lorikeet has never been common in aviculture in this country although it has a greater following on the Continent and in the USA. It is a bird that appears to me to lack the personality of most others. It is to be hoped that the breeding pool will survive in its fans' aviaries, so that the birds can have a more assured place in aviculture.

Iris Lorikeet

Trichoglossus iris iris (Plate 47)

Common names

DUTCH	Irislori
GERMAN	Irislori
FRENCH	Loriquet iris de l'est de Timor

Distribution Timor, Indonesia.
Range Is. *Population trend* D?
M-L S/V? *In the field* ?

Description Upperparts dark green;

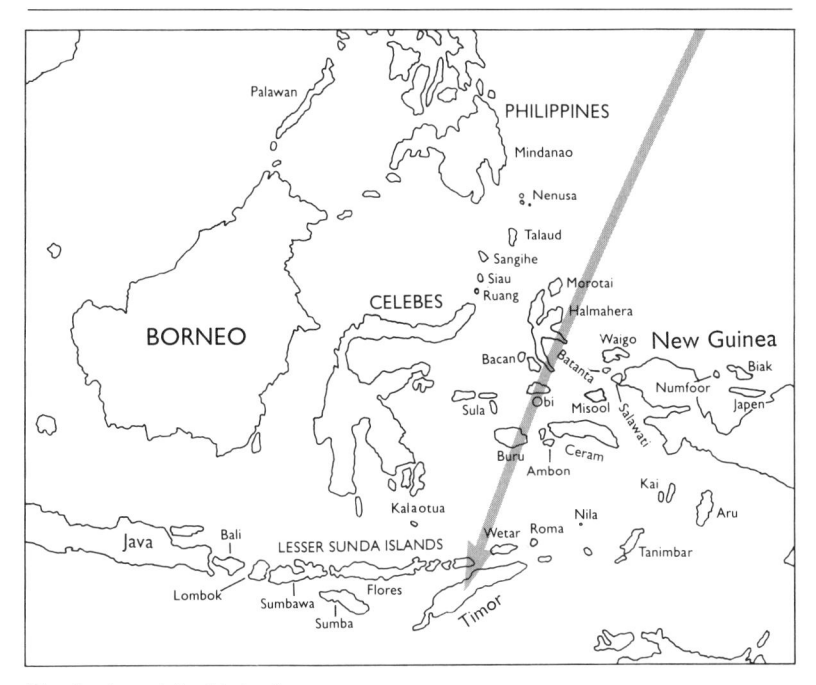

Distribution of the Iris Lorikeet

paler underparts lightly barred or scalloped with dark green; forehead and forecrown red; hind crown dark green-red-purple with a purple band from the eye to the sides of the hind neck, as well as some pink throat feathers; dusky yellow nuchal collar; beak and iris orange; legs grey.
Distinguishing features Red crown, purple streak and scalloped front.
Status a-b Probably vulnerable; only small numbers in aviculture.
Maturity 18–20 months.
Length 20cm (8in).
Weight 55–65g (2–2¼oz).
Call Quiet.
Management Quite hardy; requires a varied diet including some seed.
Nest-box B, D, F, G, H.
Eggs 2. *Incubation* 23 days.
Ring size 5mm (³⁄₁₆in) 'N'.
Fledging 9½ weeks.

Practical experience These little lorikeets, which are great characters, have always been popular but have never come into aviculture in large numbers; not being the most prolific breeders, they are still somewhat of a rarity. They require management and a diet more like that of *N.m. muschenbroekii* and are just as avid chewers, despite their more delicate beaks. In October 1994 I received some from J & A van Oosten in the USA. They settled well, seem hardy and very intelligent. (*T. rubripileum*, also from Timor, is not now thought distinct.)

There is one possibly doubtful subspecies, *T.i. wetterensis*, from Wetar Island.

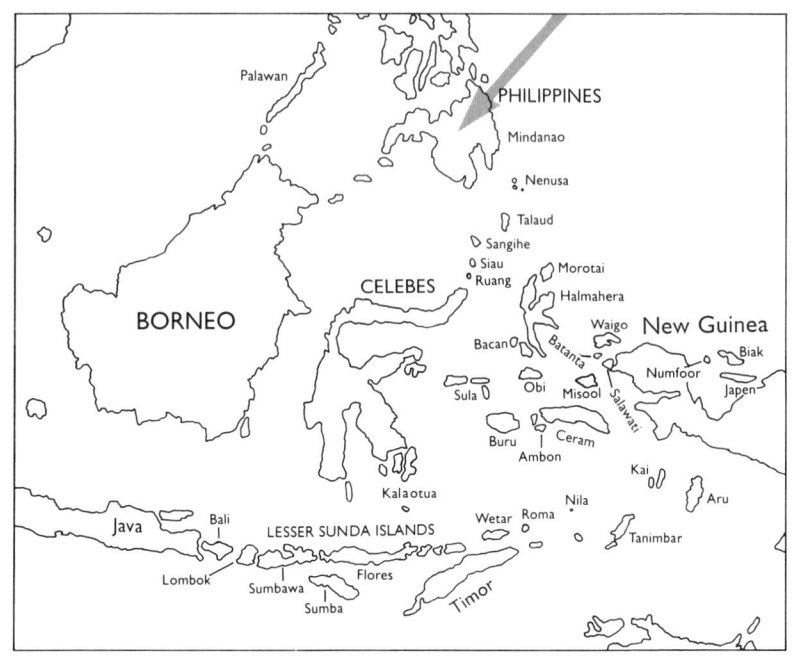

Distribution of the Mount Apo Lorikeet

Mount Apo Lorikeet

Trichoglossus johnstoniae
(Plate 48)

Common names
SYNONYM	Mrs Johnstone's Lorikeet, Mindanao Lorikeet
DUTCH	Johnstonlori
GERMAN	Apolori
FRENCH	Loriquet de Mme Johnstone

Distribution Southern Philippine island of Mindanao.
Range Is. *Population trend* D?
M-L V. *In the field* ?

Description Upper parts green; underside yellow, scallop-edged with green; forehead, cheeks and throat deep pink; maroon stripe extends from the lores to behind the eye; ear coverts yellowish; undertail and wings yellowish-green; beak orange.

Distinguishing features Deep rose-pink on parts of the head are unique.
Status a-b Under threat; rare.
Maturity 12–16 months.
Length 18cm (7in).
Weight 60–65g (2⅛–2¼oz).
Call Quiet.

Management Found to be quite easy, by the few aviculturists in the Philippines, the USA and Europe, who have them.
Nest-box A, G, H; an L-shaped box is used in the Philippines.
Eggs 2. *Incubation* 23 days.
Ring size 5.4mm (⁷⁄₁₆in).
Fledging 9 weeks.

Practical experience Roger Sweeney,

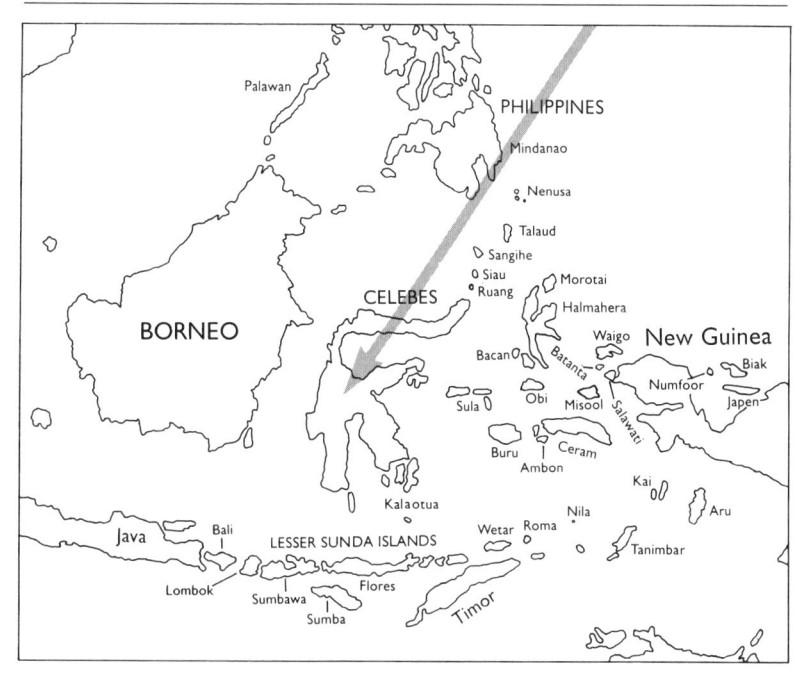

Distribution of the Ornate Lorikeet

who now works at Birds International Inc. (BII) with Tony de Dios in the Philippines, says:

> The range of the Mount Apo Lorikeet is now very restricted. It was formerly protected by National Park status, but even the National Park itself is under threat from industrial development and a power plant has already been initiated in this region. Aviculture of this species has much to commend it, providing that a captive population can be enlarged in a well-managed fashion. With all the birds available in aviculture coming from a limited number of breeding pairs, much care will have to be taken with future pairings. They are possibly dimorphic, and adult feathering is evidenced in the nest. These lorikeets have been housed in various ways, but preference is given there to suspended aviaries. They are fed on a diet of nectar, fruit, fructivorous pellets and a small amount of sprouting millet. Rearing takes place throughout the year – emphasis being put on parent rearing. I heard from Jon van Oosten in Seattle, that by the winter of 1994–95, his pairs had proved to be free and easy breeders, needing no special management.

The subspecies *T.j. pistra* is no longer considered distinct from the nominate race.

Ornate Lorikeet

Trichoglossus ornatus (Plate 39)

Common names

SYNONYM Ornamental Lorikeet

DUTCH   Ornaatlori
GERMAN   Schmuck Lori
FRENCH   Lori orné

Distribution Sulawesi and most of its larger satellite islands, where it is found to be common on lightly wooded slopes up to 1000m (3300ft). It avoids dense forest and is to be found in the company of the Yellow and Green Lorikeet (*T.f. flavorides*).
Range Is. *Population trend* S.
M-L S. *In the field* ?

Description Referred to as a lory as it has a comparatively short tail; is also the only member of the genus to have a pure yellow underwing with no barring. Forehead and crown purple; a streak of purple runs through the eye to the upper ear coverts; yellow patch, or band, but not a collar, on each side of the neck behind the ear coverts; cheeks and lower ear coverts red; breast red with heavy purple barring; abdomen green streaked with yellow; iris and beak orange.
Distinguishing features Purple crown, red cheeks, yellow neck patch, shortish tail and plain yellow underwing.
Status a-b Possibly declining in both.
Maturity About 2 years.
Length 25cm (10in).
Weight 110–130g (3⅞–4⅝oz).
Call Medium.
Management As for other medium-sized *Trichoglossus* ssp.
Nest-box A, C, E, H.
Eggs 2 (often laid at 3–4 day intervals).
Incubation 25–26 days.
Ring size 6mm (¼in) 'R–S'.
Fledging 8–9 weeks.

Practical experience These lorikeets, while popular, do not breed as freely as some other *Trichoglossus* spp. There is, however, a sustainable gene pool in captivity.

One of the first lories I ever had was of this species, back in 1967. A dealer whom I visited in order to buy some tanagers almost begged me to take the Ornate off his hands. I had not seen one before, nor did I see one again for a few years. I housed it in a large planted aviary with a collection of softbills. It never harmed the birds or the plants, which, with what we know today, seems almost unbelievable, even allowing for it being a single bird. An added bonus was that it became very tame and gentle. It was some time before I was able to acquire a companion for it.

I regret to say that breeding did not figure hugely (if at all) with me then. Nor did I have the correct housing for the different species. I provided nothing other than the general diet required for a species. Selfishly, I just enjoyed having and looking at my birds. In short, in those unenlightened days, I was purely a collector.

Cherry-red Lorikeet

Trichoglossus rubiginosus

Common names
SYNONYM   Ponape Lorikeet, Caroline Lorikeet
DUTCH   Ponapelori
GERMAN   Rotnackenallfarblori
FRENCH   Loriquet cerise

Distribution Ponape, in the eastern Caroline Islands. As long ago as 1881 it was described as being fearless in its approach to houses and was considered a pest among fruit trees.
Range Is. *Population trend* S.
M-L S. *In the field* F.

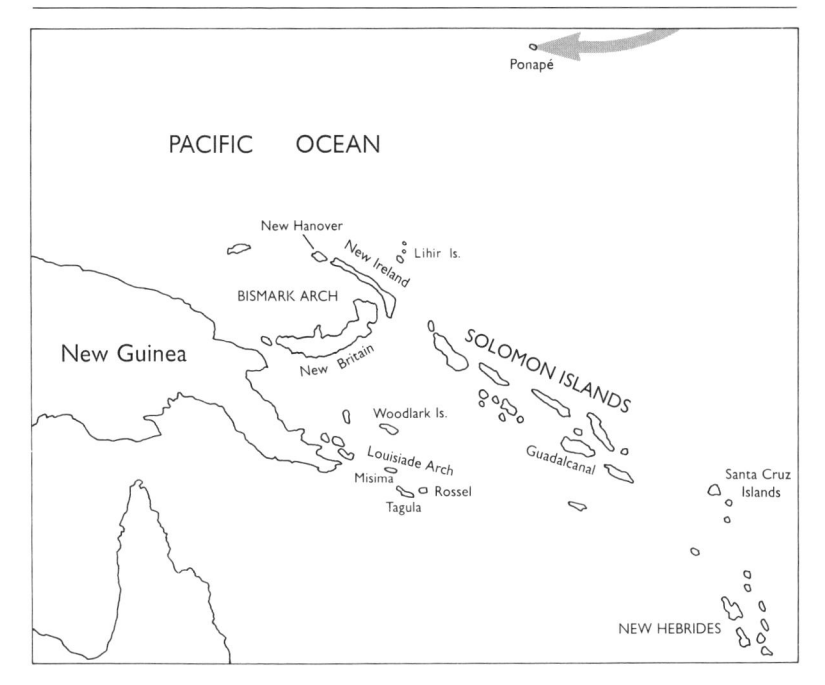

Distribution of the Cherry-red Lorikeet

Description Distinctive; almost entirely dark red, except for the flight and tail feathers which are olive-brown; body feathers lightly and variably barred with black, the same colour as underwing.
Status a-b Virtually unknown in the wild or aviculture. Although a few specimens arrived in the UK in the 1960s, and in the USA in the 1970s (two being bred at Los Angeles Zoo), little knowledge has been gained since the late 1800s. It was no doubt known at one time because I was able to obtain a painting of it from that period – when it was still classified as *Coryphilus ruginosus*. There is now a faint hope that a few may appear in aviculture before long.
Length 24cm (9½in).

Varied Lorikeet

Trichoglossus versicolor (Plate 50)

Common names
SYNONYM	Red-capped Lorikeet
DUTCH	Bonte Lori
GERMAN	Buntlori
FRENCH	Loriquet versicolore

Distribution Across North Australia from the Kimberleys in the west to the coast of Queensland in the east. It is found in all types of country where there is suitable food; especially favoured are flowering gums and paperbarks, which grow along the banks of creeks where it has been noted gleaning insects from among the leaves.
Range M. *Population trend* S. *M-L* S. *In the field* F.

LORIES AND LORIKEETS

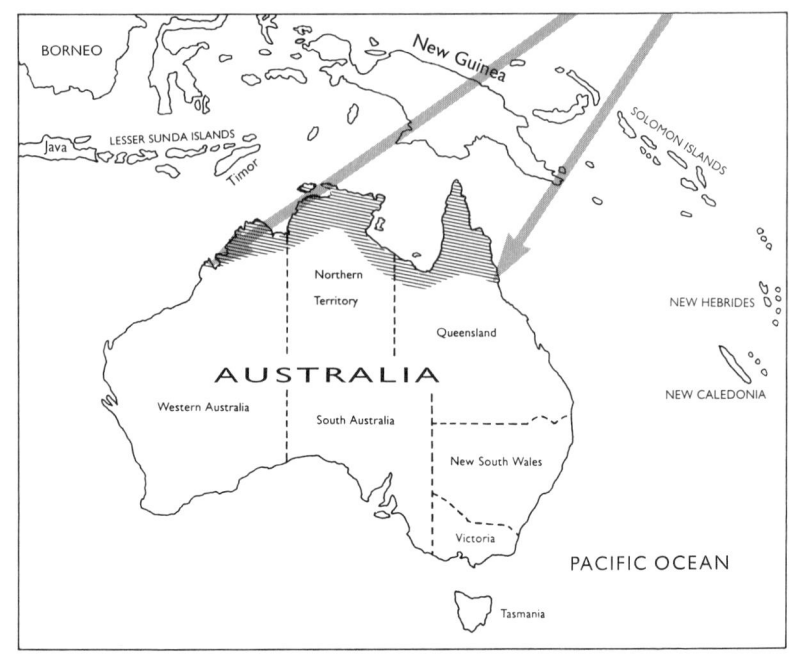

Distribution of the Varied Lorikeet

Description Dimorphic. The general colour is grass green with forehead, crown and lores crimson; back of head and sides of neck turquoise blue; ear coverts yellow; chest rust-mauve in the cock; abdomen light green – all streaked yellow; conspicuous white eye ring. Hen is much smaller, as is her red cap.
Distinguishing features Unique colouring.
Status a-b Secure in both.
Maturity About 1 year.
Length 19cm (7½in).
Weight 60g (2¼oz).
Call Low-pitched but shrill, chattering or screeching.
Nest-box B (with a spout entrance), D, G, H.
Eggs 2–5 (at 3–5 day intervals).
Incubation 22 days.
Ring size 5–5.5mm (³⁄₁₆in) 'N'.

Fledging 5½–6 weeks.

Practical experience This lory is unknown outside Australia. Its classification is not universally agreed. Joe Forshaw classifies it in *Trichoglossus*, Rosemary Low in *Glossopsitta*, and Stan Sindell, who has kept and bred these birds regularly in his aviaries and thinks, with further research, that they may be found to be migratory, believes they should be retained in their original genus *Psitteuteles*. He thinks this because of their:

(1) Dimorphism.
(2) Clutch size (3–5 eggs).
(3) White peri-orbital ring.
(4) Colouring.
(5) Behaviour.

Freshly-caught specimens, even in Australia's climate, need a period of quarantine to avoid chilling at night. It is an easy aviary subject. It is not aggressive, even in a mixed collection, and will breed at any season. Amazingly the first breeding to gain the Avicultural Society award in 1936 was in the UK. The Australian Avicultural Society award for a first breeding was given in 1965.

27 Vini

Species	Subspecies	English name	Availability
australis	–	Blue-crowned Lorikeet	
kuhlii	–	Kuhl's Lorikeet	–
peruviana	–	Tahitian Blue Lorikeet	*
stepheni	–	Stephen's Lorikeet	–
ultramarina	–	Ultramarine Lorikeet	–
5	0	5	

The *Vini* lories all being island birds and having scattered habitats, have always been a rarity and all are being threatened to the verge of extinction. In aviculture numbers have always been the small; only the Blue-crowned Lory (*Vini australis*), currently the least threatened and with a chance of being seen again in aviculture, and the Tahitian Blue Lory (*Vini peruviana*) are known at all. Only a very few people have been fortunate to have had some experience with *Vini peruviana*, albeit for a short while. It is never likely to be seen again in aviculture after the few remaining specimens are lost.

It is to be hoped that the knowledge gained of their personality and management requirements may be put to good use, as and when further relocation opportunities occur, as in the case of the Ultramarine Lory (*Vini ultramarina*). (see Chapter 13.)

The *Vini* lories have two distinguishing features apart from being tiny and quite beautiful.

(1) narrow elongated feathers of the crown of the head.
(2) slender beak.

Blue-crowned Lorikeet

Vini australis

Common names

SYNONYM	Blue-crested Lorikeet, Samoan Lorikeet
DUTCH	Blauwkap Lori
GERMAN	Blaukappchenlori
FRENCH	Lori vini à crête bleue

Distribution Discontinuous throughout Samoa, Tonga, Aututaki in the Cook Islands, and some small islands of the Tuamotu and Society Islands. In Fiji it is represented only in the southern Lau group of islands. The absence from the rest of the islands is thought to be due to competition with the Collared Lory (*Phigys solitarius*). It is a swift-flying inter-island bird, content with many types of habitat but preferring areas of mango and cheese-nut trees, coconut palms and

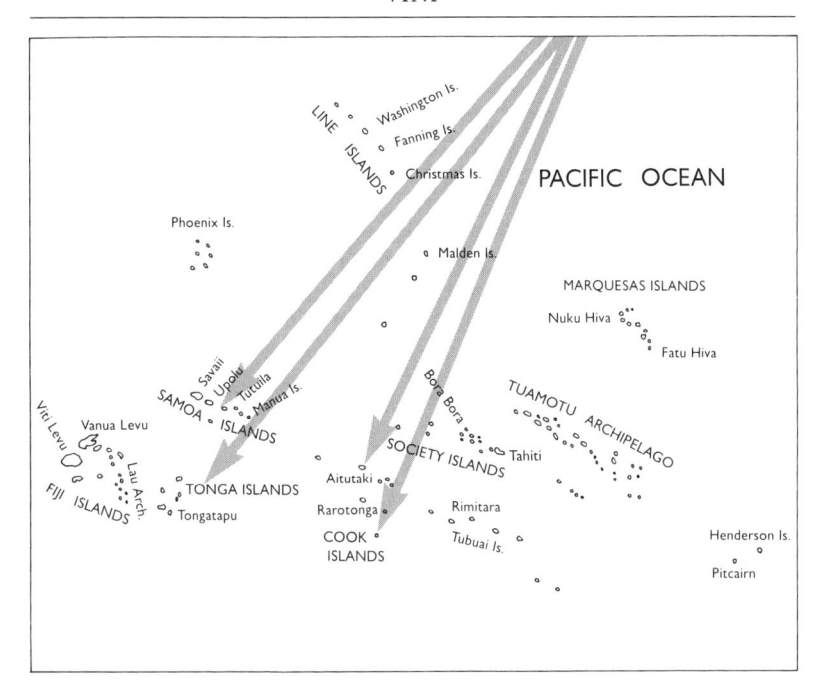

Distribution of the Blue-crowned Lorikeet

hibiscus where it searches the underside of leaves for insects.
Range Is. *Population trend* D?
M-L V/S. *In the field* C.

Description Bright emerald green with a large red bib from the eye and beak to the upper chest, and an abdominal patch; streaked crown; lower abdomen and thighs purple-blue; beak and feet orange.
Status a-b Still common through much of its range but decreasing on Tonga due to introduced predators, such as rats (it has been noted not only nesting in holes in trees but also burrowing). Another threat is thought to be pesticides used in the banana plantations. It is virtually unknown in captivity, although San Diego Zoo had five in 1970 and it has been bred in Switzerland.

Maturity 6–9 months.
Length 19cm (7½in).
Weight 35–45g (1¼–1½oz).
Call Shrill lisping 'tse tse'.
Nest-box A horizontal nest 7.5cm square by 90cm high (3in square by 36in high) was successfully used in Switzerland.
Eggs 1–2. *Incubation* 23 days.

Kuhl's Lorikeet

Vini kuhlii

Common names
Synonym	Ruby Lory, Kuhl's ruffled Lory
Dutch	Kuhl's Lory
German	Rubin lori
French	Lori vini rubis

Distribution Rimitara and Tubuai

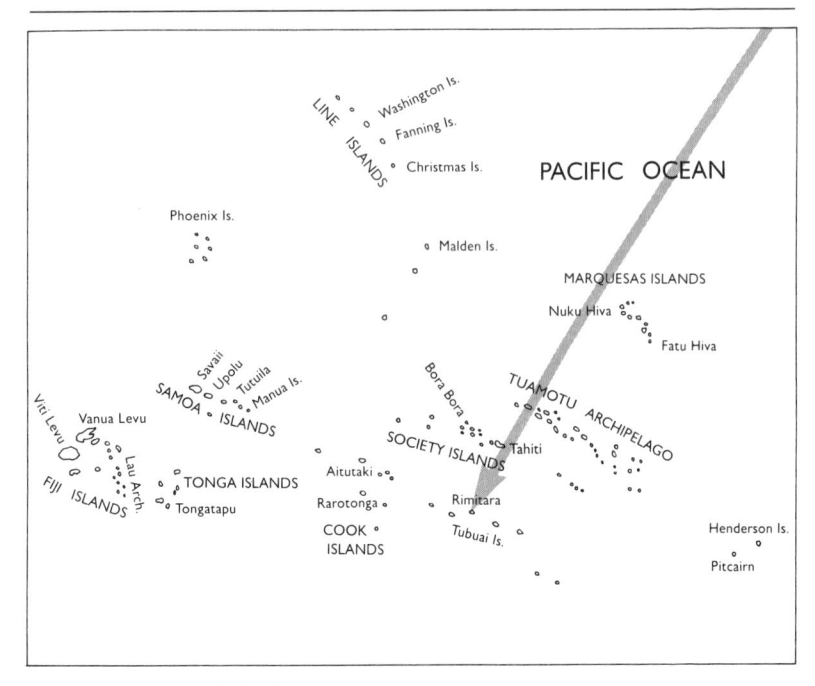

Distribution of Kuhl's Lorikeet

Islands. It has also been introduced to Washington, Fanning and, latterly, to Christmas Island. It is a bird of the valleys where it frequents coconut palms and also deep forest. More fieldwork is required to determine whether in fact it is extinct. Predation by rats has been the main threat.
Range Is. Population trend D?
M-L E. In the field F.

Description Green upperparts turning to yellowish on the lower back and rump; crown green streaked with a lighter green, behind which the occiput is deep mauve; entire front scarlet with some yellow on the flanks, and purple thighs; tail scarlet above and greyish below, with undertail coverts of greenish-yellow; underwing coverts green; beak orange, legs orange-brown and iris red.

Status a With few exceptions never known in aviculture.
Length 19cm (7½in)

Tahitian Blue Lorikeet

Vini peruviana

Common names

SYNONYM	Indigo Lorikeet, White-throated Lorikeet
DUTCH	Saifier Lori
GERMAN	Saphirlori
FRENCH	Lori blanc et bleu de Tahiti

Distribution The Society Islands (although on Tahiti itself, the largest of these, it is believed to be extinct), the most western of the Tuamotu Islands, and on Aitutaki in the Cook Islands. It was once found on at least

VINI

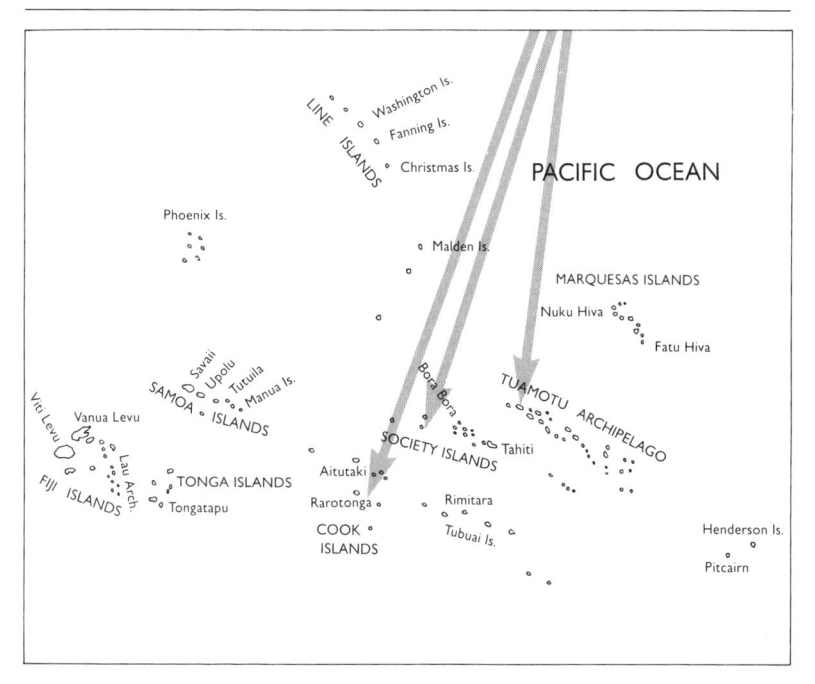

Distribution of the Tahitian Blue Lorikeet

23 islands, but is now extinct on 15 of these.
Range Is. *Population trend* S?
M-L E. *In the field* C.

Description Dark violet-blue, with a large white bib, coral beak and orange feet.
Distinguishing features Cannot be confused with the only other predominantly blue lory (*Vini ultramarina*), which is a pale turquoise blue.
Status a-b Numbers thought to be stable although there is a need for fieldwork. The threat is not only from loss of habitat, but from the introduction of rats to these low-nesting birds and, probably, from the introduction of Swamp Harriers, as well as the arrival of a mosquito which spreads avian malaria. Now all but extinct in aviculture.

Maturity 18 months.
Length 14cm (5½in).
Weight 31–34g (1–1¼oz).
Call Quiet, rasping.
Management Difficult; very delicate, needing a constant heat preferably 18°C (65°F); very susceptible to stress and aggressive amongst themselves.
Nest-box Natural log 7.5cm square by 30cm high (3in square by 12in high) was chosen in the UK.
Eggs 2.
Incubation 25 days (starting with the first egg).
Ring size 4.2–4.5mm (³⁄₁₆ in) 'L–M'.
Fledging 9 weeks.

Practical experience Most of the information on this species has been gained from a long breeding programme at San Diego Zoo where

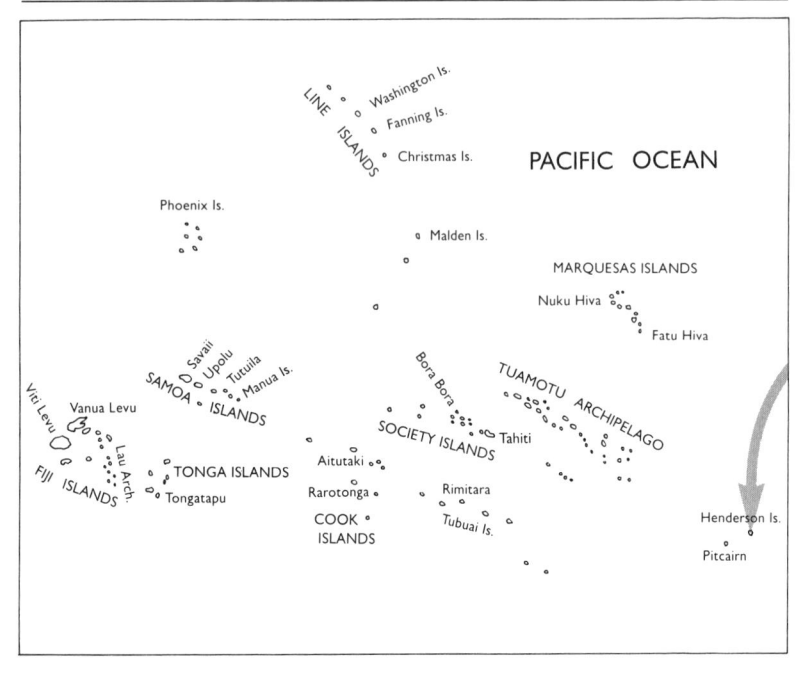

Distribution of Stephen's Lory

there have been regular breedings. Rosemary Low (1985), who has bred a number of Tahitian Blues in the UK, describes how she was extremely fortunate to have been approached about the possibility of quarantining, in the UK, an illegal shipment of these lories which had found its way into the USA and been confiscated. It appeared that, because of bureaucracy, they would have to be destroyed. Rosemary, needless to say, welcomed the challenge but found them far from easy because of their highly stressed and aggressive temperaments. Her lorries, like those in consignments to the UK earlier this century, would appear well one day and then suddenly die for no apparent reason. Diet appears to have been standard for small lories. Most chicks had to be at least partly hand-reared but this did not stop them, in turn, from reproducing.

Stephen's Lory

Vini stepheni

Common names
SYNONYM Henderson Islands Lory
DUTCH Stephen's Lori
GERMAN Stephenlori
FRENCH Lori vini de Stephen

Distribution Henderson Island (a small raised reef) in the Pitcairn Group, the easternmost area for lories within the Pacific distribution.
Range Is. Population trend S?
M-L E. In the field F.

Description Green above with a paler shaft streaking on the crown;

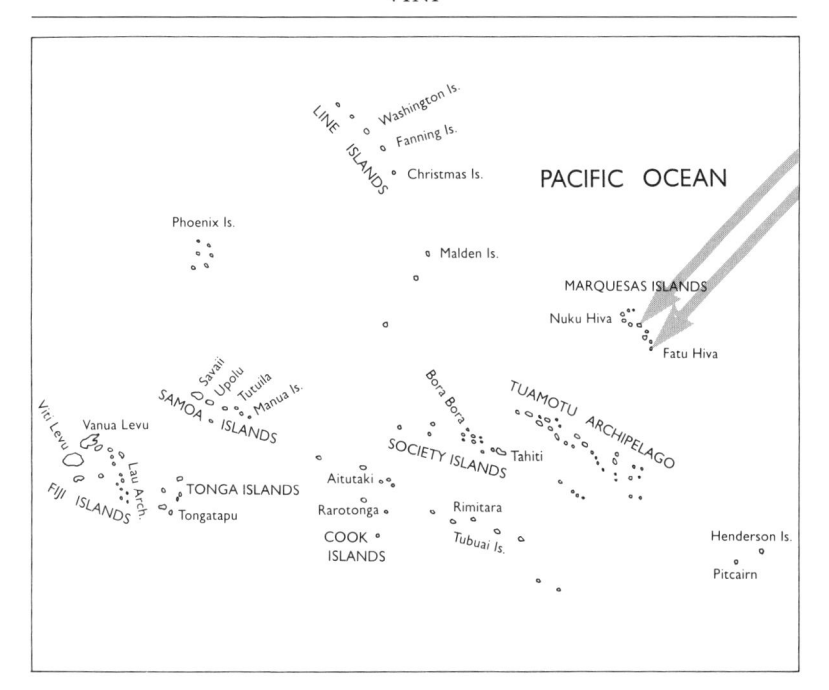

Distribution of the Ultramarine Lorikeet

underparts scarlet with a band of green-purple across the breast; thighs and abdomen purple; tail is greenish-yellow, as are the undertail coverts; underwing coverts red and green; beak and legs orange; iris yellowish.
Status a Almost nothing is known.
Status b Unknown in aviculture.
Length 19cm (7½in).

Ultramarine Lorikeet

Vini ultramarina

Common names
SYNONYM   Marquesas Lorikeet
DUTCH   Smaragd Lori
GERMAN   Smaragdlori
FRENCH   Lori bleu des Iles Marquises

Distribution The Marquesas Archipelago. (Its distribution included mainly the islands of Nuka Hiva, Ua Pou, and Ua Huka but it has now been extirpated from all but the latter island.
Range Is. *Population trend* D. M–L C. *In the field* C, R.

Description Totally distinctive colouring: forehead deep turquoise to sky blue; upperparts, rump and tail coverts sky blue and tail blue tipped white; crown mauve streaked blue; lores and cheeks white; face and upper breast white and mauve; abdomen and undertail coverts mauve; underwing coverts bluish; a patch of white above the thighs and the beak; iris and legs pale orange.
Status a An expedition in 1991 found no specimen on Nuka Hiva and Ua Poa. It is believed that the introduction of the Common Mynah and Great

Horned Owl has been a contributing factor, but the rapidly increasing population on Nuka Hiva and the building of an international airport are probably the main reasons. The proposal to construct a wharf on Ua Huka may well cause this locally favoured bird to release its last natural but tenuous strangle-hold on survival. (For further details of the recent translocation of seven Ultramarine lorikeets, which could prove to be the model for similar management of other endangered lories, see Chapter 13.)

Status a Virtually unknown in aviculture.

Length 18cm (7in).

Bibliography

References cited

2 early historical sightings
Anon. (1789) *The Voyage of Governor Phillip to Botany Bay.*
Brown, P. (1794) *New Illustrations of Zoology.*
Gray, G. R. (1865) *Jottings.*
Mivart, St. G. (1896) *The Loriidae: A Monograph of the Lories or Brush-tongued Parrots composing the family Loriidae* Porter, London, UK.

3 Habitat
Edmunds, R, & Hughes, N. (1991) *The Trees of Paradise* Green Press, 20/34 Big Rock Drive, Malibu.

13 Conservation
Kuehler, C. & Lieberman, A. (1993) 'French Polynesia' *Psitta Scene* Vol. 4, No. 4.
Lambert, R. (1993) The status and trade in North Moluccan parrots with particular emphasis on *Cacatua alba*, *Lorius garrulus* and *Eos squamata Bird Conservation Int.* Vol. 3, No. 2.
Mills, S. (1993) 'Species brought off the endangered list' *BBC Wildlife* Vol. 3, No. 2.
TRAFFIC (1993) *Traffic Bulletin* Vol. 13, Nos 1 and 3; Vol. 14, No. 1.

14 First Aid
Burr, E. (ed) (1987) *Diseases of Caged Birds*, TFH Publications, New Jersey, USA.

Raethel, H.-S. (1983) *Bird Diseases* TFH, USA.

17 *Chalcopsitta*
Low, R. (1993) 'The Rajah Lory' *Lory J. Int.* No. 3.
Loman, B & Loman, H. (1992) 'The Cardinal Lory' *Lory J. Int.* No. 2.
Beehler, B. M., Pratt, T. K. & Zimmerman, D. A. (1986) *Birds of New Guinea* Princetown University Press, New Jersey, USA.

18 *Charmosyna*
Clayton, G. (1993) 'The Josephine Lorikeet' *Parrot Soc. Mag.* June.
Dahne, H. (1992) 'The Fairy Lorikeet', *Int. Lory. Soc. Bull.* June.
Hubers, J. (1993) 'The Josephine Lorikeet' *Lory J. Int.* No. 1.
Michorius, H. J. 'The Multistriated Lorikeet', *Lory J. Int.* 1993
Watling D. (1982) *Birds of Fiji, Tonga and Samoa* Milwood Press, Wellington, New Zealand.

19 *Eos*
Forshaw, J. M. & Cooper, W. T. (1989) *Parrots of the World* Blandford, London.

21 *Lorius*
Oderkerken P. (1992) The Purple-Bellied Lory' *Lory J. Int.* No. 1.
Forshaw, J. M. (1973) *Parrots of the World* Lansdowne, Melbourne.

26 *Trichoglossus*

Hubers, J. (1993) 'The Yellow and Green Lorikeet' *Lory J. Int.* No. 4.

Forshaw, J. M. (1973) *Parrots of the World* Lansdowne, Melbourne.

Low, R. (1977) *Lories and Lorikeets* Paul Elek, London, UK.

27 *Vini*

Low, R. (1985) 'Breeding the Tahitian Blue Lory' *Avicult. Soc. Mag.* Vols 1–2.

Further reading

Coates, B. J. (1985) *The Birds of Papua New Guinea*. Dove Publications Alderley, Australia.

Collar, N. & Andrew, P. (1993) *Birds to Watch. The ICBP Check of Threatened Birds* International Council for Bird Preservation.

Forshaw, J. M. & Cooper, W. T. (1989) *Parrots of the World* Blandford, London.

Harman, I. (1981) *Australian Parrots in Bush and Aviary* David & Charles, Newton Abbot, UK.

Howard, R. & Moore, A. (1991) *A Complete Checklist of Birds of the World* Revised ed, Academic Press.

McKay, R. D. (1976) *New Guinea: the World's Wild Places* Time-Life, Amsterdam, Netherlands.

Russ, D. K. (1991) *Speaking Parrots* Revised ed. (J. Blake), Beech Publishing, Alton, UK.

Index of Scientific Names

Index entries are to page numbers, those in *italic* refer to plate illustrations.

Charmosyna spp. 36, 55–6, 142–3
Chalcopsitta a. atra 29, 131–4
Chalcopsitta a. bernsteini 134
Chalcopsitta a. insignis 27, 134–5
Chalcopsitta a. spectabilis 134
Chalcopsitta cardinalis 19, 135–7
Chalcopsitta d. duivenbodei 26, 137–8
Chalcopsitta d. syringanuchah 138
Chalcopsitta s. chloroptera 141
Chalcopsitta s. rubrifrons 141
Chalcopsitta s. sintillata 28, 139–41
Chalcopsitta spp. 131
Charmosyna amabilis 143
Charmosyna diadema 160
Charmosyna j. cyclopum 147
Charmosyna j. josephinae 147
Charmosyna j. sepikiana 18, 104, 144–7
Charmosyna margarethae 147–8
Charmosyna meeki 159
Charmosyna multistriata 40, 148–9
Charmosyna palmarum 160
Charmosyna p. goliathina 3, 4, 149–52
Charmosyna p. papou 152
Charmosyna p. pulchella 1, 2, 152–4
Charmosyna p. rothschildi 154
Charmosyna p. stellae 152
Charmosyna p. wahnesi 152
Charmosyna pl. intensior 156
Charmosyna pl. ornata 156
Charmosyna pl. pallidor 156
Charmosyna pl. placentis 6, 154–6
Charmosyna pl. subplacens 156
Charmosyna r. kordoana 159

Charmosyna r. krakari 157
Charmosyna r. rubrigularis 156–7
Charmosyna r. rubronotata 5, 157–9
Charmosyna toxopei 160
Charmosyna wilhelminae 159–60

Eos spp. 161
Eos b. bernsteini 163
Eos b. bornea 23, 161–3
Eos b. cyanothus 163
Eos b. rothschildi 163
Eos cyanogenia 7, 102, 164
Eos h. challengeri 98, 166
Eos h. histrio 20, 98, 164–7
Eos h. talautensis 102, 166
Eos reticulata 10, 99, 102, 103, 167–9
Eos s. atrocaerulea 171
Eos s. obiensis 25, 171–2
Eos s. riciniata 171
Eos s. squamata 24, 99, 170–1
Eos semilarvata 169

Glossopsitta spp. 173
Glossopsitta concina 45, 173–4
Glossopsitta porphyrocephala 51, 174–6
Glossopsitta pulsilla 49, 176–7

Loriinae 11, 97, 128
Lorius spp. 178
Lorius albidinuchus 193
Lorius amabilis 193
Lorius chlorocercus 17, 178–80
Lorius domicellus 11, 102, 103, 180–2

243

INDEX

Lorius g. flavopalliatus 16, 102, 184–6
Lorius g. garrulus 15, 103, 182–4
Lorius g. morotaianus 102, 184
Lorius g. obiensis 184
Lorius h. devittatus 187
Lorius h. hypoinochrous 186–7
Lorius h. rosselianus 187
Lorius l. cyanauchen 189
Lorius l. erythrothorax 14, 52, 190–1
Lorius l. jobiensis 12, 52, 191–2
Lorius l. lory 13, 52, 187–90
Lorius l. salvadorii 189–90
Lorius l. somu 190
Lorius l. viridicrissalis 190
Lorius tibialis 193

Neopsittacus spp. 194
Neopsittacus m. major 197
Neopsittacus m. medius 197
Neopsittacus m. musschenbroeki 46, 194–7
Neopsittacus p. alpinus 198
Neopsittacus p. pullicauda 197–8
Neopsittacus p. socialis 198

Oreopsittacus spp. 199
Oreopsittacus a. arfaki 199–200
Oreopsittacus a. grandis 200
Oreopsittacus a. major 199–200

Phigys spp. 201
Phigys solitarius 23, 201–2
Pseudeos spp. 203
Pseudeos fuscata 8, 9, 203–4
Psittacidae spp. 11, 15

Trichoglossus spp. 205–6
Trichoglossus chlorolepidotus 43, 206–7
Trichoglossus euteles 42, 207–8
Trichoglossus f. flavoviridis 41, 208–9
Trichoglossus f. meyeri 44, 209–10

Trichoglossus goldiei 38, 210–12
Trichoglossus h. brooki 214
Trichoglossus h. caeruleiceps 214
Trichoglossus h. capistratus 32, 53, 215–17
Trichoglossus h. deplanchii 214
Trichoglossus h. djampeanus 215
Trichoglossus h. flavicans 214
Trichoglossus h. flavotectus 53, 217–18
Trichoglossus h. forsteni 35, 53, 219–20
Trichoglossus h. fortis 215
Trichoglossus h. haematodus 33, 53, 212–15
Trichoglossus h. massena 35, 53, 218–19
Trichoglossus h. micropteryx 214
Trichoglossus h. mitchelli 36, 53, 98, 102, 220–1
Trichoglossus h. moluccanus 30, 53, 221–3
Trichoglossus h. nigrogularis 53, 214
Trichoglossus h. rosenbergii 53, 103, 214–15
Trichoglossus h. rubritorquis 31, 53, 223–5
Trichoglossus h. stresemanni 215
Trichoglossus h. weberi 21, 104, 225–6
Trichoglossus i. iris 47, 226–7
Trichoglossus i. wetterensis 227
Trichoglossus johnstoniae 48, 228–9
Trichoglossus ornatus 39, 229–30
Trichoglossus rubiginosus 16, 230–1
Trichoglossus rubripileum 227
Trichoglossus versicolor 50, 231–3

Vini spp. 202, 234
Vini australis 234–5
Vini kuhlii 235–6
Vini peruviana 102, 236–8
Vini stepheni 238–9
Vini ultramarina 239–40

Index of Common Names

Page numbers in *italic* refer to plate illustrations.

Alpine Lorikeet 197–8
Amboina Rotlori *23*, 161–3
Apolori *48*, 228–9
Arfak Alpine Lorikeet 199–200
Arfakbergzierlori 199–200
Arfaklori 199–200

Belbburst Allfarblori *53*, 217–18
Bernstein's Lory 134
Bernstein's Red Lory 163
Biak Lory 189
Black-capped Lory *13*, 52, 187–90
Black Lory *29*, 131–4
Black-throated Lorikeet *53*, 214
Black-winged Lory *7*, 102, 164
Blau Kappchenlori 234–5
Blauohrlori *7*, 102, 164
Blaustrichellori *10*, 99, 102, 103, 167–9
Blauwangen Allfablori *32*, *53*, 215–17
Blauwgestreepte Lori *10*, 99, 102, 103, 167–9
Blauwkap Lori 234–5
Bloedvleklori *32*, *53*, 215–17
Blue-cheeked Lory *7*, 102, 164
Blue-crested Lorikeet 234–5
Blue-crowned Lorikeet 234–5
Blue-diademed Lory *20*, 98, 164–7
Blue-eared Lory 169
Blue-fronted Lorikeet 160
Blue-headed Lorikeet 214
Blue mountain Lorikeet *30*, *53*, 221–3

Blue-necked Lory *10*, 99, 102, 103, 167–9
Blue-streaked Lory *10*, 99, 102, 103, 167–9
Blue-tailed Lory *20*, 98, 164–7
Blue-thighed Lory 193
Bonte Lori *50*, 231–3
Braunlori *26*, 137–8
Breitbinden Allfablori *33*, *53*, 212–15
Brook's Lorikeet 214
Brown Lory *26*, 137–8
Buntlori *50*, 231–3
Buru Lorikeet 160
Buru Red Lory 163

Cardinal Lory *19*, 135–7
Carmine-fronted Lory 141
Caroline Lorikeet 16, 230–1
Challenger Red and Blue Lory 98, 166
Chattering Lory *15*, 103, 182–4
Cherry-red Lorikeet 16, 230–1
Coconut Lorikeet *35*, *53*, 218–9
Collared Lory 23, 201–2
Cyclops Lorikeet 147

Deplanche's Lorikeet 214
Devittatus Lory 187
Diadeem Lori *20*, 98, 164–7
Diadem Lorikeet 160
Diademlori *20*, 98, 164–7
Djampea Lorikeet 215
Duchess Lorikeet 147–8
Duivenbodei Lori *26*, 137–8

245

INDEX

Duivenbode's Lory *26*, 137–8
Dusky Lory *8*, *9*, 203–4
Dwerglori *49*, 176–7

Eastern Black-capped Lory 186–7
Edward's Lorikeet *32*, *53*, 215–17
Einsiedlerori 23, 201–2
Emerald Lorikeet 197–8
Emeraldlori 197–8
Erythro Black-capped Lory *14*, *52*, 190–1
Erzlori *11*, 102, 103, 180–2

Fairy Lorikeet *1*, *2*, 148, 152–4
Forsten Allfablori *35*, *53*, 219–20
Forsten, Loriquet de *35*, *53*, 219–20
Forstenlori *35*, *53*, 219–20
Forsten's Lorikeet *35*, *53*, 219–220
Frauenlori *13*, 52, 187–90

Geelborstlori *53*, 217–18
Geelgroene Lori *41*, 208–9
Geelkoplori *42*, 207–8
Geelmantellori *16*, 102, 184–6
Gekraagde Lory 23, 201–2
Gelbgruner Lori *41*, 208–9
Gelbkopflori *42*, 207–8
Gelbmantellori *15*, 103, 182–4
Gerbirgs Allfablori *30*, *53*, 221–3
Gold-banded Lorikeet 152
Golden–banded Lory 143
Goldie's Lorikeet *38*, 210–12
Goldstrichellori *1*, *2*, 152–4
Greater-streaked Lory *28*, 139–41
Green and Yellow Lorikeet *43*, 206–7
Green-naped Lorikeet *33*, *53*, 212–15
Green-streaked Lory 141
Greenie Lorikeet *43*, 206–7
Groenneklori *33*, *53*, 212–15
Groenstaartlori *17*, 178–80
Grunschwanzlori *17*, 178–80
Gualori *46*, 194–7

Half-masked Lory 169

Halfmasken-Lori 169
Halfmaskerlori 169
Handsome Lory 134
Henderson Islands Lory 238–9

Indigo Lorikeet 102, 236–8
Iris Lorikeet *47*, 226–7
Irislori *47*, 226–7

Jerryang *49*, 176–7
Jobi Black-capped Lory *12*, *52*, 191–2
Jobi Frauenlori *12*, *52*, 191–2
Jobi Lory *12*, *52*, 191–2
Jobilori *12*, *52*, 191–2
Johnstonlori *48*, 228–9
Josephinelori *18*, 104, 144–7
Josephinenlori *18*, 104, 144–7
Josephine's Lorikeet *18*, 104, 144–7

Kahl's Ruffled Lory 235–6
Kapuzen Lori *24*, 99, 170–1
Kardinal Lori *19*, 135–7
Kardinallori *19*, 135–7
Koningslori *7*, 102, 164
Kuhl's Lorikeet 235–6
Kuhl's Lory 235–6

Lilac-naped Lory 138
Little Lorikeet *49*, 176–7
Little Red Lorikeet *1*, *2*, 152–4
Long-tailed Lorikeet *3*, *4*, 149–52
Lori à bande violette 186–7
Lori à calotte noire *13*, *52*, 187–90
Lori à calotte noire de Salvadore *14*, *52*, 190–1
Lori à croupion noir *1*, *2*, 152–4
Lori à dos blanc *8*, *9*, 203–4
Lori à front jaune *28*, 139–41
Lori à nuque violette de Bechstein *24*, 99, 170–1
Lori à nuque violette d'Obi *25*, 171–2
Lori à queue verte *17*, 178–80
Lori blanc et bleu de Tahiti 102, 236–8

Lori bleu des Iles Marquises 239–40
Lori Cardinale *19*, 135–7
Lori de Duivenbodeii *26*, 137–8
Lori de Marguerite 147–8
Lori des dames *11*, 102, 103, 180–2
Lori des Molluques *15*, 103, 182–4
Lori des Moluges à dos jaune *16*, 102, 184–6
Lori histrion *20*, 98, 164–7
Lori Jobi *12*, *52*, 191–2
Lori noir *29*, 131–4
Lori orné *39*, 229–30
Lori Rajah *27*, 134–5
Lori rouge *23*, 161–3
Lori solitaire 23, 201–2
Lori strie bleu *10*, 99, 102, 103, 167–9
Lori van de Blauwe Bergen *30*, *53*, 221–3
Lori vini à crete bleue 234–5
Lori vini de Stephen 238–9
Lori vini rubis 235–6
Loriquet à collier rouge *31*, *53*, 223–5
Loriquet à cou rouge 143
Loriquet à nuque vert *33*, *53*, 212–15
Lori aux ailes noires *7*, 102, 164
Loriquet aux marques rouges *5*, 156–7, 157–9
Loriquet cerise 16, 230–1
Loriquet de Florent *51*, 174–6
Loriquet de Goldie *38*, 210–12
Loriquet de Josephine *18*, 104, 144–7
Loriquet de Mme Johnstone *48*, 228–9
Loriquet de Mont Goliath *3*, *4*, 149–52
Loriquet de Musschenbroek *46*, 194–7
Loriquet de Victoria 197–8
Loriquet de Weber *21*, 104, 225–6
Loriquet de Wetar *53*, 217–18
Loriquet des Monts Arfak 199–200

Loriquet écaillé *43*, 206–7
Loriquet iris de l'est de Timor *47*, 226–7
Loriquet joli 6, 154–6
Loriquet Multistrie *40*, 148–9
Loriquet musque *45*, 173–4
Loriquet nain *49*, 176–7
Loriquet versicolore *50*, 231–3
Loriquet vert de Sula *41*, *44*, 208–9, 209–10
Lory of Bonthain *44*, 209–10
Louisiade Lory 186–87

Margaretha's Honingpapegaai 147–8
Margarethenlori 147–8
Marquesas Lorikeet 239–40
Massena Allfablori *35*, *53*, 218–19
Massena, Loriquet de *35*, *53*, 218–19
Massena Lory *35*, *53*, 218–19
Massenalori *35*, *53*, 218–19
Meek's Lorikeet 159
Meyer's Gelbgruner Lori *44*, 209–10
Meyer's Lorikeet *44*, 209–10
Meyerlori *44*, 209–10
Mindanao Lorikeet *48*, 228–9
Mitchell Allfablori *36*, *53*, 98, 102, 220–1
Mitchell, Loriquet de *36*, *53*, 98, 102, 220–1
Mitchell's Lorikeet *36*, *53*, 98, 102, 220–1
Mitchell's Lory *36*, *53*, 98, 102, 220–1
Moluccan Lory *23*, 161–3
Moluccan Red Lory *23*, 161–3
Molukkenlori *15*, 103, 182–4
Morotai Yellow-backed Lory 102, 184
Moschuslori *45*, 173–4
Mount Apo Lorikeet *48*, 228–9
Mount Goliath Lorikeet 118, 142, 149–52, 194
Mrs Johnstone's Lorikeet *48*, 228–9
Musk Lorikeet *45*, 173–4

INDEX

Musklori 45, 173–4
Musschenbroek's Lorikeet 46, 194–7

New Britain Lory 193
New Caledonian Lorikeet 160

Obi Lory 25, 171–2
Obilori 25, 171–2
Olive-green Lorikeet 214
Orange-fronted Lory 141
Orange Geestrepte 28, 139–1
Orange-naped Lory 31, 53, 223–5
Ornaatlori 39, 229–30
Ornamental Lorikeet 39, 229–30
Ornate Lorikeet 39, 229–30

Palm Lorikeet 160
Papuan Lorikeet 3, 4, 149–52
Perfect Lory 42, 207–8
Plain Lorikeet 42, 207–8
Pleasing Lorikeet 6, 154–6
Ponape Lorikeet 16, 230–1
Ponapelori 16, 230–1
Porphyrlori 51, 174–6
Prachtgelbmantellori 16, 102, 184–6
Princess Margaret's Lorikeet 147–8
Purperkaplori 11, 102, 103, 180–2
Purperkoplori 51, 174–6
Purple-bellied Lory 186–7
Purple-capped Lory 11, 102, 103, 180–2
Purple-crowned Lorikeet 51, 174–6
Purple-naped Lory 11, 102, 103, 180–2
Pygmy Lorikeet 159–60

Rainbow Lorikeet 30, 32, 33, 35, 53, 212–15, 215–17, 217–18, 218–19, 221–2
Rajah Lory 27, 134–5
Rajahlori 27, 134–5
Red and Blue Lory 20, 164–7
Red-breasted Lorikeet 35, 36, 53, 98, 102, 219–20, 220–1

Red-breasted Lory 14, 52, 189, 190–1
Red-capped Lorikeet 50, 231–3
Red-chinned Lorikeet 156–7
Red-collared Lorikeet 31, 53, 223–5
Red-faced Lorikeet 49, 176–7
Red-flanked Lorikeet 6, 154–6
Red Lory 23, 161–3
Red-marked Lorikeet 5, 157–9
Red-necked Lory 31, 53, 223–5
Red-quilled Lory 27, 134–5
Red-spotted Lorikeet 5, 157–9
Red-streaked Lory 141
Red-throated Lorikeet 156–7
Red-throated Lory 101, 143
Rode Lori 23, 161–3
Rodeneklori 31, 53, 223–5
Rodesborstlori 14, 52, 190–1
Roodflanklori 6, 154–6
Roodkin Lori 143, 156–7
Roodstuitlori 5, 157–9
Rosenberg's Lorikeet 53, 103, 214–15
Rossel Island Lory 187
Roter Lori 23, 161–3
Rothschild's Fairy Lorikeet 154
Rothschild's Red Lory 163
Rotkinnlori 143, 156–7
Rotnacken Allfablori 31, 53, 223–5
Rotnackenallfarblori 230–1
Rotstirnlori 5, 157–9
Rubin Lory 235–6
Ruby Lori 235–6
Ruffled Lory 23, 201–2

Saifer Lori 102, 236–8
Salvadori Frauenlori 14, 52, 190–1
Salvadori's Lory 189–90
Sammetlori 27, 134–5
Samoan Lorikeet 234–5
Saphirlori 102, 236–8
Scaly-breasted Lorikeet 43, 206–7
Schimmerlori 28, 139–41
Schmuck Lori 39, 229–30
Schonlori 6, 154–6
Schubbenlori 43, 206–7

Schuppenlori *43*, 206–7
Schwarzlori *29*, 131–4
Schwarzstersslori 186–7
Sepik Lorikeet *18*, 104, 144–7
Smaragd Lori 239–40
Smaragdgualori 197–8
Smaragdlori 239–40
Somu Lory 190
Southern Green-naped Lorikeet 214
Stella Papualori *3*, *4*, 149–52
Stellalori *3*, *4*, 149–52
Stella's Lorikeet *3*, *4*, 149–52
Stephenlori 238–9
Stephen's Lory 238–9
Stresemann's Lorikeet *53*, 215
Stresemann's Lory 193
Striated Lorikeet *40*, 148–9
Sula Lorikeet *41*, 208–9
Sumba Lorikeet 215
Swainson, Loriquet de *30*, *53*, 221–3
Swainson's Lorikeet *30*, *53*, 221–3

Tahitian Blue Lorikeet 102, 236–8
Talaud Red and Blue Lory 102, 166

Ultramarine Lorikeet 239–40

Varied Lorikeet *50*, 231–3
Veelstrepenlori *40*, 148–9
Veilchenlori *38*, 210–12
Vielstrichellori *40*, 148–9
Violet-naped Lory *24*, 99, 170–1

Violet-necked Lory *24*, 99, 170–1
Violetneklori *24*, 99, 170–1
Violetstaart Lori 186–7
Viooltjeslori *38*, 210–12

Wallace's Lory 172
Weberlori *21*, 104, 225–6
Weber's Allfablori *21*, 104, 225–6
Weber's Lorikeet *21*, 104, 225–6
Weissburzel Lori *8*, *9*, 203–4
Western Black-capped Lory *13*, *52*, 187–90
Wetar Lory *53*, 217–18
Whiskered Lorikeet 199–200
White-naped Lory 193
White-throated Lorikeet 102, 236–8
Wilhelmina's Lorikeet 159–60
Witruglori *8*, *9*, 203–4

Yellow and Green Lorikeet *41*, 208–9
Yellow-backed Lory *16*, 102, 184–6
Yellow-bibbed Lory *17*, 178–80
Yellow-breasted Lorikeet *53*, 217–18
Yellow-headed Lorikeet *42*, 207–8
Yellow-streaked Lory *28*, 139–1

Zip Parrot *51*, 174–6
Zwarte Lori *29*, 131–4
Zwartkoplori *13*, *52*, 187–90
Zwartstuitlori *1*, *2*, 152–4
Zwerglori *49*, 176–7

General Index

access 31
accidents 115–16
  see also injuries
  prevention 108
accommodation 24–36
aggression 41
air, clean 110
Albertis, Luigi d' 15–16, 18
amino acids 50
appetite 39, 109
ascites 118
aspergillosis 118
assistance boxes 79
ataxia 119–20
Australia 15
aviaries
  spare 45
  types of 24–32
aviculture 14, 97
aviculturists 102–4

Banks, Sir Joseph 15
beaks 110–12
behaviour 12–13, 21–2, 40
Bevere, Pieter de 16
binding (egg) 51, 120
Birdlife Indonesia 101
Birdlife International 101
bites 115
boredom 40
breathing 109
breeders 37
breeding 68–74
  captive 101–2
Brisson 16
brooders 82–5
Buffon, Salvadori, Comte de 15, 16

bullying 40, 109

cages see aviaries
calcium 50
candidiasis 118–19
candling 70, 71, 78
capping 78
captive breeding 101–2
characteristics 11
chicks 71–4
  hand-rearing 82–93
chills 116
china eggs 78
chromosomal sexing 66
CITES (Convention on International Trade in Endangered Species) 99–100
cleanliness 88, 112
coccidiosis 119
compatibility 40–1
concussion 123
conservation 97–107
Cook, Captain 15
cover (plant) 36
crops
  impacted 123
  monitoring 89–90
Currumbin, Australia 22–3, 104–5
cuts 109, 115

dealers 37
diet 11, 47–64, 119
  see also feeding; rearing formulas
diseases 118–27
disinfecting 112
displays, mating 68–9
distribution, of lories 13
DNA sexing 66–7

INDEX

draughts 33, 109
droppings 13
drunkenness see ataxia
dust 110

Edmunds, Richard 19, 20
eggs
  binding 51, 120
  breaking 69
  china 78
  eating 69
  growth of 77–8
  hatching 80–1
  requirements for incubation 76–7
  turning 76
enteritis 121
escapees, catching 117
euthanasia 116
exercise 109–10
extinction 14, 23, 94, 98
eye infections 121

faces, scaly 125
faeces 90, 109
feather disease *see* psittacine beak
feathers 11–12
  colour changes 123
  plucking 74, 121
feeding 47–64 *see also* diet
  habits 13, 21
  hand-reared chicks 87–8
  utensils 52
Finsch, Friedrich Herman Otto 16
first aid 108–17
fits 123
fledging 74
floors, aviary 28–9
formulas, rearing 85–7
fostering 70
french moult 121–2
French Polynesia/Zoological Society of San Diego Ultramarine Project 105
frost 43
frostbite 123
fumes 124
fungus 124

Garnot 16
geographical ranges 11
Goffin/Blue-streak project 103
Gray, George Robert 16
Griffiths, Alex 22

habitat 17–20
hand-rearing 82–93
hatchers 75–6, 80
hatching 80–1
  assistance in 79–80
heat and fluid therapy (HFT) 114–15
heat (weather) 42–3
heating 29–30
HFT *see heat* and fluid therapy
historical sightings 15–16
Histrio Project 103
Hombron 16
Hughes, Nigel 19, 20
humidity
  in brooders 84–5
  for incubation 76
hygiene 42, 76

importers 37
incompatibility 41, 109
incubation 69, 75–81
incubators 75–6, 80
injuries
  cuts 109, 115
  legs, broken 115
  ring 125
  toes, broken 115–16
  wings, broken 115
International Loriinae Society (ILS) 102–3
iron 50
IUCN (International Union for the Conservation of Nature) 100
  Species Survival Commission 105–7

Jacquinot 16
Java 16

Koch, Ludwig 16

Kuhl 16

lead 124
legs
  broken 115
  scaly 125
Lesson 16
lice 123–4
light 30–1
lories
  distribution of 13
  geographical range 11
  groups and societies 37, 99–7
  historical sitings 15–16
  importing 15, 38–9
  obtaining 37–8
  topography 11, 129
  wild 21–3
Loriidae, The 16
lorikeets *see* lories
Lory Journal International 94, 103

magazines 37
magnesium 50
maintenance 45
management
  general 37–46
  hand-reared chicks 87–93
  incubators 75–6, 80
  routine care 109–15
materials, for aviaries 27–8
mating displays 68–9
medicine cupboards 113
minerals 50
mites 123–124
Mivart, St George 16
mould 124
Müller 16

nails 110–12
nests 23, 34, 35, 36, 42
New Guinea 15, 16, 17–20
New Illustrations of Zoology 15
night fright 116
noise 13
non-sitting 70

observation 39–40, 109
ornithosis *see* psittacosis

pairing 40–1
Peale 16
perches 33, 34
pesticides 124
Phillip, Captain Arthur 15, 16
phosphorus 50
plants
  for cover 36
  for nutrients 59–60
plucking, feathers 74
plumage *see* feathers
pneumonia 124
poisons 124
pollutants 110
ponds 32–3
post-mortems 117
potassium 50
powercuts 43–4, 76–7
probiotics 61–2, 90–1, 113
pseudotuberculosis 126–7
psittacine beak (PBFD) 122
Psittacine Research Center (USA) 48
psittacosis 125

quarantine 38–9, 112

RARE 102
rearing formulas 85–7
records 92
Red and Blue Project 103
regurgitation 109
repairs 45
research 48
ring injuries 125
ringing 92–3
roofing 28

safety 31
security 31–2, 95
seeds
  contaminated 124
  sprouting 60
sexing 65–7

INDEX

sightings, historical 15–16
sinusitis 125
Sharpe, Richard Bowdler 16
siting, of aviaries 26–7
Solomon Islands 20
South Pacific, species 101
spoon-feeding 89
sprinklers 32–3
stress 112
studbooks 94–6
surgical sexing 65–6
suspended aviaries 24–6

temperature
  in brooders 83–4
  for incubation 76
toes, broken or lost 115–16
tongues, brush 11, 14
topography 11, 129
TRAFFIC (Trade Records Analysis of Flora and Fauna in Commerce) 98–9, 100
transport 45, 46
  of chicks 93
  of sick birds 116
Trees of Paradise 19
trichomoniasis 126
Tupia 15
turning (eggs) 76

UK Lory Group 103
utensils
  feeding 52
  hand-rearing 88

ventilation 30–31
  in brooders 84
veterinary surgeons 108, 116
visual sexing 65
vitamins 49–50, 61
vomiting 109
Voyage of Governor Phillip to Botany Bay, The 15

Wallace, Alfred Russel 15
water 63–4, 76, 124
water filtration unit 63
weather, extremes of 42–4
weight 72–3, 91–2
winds, high 43
wings
  broken 115
  clipping 41
worms 126

yersiniosis 126–7

zinc 124
zoos 103–4